REPUBLICAN
RESCUE

SAVING THE PARTY FROM TRUTH DENIERS,
CONSPIRACY THEORISTS,
AND THE DANGEROUS POLICIES OF JOE BIDEN

CHRIS CHRISTIE

Threshold Editions

New York   London   Toronto   Sydney   New Delhi

Threshold Editions
An Imprint of Simon & Schuster, Inc.
1230 Avenue of the Americas
New York, NY 10020

First Threshold Editions hardcover edition November 2021

THRESHOLD EDITIONS and colophon are trademarks of Simon & Schuster, Inc.

For information about special discounts for bulk purchases, please contact Simon & Schuster Special Sales at 1-866-506-1949 or business@simonandschuster.com.

The Simon & Schuster Speakers Bureau can bring authors to your live event. For more information or to book an event, contact the Simon & Schuster Speakers Bureau at 1-866-248-3049 or visit our website at www.simonspeakers.com.

Interior design by Jaime Putorti

Manufactured in the United States of America

10 9 8 7 6 5 4 3 2 1

Library of Congress Cataloging-in-Publication Data is available.

ISBN 978-1-9821-8751-4
ISBN 978-1-9821-8753-8 (ebook)

For my children, Andrew, Sarah Anne, Patrick, and Bridget:
This book was written in the real hope that it will contribute
to getting our country back on track so that each of you can
enjoy the opportunities that this extraordinary American life
has given to me and your mother.

CONTENTS

Introduction   *1*

PART I: DONALD AND ME

1 Help Wanted   *9*
2 Task Force   *27*
3 Early Warning   *41*
4 Debate Prep   *55*
5 Show Time   *67*
6 Getting It   *81*
7 Intensive Care   *93*
8 Losing It   *109*

PART II: CRAZY TALK

9   Right Way   *131*
10 History Lesson   *145*
11 Born Where   *161*
12 Pizza Time   *177*
13 Q Amok   *189*
14 Lies Plural   *203*

PART III: WINNING AGAIN

15 On Education   229
16 On Crime   237
17 On Business   245
18 On Media   253
19 On Threats   261
20 On Enemies   269
21 On COVID   277
22 On Elections   281

Conclusion   287
Acknowledgments   291

REPUBLICAN
RESCUE

INTRODUCTION

Winning is good. Losing is horrible. And nothing in politics is truer. Believe me, I know.

And now, two painful realities have gotten me writing again. The first comes from the losses that my party, the Republican Party, suffered over the past three years, losses we urgently need to turn into wins. We lost the House of Representatives in 2018. The Democrats picked up 41 seats that year and—*talk about painful*—the ultraliberal Nancy Pelosi became Speaker of the House. That November, the Democrats also snatched governorships in Illinois, Wisconsin, Michigan, Nevada, New Mexico, Kansas, and Maine, all states we'd won two years earlier. Then, in 2020, the electoral map went from bad to perverse. We lost the U.S. Senate by a painfully slim margin. Suddenly, the future of the republic was resting at least temporarily in Chuck Schumer's untrustworthy hands.

I liked it a whole lot better when his job title included the word *minority*.

And worst of all, we also lost the White House in 2020. I hate to even type those words, but there they are.

Very few people were as publicly invested in the success of Donald Trump as I was. As governor of New Jersey, I was the first major political figure to endorse him in 2016, after I ended my own campaign for president. I prepared him for the debates that fall by playing Hillary Clinton. No one could call that typecasting! From start to finish, *that was an acting job*! I chaired the Trump presidential transition committee. Through his time in the White House, I constantly gave him my best advice, some of which he even followed and some of which I'm confident in his private moments he wished he had. I headed his Opioid and Drug Abuse Commission, which led to one of the biggest successes of the administration, the bipartisan legislation that was passed to deal with the opioid crisis. He asked me to be his chief of staff. And I played a mean Joe Biden in the 2020 debate prep. Few people were rooting harder for Donald Trump to win than I was.

Another important point to note right at the start: There is nothing in this book that I have not said directly to Donald Trump. We have been friends for twenty years and still are friends. But friends have disagreements. And President Trump knows that I tell it like it is—in public and private—and it should be no different even when you are talking to an old friend . . . who just happens to be POTUS.

But losing hurts. Despite the pain, we have to live in the real world, not the world as we wish it to be.

How bad was it? Well, the last time the Republican Party surrendered the House, the Senate, and the White House in two years, Herbert Hoover was in the Donald Trump role. After that, Democrats held the White House for 28 of the next 36 years and the House of Representatives for 48 of the next 52. The Senate tally was only slightly less bleak.

I don't think America can withstand another Republican dry spell like that one. I know *I* can't. I don't want a repeat of the aftermath of Herbert Hoover.

Let's be clear: Political parties have one purpose and one purpose only, and that's to produce victories. It's those victories that allow us to shape the future and make the country a better place. So, it's never just a Republican victory. It's also America's. Platforms, fund-raising committees, flashy conventions, soaring speeches, and all the rest of it—they matter only to the extent that they help secure the next win and the next chance to change America for the better. Losing political parties need to change their ways in order to once again become winning parties. Everything else is a big waste of time.

We need to ask ourselves: Why did we lose? And what do we need to do differently to make sure we win? To share those vital answers is the first reason I decided to write this book. The second reason is Joe Biden and the Democrats, and the dangerous policies they are now busy imposing on all of us.

With each new burst of runaway spending, with each new lurch to the left, with each new calling election integrity "Jim Crow 2.0," with each new imposition of critical race theory in the classroom of an unsuspecting child, with each new reversal of Trump administration policy, and with each new assault on the values that everyday Americans cherish, the pressing need for a Republican rescue becomes more severe. But before Republicans can rescue America, we also need to rescue ourselves.

This is no academic exercise. The stakes could hardly be any higher. And the time is short. As the radical policies of the Biden-Harris administration push our country ever closer to the point of no return, becoming a government-centric, anticapitalist society that no longer rewards innovation and ambition, no longer protects individual liberty and freedom, we must keep sounding the alarm. We must also make a clear-eyed assessment of what got us into the mess we're in and how we can get out of it.

As Republicans, we need to free ourselves from the quicksand of endless grievances. We need to turn our attention to the future and quit wallowing in the past. We need to face the realities of the 2020 election and learn—not hide—from them. We need to discredit the extremists in our midst the way William F. Buckley and Ronald

Reagan once did. We need to renounce the conspiracy theorists and truth deniers, the ones who know better and the ones who are just plain nuts. We need to give our supporters facts that will help them put all those fantasies to rest so everyone can focus with clear minds on the issues that really matter. We need to quit wasting our time, our energy, and our credibility on claims that won't ever convince anyone or bring fresh converts aboard.

We need to learn to win again.

The only way to push back against policies we know are wrong is to focus on alternatives that the American people will see are right, then ride those ideas to victory. Nothing else is going to win Congress for the Republicans in 2022 or the White House in 2024.

Enough with the wishful thinking and self-delusion. The infighting has to end. So does the wallowing in the past. We need to be the party that embraces the truth even when it's painful. Grievances and conspiracy theories always die hard. But they can only live in the darkness. Their days are numbered once the light of truth shines down.

One of the great things about public life in this country of ours is the twenty-four-hour-a-day, seven-day-a-week open marketplace for ideas. In a life defined by passionate engagement, it's always a thrill for me to stand "in the arena"—Teddy Roosevelt's potent phrase—deliver my strongest insights, and be heard. I will always speak plainly, boldly, and bluntly, and I intend to do so here. Not everyone will agree with every syllable—and wouldn't that be boring? But everyone knows I never pull my punches. I call things as I see them. And I let the chips fall where they may. I will always be for telling my fellow citizens the hard truths.

This battle will not end without prodigious struggle. The Democrats will not be defeated without sound alternatives to their flawed ideas. Hating the other side is not enough. Calling them wrong is not enough. Pretending we won when we lost is a waste of time and energy. We have to clear out the brush, on our own side and on theirs, before the fresh planting can begin. And that's exactly the job ahead.

It can't be done with vague generalities. Slogans aren't nearly enough now. The time for snappy platitudes is past. We need to get specific on every page. Specific about what happened in the final year of the Trump administration. Specific about the grievances and falsehoods that have stalled our party. Specific about the alternatives to the radical, out-of-touch Biden program that Americans in large numbers will rally around. And most of all, specific about the route to victory again.

Hold on tight now. The fun has only begun. We don't have to be about yesterday. We must be about tomorrow. That's the road to victory.

PART I

DONALD AND ME

CHAPTER 1

HELP WANTED

I got a call from Kellyanne Conway. This was early December of 2018.

"I think he's going to get rid of General Kelly very soon," she said, "and he's been talking to me about asking you to be chief of staff. I don't know if he's going to do it or not. But you'd better start thinking about what you want to say if he does."

Kellyanne didn't miss much. A veteran Republican pollster, she had managed Donald Trump's successful 2016 campaign and was now counselor to the president. She grew up Kellyanne Fitzpatrick near the Atco drag strip in South Jersey's Camden County, playing field hockey and working eight summers on one of the area's remaining blueberry farms. Her family, like mine, was part Irish and part Italian. Though she'd graduated from George Washington University law school and spent a couple of decades as a high-level political operative and cable-news talking head, to me she was still a plainspoken Jersey girl. She was also my best friend in the Trump White House, besides the president himself.

Trump had made no secret of his frustration with John Kelly, the retired four-star Marine general and former head of the U.S. Southern Command who'd run the White House staff for fourteen months by then. From what I'd been hearing, Trump hadn't only been keeping Kelly in the dark on key decisions. The two men were barely speaking anymore. For his part, Kelly seemed to have concluded that the president was not up to his definition of a commander in chief. Kelly never said this in so many words, but his body language was unmistakable. The impatient eye rolls. The rocking back and forth as Trump spoke. Whatever respect had been there initially, it was long gone. The midterm elections hadn't gone well for the Republicans. Democrats had won control of the House of Representatives with a massive 41-seat gain. Though the Republicans kept their Senate majority and actually added two seats, the high-turnout election had devolved into an angry referendum on the personality of Donald Trump. With his eyes now turning to his own reelection in two years, he was itching to shake up his cabinet and White House staff.

He'd already settled on Bill Barr to replace Jeff Sessions as attorney general, which was a big disappointment to me. Ever since I'd helped Trump get elected, I'd always said that attorney general was the one job I would accept from him. He'd offered me just about every other position this side of White House chef. Secretary of labor. Secretary of homeland security. Ambassador to the Vatican. Ambassador to Italy. He figured I'd be a good fit at the Vatican since I am Catholic. He thought of me for ambassador to Italy because my mother was Italian. I don't think the analysis went any deeper than that. Trump didn't overanalyze choices like these.

He'd even asked if I wanted to be chairman of the Republican National Committee *part-time*—while I stayed on as governor of New Jersey. I'd said "no, thank you" to all of it. For me, it was attorney general or nothing, as I kept telling the president. I really wasn't interested in anything else.

But what about chief of staff? The person who actually *runs* the White House, in a normal White House anyway. That might be interesting. Setting the daily agenda. Overseeing the president's schedule and controlling access to him. Corralling the cabinet. Keeping the senior staffers from trying to kill each other. That job was especially important, I knew, in a White House as seat-of-the-pants as this one, where the president wanted to run everything himself. Reince Priebus, Trump's first chief of staff, had failed to master the difficult managing-up part. Now General Kelly had stumbled, too.

After I got the heads-up call from Kellyanne, I heard nothing for more than a week. I was back home in New Jersey, doing what I'd been doing since I'd stopped being governor in January and had decided against moving down to Washington: building my consulting and law businesses. Trying to help my clients. Sharing my political commentary with George Stephanopoulos on ABC. Serving on boards of directors. Making real money for the first time in my life. This isn't called "freelancing" anymore, I was told. It's a "portfolio career," meaning you do a lot of different things for a lot of different people who believe you still have the knowledge, the power, and the experience to get stuff done.

All was going well.

Then, on December 12, I got a call from Donald Trump's personal secretary Molly. "The president would like to see you tomorrow evening at the residence for a conversation," she said.

"What about?"

"He didn't tell me," she answered. "He just wants you to come to the White House, and the meeting will be up in the residence."

"Okay," I said. "I'll be there."

I made a reservation for the next afternoon on the Amtrak Acela train to Washington.

Was this the follow-up to what Kellyanne was talking about? Or something totally different? With Trump, I knew it could be anything. His mind was constantly jumping from topic to topic, especially when the topics involved hiring and firing the people who reported to him. Especially the firing part. He'd think about firing someone, poll his friends for their opinions, think about not doing it, then think about doing it again—and truly, you could never really be sure how, when, or where he would land.

That was just Trump.

All I knew was what Kellyanne had told me and that I hadn't heard another word about it since. "If I had a guess," I said that night to my wife, Mary Pat, "I think he's offering me chief of staff. What do you think I should do?"

Mary Pat had been through this drill with me before. As usual, she threw the decision back at me. "Do whatever you want to do," she said, "but I'm not coming to Washington with the kids. We need to stay in New Jersey."

We have four busy children, two boys and two girls. Our younger son, Patrick, was a senior in high school. Our younger daughter, Bridget, was a sophomore. "We can't go anywhere," Mary Pat said. "And this is a twenty-four-seven job. If you go, you're gonna go down there and live on your own. Whenever you can come back and see us, you'll come back and see us. But if I were you, I wouldn't make a decision on the spot if he offers it. Tell him you've got to come back and talk to me, and we'll figure it out."

"Agreed," I said.

Before I left home for the train station, I knew there was only one person to call.

The great James A. Baker III.

To me, Baker was the wisest of Washington wise men. He'd been secretary of the Treasury under Ronald Reagan, secretary of state for George H. W. Bush, and chief of staff—the *gold-standard* chief of staff—for both presidents. No one else had Baker's unique mix of Princeton-rugby polish, Marine Corps confidence, insider-Washington savvy, and Texas common sense—or, at age eighty-eight, his eternal aura of yes-I-really-have-seen-and-done-it-all. If anyone could help to steer me on this one, it was James Baker.

When I called his office at the Baker Botts law firm, he got right on the phone. "I need your advice," I told him.

"Well," he said in that laconic way of his, "if you're calling me, that means you're about to be offered the worst fuckin' job in Washington."

"I think I am," I said.

I'm not quite sure how he knew that. I didn't ask. I just fell back on my default assumption: Jim Baker knows everything.

He was generous with his advice. "There are some things you should demand before you agree to take the job," he said. I grabbed a pen and a legal pad. I wrote furiously as he ticked off the things I should ask for, taking notes as carefully as I could.

Here's what I wrote on my pad:

1. Chief of staff gets to staff the White House.

2. I get to manage the staff with the exception of Jared and Ivanka. On Jared and Ivanka, POTUS gets to determine role. Chief of staff needs to be fully informed of their activities.

3. Walk-in rights for Chief of Staff to any White House meeting—presidential or otherwise.

4. Walk-in rights for staff determined by Chief of Staff with the exception of the family of POTUS.

5. Chief of Staff controls his public appearances with assumption being Chief of Staff is a behind-the-scenes player—*not* a TV star.

6. Chief of Staff has representative at campaign and convention for planning and coordination purposes.

7. All disputes/disagreements between CoS and POTUS to be settled in private. No public statements of dissatisfaction or criticism.

8. Ability to go home on weekends to see Mary Pat and the children.

9. Attorney paid for by the RNC to advise me personally on various issues.

"Type it up," Baker said. "And make him sign it. Keep it in your desk drawer. And attach to it an undated but signed resignation letter. The resignation letter should say, 'Dear Mr. President: Due to the fact that we have not been able to keep our agreement upon which I accepted this job in the first place, I hereby tender my resignation as White House chief of staff.'"

That was a lot to write down, but I think I got all of it. And Baker delivered all those points right off the top of his head. And I had to take it seriously, he said.

"If he ever breaks one of the agreements he's made on this list, detach the letter from the list, walk it in, hand it to him, and walk out. He has to know that you're gonna do that. You can't threaten it. You just have to do it. If you're going to take the job, you have to be committed to doing it just that way."

I told Baker I really appreciated his suggestions, all of which sounded wise to me. He left me with one last thought.

"Governor," he said, "do what you think is best, and anything you ever need from me, I'm here to help. But I'll tell you this. If you take this job, you're the greatest American patriot since Paul Revere."

No, no one could ever accuse James Baker of holding back.

"I hear you, Mr. Secretary," I said. "I hear you."

"That's all," he said. "That's all, my friend."

*   *   *

The Amtrak train was just pulling out of Trenton when my phone rang. It was Rudy Giuliani, the former mayor of New York City, the president's personal lawyer, and so much more. He and Trump had a relationship so long and complicated, it cannot possibly be summed up in a few lines. But the two of them spoke regularly. And though he often complained about Rudy, he also listened to a lot of what Rudy said.

"He's offering you chief of staff tonight," Rudy said to me right after *hello*. "I just got done talking to him. He's offering it to you. What are you gonna do?"

"I really don't know," I answered.

"Okay, well, you've got a little time on the train to figure out what you're going to say. But I think that's going to be the question."

It was Rudy's call that wiped any lingering doubt from my mind. I hadn't been summoned to the White House for idle conversation. Kellyanne hadn't read too much into Trump's latest personnel complaints. He'd called me down to Washington to talk to me about being his chief of staff. But I still didn't know what I was going to say. I had Kellyanne's heads-up, which I was grateful for. I had Mary Pat's reaction, which was important to me. I had Baker's points. I had Rudy's clarification. What else did I need?

When I got to the White House gate, several dozen people were milling outside. This being December 13, the White House holiday parties were now in full swing. Afternoon parties. Evening parties. Different groups were invited to come at different times. I didn't linger long enough to figure out whose turn this was. As soon as I came in off the sidewalk, one of the agents stopped me and steered me in a different direction. To me, that was the final confirmation of what I already knew. *They don't want me being seen here. I'm going to be offered this job.*

The agent walked me into the house and up to the south side of the second floor, where the residence is, then through the Center Hall and into what is known as the Yellow Oval Room. First used as a drawing room by President John Adams, it's had many different uses over the past two-plus centuries. It's been a library, an office, and a family parlor. More recent presidents, including Trump, have used it for small receptions and for greeting heads of state immediately before state dinners. The southwest window has a swing-sash door to the Truman Balcony. Double doors on the west side lead to the president and First Lady's bedrooms.

This is the innermost of inner White House sanctums—unless the president invites you to jump on his bed.

As I walked into the room, Melania stood to greet me. I hadn't known the First Lady was going to be joining us. "He had to take a phone call," she said. "He'll be here in a second."

I sat on the sofa across from her and set my briefcase down. Melania could not have been more welcoming. She and I chatted for a few minutes. My family. Her family. No business. Just a couple of old friends catching up. I'd had laryngitis and my voice still sounded scratchy. She insisted on getting me some tea with honey.

The tea arrived, and then Donald bounded in with his usual energy and volume. He was not a guy who believed in quiet entrances . . . anywhere.

"What's with the briefcase?" he said to me.

"Well," I answered, "this is a business meeting. So I'm here to do business."

"Oh," he said, drawing out the *ohhh* into a couple of syllables. "So we've got a briefcase? What? Are we going to take notes?"

"Yes, we are," I said.

I'm not sure why the briefcase struck him, but clearly it did. That's just Trump, I suppose, the Donald I'd gotten to know, instinctively commanding the room. He fixates on things. "Okay," he said. "Well, Melania, this is a business meeting. This is a big business meeting."

That's when he sat down and started pitching me on the chief of staff job.

"John Kelly's gotta go," he said. "We're not getting along anymore. He's not the right fit. He doesn't understand politics. We're now getting into the last two years of my first term, and you are just the guy to lead me to reelection. To be running the White House and then coordinating the activities for the campaign. You understand politics. You're smart. You're the guy to do this."

I liked the way all that sounded, of course. But I knew there was more to the conversation than incoming flattery.

"Well, Mr. President," I said, "before you go any further, I have a number of conditions."

I didn't say *demands*. I called them *conditions*. That sounded better, I thought. He didn't seem taken aback. I explained.

"These are conditions that, if they aren't met, it would make no sense for me to take this job because, without them, I couldn't operate effectively for you."

I opened up my briefcase and fetched the legal pad. "Here's the business meeting," Trump said teasingly.

"Here we go. We're gonna do business now. Chris is taking his notes out."

I just nodded.

So I went through the list that Baker had given me.

The right to pick the staff and to manage them. The Jared and Ivanka carve-out. The walk-in rights—mine and the staff's.

Yes, yes, yes, and yes. He agreed to all of those.

Then I got to condition number five, deciding on my own media appearances. That's when Trump shot up straight in the chair.

"No, no, no, no, no," he erupted. "*I* control those."

Uh-oh. Trouble.

I did my best to explain.

"Mr. President," I said. "As White House chief of staff, the only way you get yourself in trouble is if you become too much chief and not enough staff. I don't want to be an out-front public figure in the administration, on TV all the time. I want to be able to work the media behind the scenes for you. I want to be able to do it quietly but persistently and effectively to try and shape the stories you get. And if I'm getting thrown out on the lawn every day to make statements and stuff, my effectiveness is going to be much less."

"No, no, Chris," he countered. "I decide when you go on TV. That's the way this works."

"That's a problem for me," I said.

"Well, go through the rest of them," he said, "and we'll see how we do."

And I did.

My representative on the reelection campaign and the convention. The disagreements settled in private. The weekend home visits. The lawyer on retainer.

Without hesitation, he said yes to all of those.

Melania had been sitting quietly, just listening. For the first time since Donald and I started talking, she spoke up. "I have a question for the governor," she said.

"Sure. What?" Trump asked.

"How are you going to handle Jared and Ivanka?"

He shot her a look that I would describe as the visual equivalent of . . . *whaaat?!*

"What are you asking questions like that for?" he said. "I told you I've dealt with Jared and Ivanka. They're totally supportive of what I'm doing here. I know what I'm doing. This is not going to be a problem for Chris. Why are you bringing that up?"

Melania held her ground. "Donald," she said calmly, "I didn't ask you. I asked the governor."

"I'm not gonna handle them," I replied.

"What do you mean?" she asked.

"I told the president during the transition that I thought it would be a huge mistake to bring any direct family members onto the White House staff," I said, turning then to Trump. "Mr. President, you chose the exact opposite, to bring Jared and Ivanka in and give them high-profile jobs. You know I didn't think that was a good idea because I don't think you should ever hire somebody you can't fire, and you can't fire people you have to have Thanksgiving with."

Trump didn't interrupt me there. So I went on.

"Since you decided to do that, I can't have them answer to me because they *won't* answer to me. Because if I give them an answer they don't like, they're just going to come upstairs to the residence after work is over and convince you otherwise. So I don't want them to report to me. The only way I'll do this is if they report to you. All I'll ask is that, once a week, they each send me an email letting me know what they plan on working on the next week so I make sure nobody else on the staff is stepping on their toes or duplicating their work."

And the president seemed okay with that. More than okay. "That's a great idea," he said. "I like that. That's good. I can do that."

Then Trump changed the subject. "What about the book?" he wanted to know.

As Trump was aware, I had recently finished writing a book called *Let Me Finish*. In the book, I talked about my colorful upbringing in New Jersey and my time as the state's chief federal prosecutor and two-term governor. There was also a lot in the book about Donald Trump. After my own run for the Republican nomination in 2016, I'd been the first major officeholder in America to endorse him for president. I made speeches for him. I prepped him for the debates with Hillary Clinton. At his request, I chaired his transition team, drawing up a detailed plan for the new Trump presidency. Cabinet appointments. Policy initiatives. Executive orders. Everything the new administration needed to get off to a rousing start. Sadly, Steve Bannon, the campaign's senior strategist, and Jared Kushner, Trump's son-in-law, tossed the entire plan in a dumpster and got me fired as transition chief. And that got the new administration off to an unnecessarily rocky start.

It all stemmed from an ancient resentment. When I was the United States attorney in New Jersey, I had prosecuted Jared's father in a sordid family tax-and-fraud case and sent the father to federal prison. I wrote honestly about all of this in *Let Me Finish*, how bitter feelings from the past had come back to haunt a new presidency. Some people came out well in the telling. Some people did not.

The book wasn't out yet as I sat down with the president that night, and no one in the White House had seen it, including Trump. But the book was already at the printer and was due in stores in a little more than a month.

Awkward timing? Yes, it was.

"Is the book critical of me?" Trump asked.

"The book is honest about you," I said.

"But is it critical?"

"No, sir. I wouldn't call it critical. But it's honest about the interactions we had and what went on."

"Is it critical of anyone?" he asked.

Obviously!

"Yes," I said. "It's critical of Steve Bannon. It's critical of Jared. Those are the two biggest ones I'd say it's critical of."

"How bad is it?"

"Well," I said. "I just tell the truth, sir. I blame Jared for having me fired as the head of the transition and for never having wanted me to be in charge at all. And I say that I think he causes a lot of problems around here because he plays outside his area of expertise."

Jared was prepared for that, and so was he, Trump said. "We knew about the book, and he figured it was going to be bad about him. I've already spoken to him about it, and I don't think that's going to be a big deal. Do you have a copy of the book for me to look at?"

"Not with me."

"Maybe I should look at it before we go through with this," he said.

"It's not going to matter," I told him. "I told you exactly what it says. And quite frankly, Mr. President, I don't want it out there. My publisher doesn't want it out there. If I gave it to you, it might fall into the wrong hands."

He just smiled. And we were done.

"I've got to go down to the Christmas party," he said as he got up from his chair.

"Okay."

"So, it's gonna be great, Chris," he said to me. "You and I back together again. We're going to be great. I'm gonna get reelected, and you're gonna be a big part of the reason why."

"Mr. President," I said, "you know Mary Pat. You don't think for a second I can go back home tonight and say to her, 'By the way, I just accepted the second-most important job in the federal government, and you and I never talked about it.' You don't think I can do that, right?"

It was Melania who stepped in, and I appreciated it. "Oh, no," she said. "Not with Mary Pat. You will not do that."

"Exactly, Melania," I said, turning back to the president. "So let's talk tomorrow morning. I promise I'll give you an answer tomorrow morning."

We shook hands. COVID was more than a year away. People still shook hands. And off he went to the party.

"You know your way around here," Melania said to me with a smile as I put my legal pad back in the briefcase. "You can let yourself out."

The media like to portray Melania as chilly and aloof. In my experience, she's always been friendly, warm, and down-to-earth. I know that conflicts with her public image, but it's the Melania I have known since I first got to know Donald Trump.

I was an hour or so into my late-night Acela ride back to New Jersey when my phone suddenly blew up.

Reporters. A lot of them.

I figured I would just ignore the onslaught. For two reasons: I was on the train, and also I didn't know what they were calling about. But from the texts and the emails that were also pouring in, I quickly discovered that Jonathan Swan, a well-wired reporter for the political website Axios, had just posted a story about me.

"Scoop," the headline read. "Trump meets Chris Christie to discuss chief of staff job."

Holy crap! How did Jonathan get that so fast?

Now the other reporters were chasing his scoop. According to the report, "President Trump met with Chris Christie" and "considers him a top contender to replace John Kelly as chief of staff, a source familiar with the president's thinking tells Axios."

This was more than friendly chitchat, the story made clear. "Behind the scenes: Trump has met with a couple of others, but the way he's discussed Christie to confidants makes them think he's serious. Christie is 'tough; he's an attorney; he's politically-savvy, and one of Trump's early supporters,' the source said. 'The former New Jersey governor's legal background may also come in handy next year.'

"Between the lines: Christie is used to being a principal, and it's unclear how he would handle playing second fiddle. Also, he is not a friend of the Kushners. (As U.S. attorney for New Jersey, Christie sent Jared's father to prison.)"

Well, that pretty much summed up the current state of play, didn't it?

Still, I couldn't help but wonder as the train pushed north through Wilmington and Philadelphia. There were only three people in that room at the White House. I knew I didn't leak the story. It seemed highly unlikely to me that Melania did. Who was left? Did Trump really have someone leak that story even before I'd gotten off the train?

Mary Pat and I spoke when I got home. I talked to her about Baker's list and Trump's almost-agreement and his anxious questions about the book. I went to bed thinking I probably wasn't going to take the job because he couldn't agree to all of the conditions that Jim Baker had laid out.

I can't be stupid here, I said to myself. *I have to listen to Baker's advice.*

At seven thirty in the morning, my phone rang again. It wasn't a reporter this time. It was Jared Kushner's soft voice.

"I know about your meeting last night with the president," he said. "And I know what he's offered you. And I'm fine with it. I'm looking forward to it. I'll be supportive of you and supportive of everything you do to help make the president more successful."

"Thank you," I said. "I appreciate that. But I haven't made any final decision."

"What are you going to do?" Jared asked.

I certainly didn't want to go there. Not with Jared. "When I make that decision," I said, "I'd rather communicate that directly to the president, if you don't mind. But thanks for the phone call."

About forty minutes later, Mary Pat's phone rang. It was Ivanka, Jared's wife and the president's first daughter.

All I could hear was Mary Pat's side of the conversation, but she described the back-and-forth to me as soon as she hung up.

After some introductory niceties, Ivanka had said to Mary Pat: "My dad's offered the governor chief of staff. I know there have been problems between the governor and my husband's family in the past. But you have my word, wife to wife, mother to mother, that I will make sure that nothing like that happens if the governor comes here. I'll make sure he has every chance to be successful. I hope you'll encourage him to take the job."

Mary Pat had been taken aback by that. She assured her she would discuss it with me and got off the phone without making any commitments.

By that point, I had pretty much decided there was no way I was going to take this job. And the high-pressure campaign from the next generation, especially Ivanka's call to Mary Pat, wasn't about to convince me otherwise. I didn't need to be the next Paul Revere.

I called Molly at the White House and said to her: "I need to speak to the president."

"He's not downstairs yet," she said. "But let me reach out to him. I know he's expecting your phone call."

As soon as I hung up with Molly, Kellyanne Conway was on the phone. She'd just heard the chief of staff job had officially been offered and urged me to say yes. I didn't tell her for certain I wasn't going to take it, but I gave her every indication so she wouldn't be blindsided when I told the president no. I told her how much I appreciated her early heads-up.

A few minutes after that, Trump was on the line.

"Mr. President," I said, "I've considered everything we spoke about last night. But I just don't think this is the right time for me to do this. So I'm not gonna do it."

Long pause.

"That's not the answer I was expecting to hear," he said.

"I understand that, sir. I'd like to put out a statement right away that says I've withdrawn from consideration so it doesn't appear as if I've turned you down publicly."

"That would be great," he said. "I'd appreciate it if you would do that."

"No problem," I said. "I'll do that as soon as we get off the phone. One thing did intrigue me, though."

"What?"

"That Jonathan Swan story last night."

"What about it?" the president asked.

"Well, there were only three of us in the room. I can tell you for sure I didn't leak it."

He cut me off there. "No, I did," he said.

"Really?" I said. "Who did you have leak it for you?"

"It was a great story, right? It was good for you and good for me. It was good."

"Yeah," I said, "but who did you have do it?"

"I did it myself," he said. He sounded very proud when he said that.

If I had any doubts about my decision, at that moment they entirely disappeared.

CHAPTER 2

TASK FORCE

Every time I said no to one of Donald Trump's job offers, I figured that would be the last one I would ever receive. I certainly didn't expect another one when I turned down the job of chief of staff.

Little did I know.

The chief of staff job went instead to Mick Mulvaney, a former Republican congressman from South Carolina and leader of the House Freedom Caucus. Soon after Trump took office, the staunch fiscal conservative joined the administration as director of the Office of Management and Budget and then, without quitting that job, also became acting director of the Consumer Financial Protection Board, an agency he had railed against constantly as a congressman. When he was named Trump's acting chief of staff in January 2019, Mulvaney still hung on to the budget job.

It was a good idea, hedging his bets like that. Mulvaney would last fourteen months as White House chief of staff before being shipped off to Belfast as U.S. special envoy for Northern Ireland. Mark Meadows, a former Tea Party congressman from North Carolina and founding member of the Freedom Caucus, would become Trump's fourth staff chief.

No, nothing is forever with Donald Trump.

Just as Meadows was about to replace Mulvaney, the president and the First Lady made a whirlwind, thirty-six-hour state visit to India, February 24–25. It was just the kind of foreign travel that Trump loved most: in and out in a hurry on Air Force One and an itinerary packed with grand pageantry. Indian prime minister Narendra Modi really put on a show, including a sunset tour of the Taj Mahal and a mass rally at the world's largest cricket stadium in Ahmedabad. One hundred thousand adoring Indians cheered the American president. Almost all of them had on matching white caps bearing the words "Namaste, Trump," a Sanskrit phrase that means "I bow to you, Trump" or simply "hello, Trump." But when the president got back to Washington, the glow from India didn't last long. The World Health Organization hadn't yet declared the novel coronavirus (COVID-19) a global pandemic. That was still two weeks off. But the president was already being pounded by Democrats and the media for not taking the deadly virus seriously enough. Some of his early quotes were already coming back to haunt him.

"We have it totally under control," he'd said on January 22. "It's one person coming in from China. It's going to be just fine."

"China has been working very hard to contain the coronavirus," he'd said on January 24. "The United States greatly appreciates their efforts and transparency. It will all work out well."

The president did announce travel restrictions on China that went into effect on February 2, a month after the Chinese government first revealed the outbreak. He described the measures as a "ban" that "closed the country," though they blocked U.S. entry only for foreign nationals who had visited China in the previous fourteen days. U.S. citizens and permanent residents were still free to come and go. But it was something, and Trump had done it, and he cited it often when he was accused of not doing enough.

"Looks like by April, you know in theory when it gets a little warmer, it miraculously goes away," he said on February 10.

I understood where the president was coming from. He didn't

want to alarm the American people. He didn't want to take drastic measures that might harm the nation's economy. And personally, his entire brand involved projecting self-confidence. The mask wearing, the crowd avoidance, and the school-and-business shutdowns that public health experts were now calling for—it all sounded weak to Trump.

He was just back from India when I heard from him again. I was in my office when he called.

"I got an idea I want to run by you," he said to me.

"Sure."

Almost a month earlier, Trump had set up a White House Coronavirus Task Force, chaired by Secretary of Health and Human Services Alex Azar. But the task force wasn't doing much, according to Trump, and he wasn't convinced Azar was the right person to be in charge.

"Do you think you'd be willing to come down here and run the COVID task force for me? There's nobody better at dealing with a crisis than you are. Hurricane Sandy, you were the best! Everybody acknowledges that. There's never been a governor who's handled things like you have. Would you be willing to do it for me?"

I was a little surprised to hear him refer to COVID as a crisis, given some of his recent comments. But that was a good sign, wasn't it? Maybe the president was starting to see how huge a threat this was.

"The answer is I probably would be," I told him. "Let me just run it by Mary Pat and make sure that she's supportive."

"Okay," he said. "I'll call you back in a couple of hours. I'll do some more thinking about it too, and you talk to Mary Pat."

Technically, he didn't offer the position to me. He brought it up and said, *Would you consider it?* and I said, *Yeah, I probably would. Let me talk to Mary Pat.* And he said, *Let me think about it some more.*

Mary Pat was at home in Mendham. The office is in Morristown, a fifteen-minute drive. I asked her to come down so we could talk face-to-face. Once she arrived, I said to her: "There's no way I can say no to this. This virus is, I think, a huge national crisis. No one's figured it out yet. But I'm telling you, it's going to be bad. If the president wants me to do this, I have to. I can't say no."

Enough said. Mary Pat was on board. I had no other conditions this time.

I talked to Rich Bagger. A longtime pharmaceutical executive who'd served as chief of staff when I was governor, Rich had joined our consulting firm, Christie 55 Solutions, two months earlier. "If you have to do this, then go do what you need to do," he said. "I'll keep the business going."

Two hours later, Trump was back on the phone.

"I've made a decision," he said. "I think this job is too small and too temporary for you. I want you to be completely available to me for the campaign to help me get reelected. So I've decided to give it to Pence."

Other than me and Pence, he said, he had considered one other person to replace Azar as task force chairman, Dr. Scott Gottlieb, a well-respected physician with considerable government experience who'd been commissioner of the Food and Drug Administration for the first two years of the term. "But I'm leaning toward Pence," Trump said.

"Okay, that's fine with me, Mr. President."

"I don't want you to be disappointed."

"I'm not. This is totally your call. I'm happy to help any way you'd like me to."

And that's where we left it, right there.

That same afternoon, February 26, Trump named Vice President Mike Pence to head the White House COVID Task Force. "Because of all we've done, the risk to the American people remains very low," the president said in announcing the move. "We're going very substantially down, not up."

Questioned by reporters about the fresh alarm from public health experts, Trump continued to downplay the threat. Asked about the fifteen U.S. cases that had been reported so far, the president said: "The fifteen within a couple of days is going to be down to close to zero." He brushed off concerns that too few Americans were tested. "Well, we're testing everybody that we need to test. And we're finding very little problem. Very little problem," adding, "This is the flu. It's like the flu."

But as the president spoke, the outlook was already darkening.

So far, the COVID cases in the United States had all been connected to foreign travel. But that day, the U.S. Centers for Disease Control and Prevention identified a patient in California as the first case of "community spread." He hadn't traveled anywhere. Clearly, this was not just about China anymore. Three days later, a coronavirus patient died in Washington State, the nation's first known COVID death.

Despite the optimism from the White House, others in Washington were far more worried than the president appeared to be. The Federal Reserve, concerned about potential damage to the U.S. economy, slashed interest rates half a percentage point on March 3, the first emergency rate cut in twelve years. Pushing to increase coronavirus testing, the CDC said the next day that clinicians should now "use their judgment" if a patient should be tested.

Clearly, this wasn't just an American problem. Nations were scrambling around the world. On March 11, the World Health Organization declared COVID-19 a pandemic, citing "alarming levels of spread and severity" and also "alarming levels of inaction."

It's not fair to say the president did nothing, as some Democrats and media critics were claiming. On March 11, he added Europe to the restricted-travel list. On March 13, he declared COVID a national emergency, which freed up federal funds. But as I watched in frustration from the sidelines, the crisis was plainly growing worse every day. And he seemed to think that more severe measures might rattle the economy or make him look weak.

More drastic action clearly needed to be taken.

Public health officials were going from concerned to worried to apoplectic. Families, schools, and businesses were putting in their own measures. State and local governments, including some Republican governors, were saying they couldn't wait for Washington. Sixteen states had closed schools already. Carnival, Royal Caribbean, and Norwegian cruise lines had just postponed all their outbound trips for thirty days. New York governor Andrew Cuomo announced a Broadway shutdown of all thirty-one shows until April 13. *Last Week Tonight, Real Time with Bill Maher, The Daily Show with Trevor Noah,* and *Ellen DeGeneres* all suspended production. And all the late-night shows decided, *No studio audiences.* That first night was a bit odd. Stephen Colbert refused to do *The Late Show* and instead aired the rehearsal. He drank bourbon throughout. *Jimmy Kimmel Live!* was guest-hosted in an empty theater by Democratic presidential candidate Pete Buttigieg.

I called Steve Mnuchin, the former Goldman Sachs partner and Hollywood producer who was now the Treasury secretary, definitely one of the worldlier people in the administration, to tell him they needed to get more aggressive in their COVID responses. Having responded to the largest crisis in New Jersey history, Hurricane Sandy, I felt like I knew a bit about how to handle a crisis in public. Mnuchin's basic job was to make sure the American economy thrived. He said he thought I was overreacting.

"Stephen," I said to him, "the sports are getting ready to close in a matter of weeks. They're not going to be able to do this." This was more than conjecture on my part or something I'd just picked up reading the sports pages or watching ESPN. My older son, Andrew, was the coordinator of amateur and international scouting for the New York Mets. Believe me, I was hearing about COVID and the professional sports world every single day.

"The only question," I told Mnuchin, "is are you going to look like you're leading or following? On this stuff, you're gonna want the people to think that you're doing absolutely everything you can do to prevent people from getting sick and dying. There's no risk of overreaction here, certainly not initially. We can be very aggressive in the beginning and pare it back if we've overreached. But we need to do this."

He didn't buy it, either.

I spoke to Alex Azar, the secretary of health and human services. Though he was no longer running the task force, he was still in charge of America's public health system. He had authority over the CDC and the National Institutes of Health, two key agencies in the nation's COVID response.

Azar agreed with me. But he told me he didn't think the president was going to buy it. "I would do all of that," he said. "But the president isn't there yet."

After Azar, I had no one else to call.

That's when I decided I had to speak up publicly. I couldn't sit quietly. I couldn't just make phone calls to Washington. I had to be on the record about this growing threat. Unless the administration changed its course, unless the president turned up the urgency and changed his tone, this was going to end badly. Very badly. For the president. For the nation. For everyone.

I had mentioned my growing concern in a couple of interviews and in my Sunday morning appearances on ABC. But I thought I needed to write something that everyone in Washington would notice, including the president. I wanted to lay out the specifics about what I was convinced needed to be done.

So I wrote an op-ed for the *Washington Post*. The piece ran on March 16, three days after Trump had declared the national emergency without taking any of the necessary follow-up steps. And then I wrote three more op-eds after that. Explaining exactly what I believed the nation and its leaders should do now. It wasn't that my views were all that original. But I hoped the president would listen to me in a way he wasn't listening to others. I tried to be as plain as I could be.

The first piece was headlined: "What Trump must do now to reduce the coronavirus risk."

No equivocating there.

I didn't bash the president. I tried to give him a name to look up to, touting his desire "to protect public health and our economy," adding, "The travel bans from China and Europe have turned off the flow of people from world virus hot spots." I knew he was proud of that. Why not give him credit? But "more must be done," I emphasized. "I fear Americans are not yet taking this virus seriously enough."

In the piece, I wrote about the lessons I'd learned in 2012 from Superstorm Sandy. I cited the importance of "setting the right tone before the hurricane hit" and taking "the most aggressive measures needed to be taken to protect lives."

COVID was way worse, I wrote. "The steps we take—or fail to take—in the coming days will determine just how lethal the disease will be in terms of citizens' lives and the health of our economy."

I singled out the specific actions that Trump absolutely needed to take immediately.

Close schools: "The president should direct governors to close all educational institutions, K–12 and higher education, until at least May 11."

Protect our hospitals: "The stress on our health-care system is not yet calculable, but we should prepare for the worst," including turning other medical facilities into COVID-only care facilities.

Use FEMA money to purchase "ventilators, masks, hospital beds, and other medical supplies to address the coming crisis. None of this will be wasted; they can and should be stored for any future crisis."

Finally—and this was the most controversial at the time: "The president should also direct governors to prohibit attendance at public facilities, including restaurants and bars, until at least May 11, in accordance with CDC guidelines. Exceptions should be made for supermarkets and pharmacies. Public gatherings pose the biggest threat for community spread. There are still too many Americans going out to restaurants, bars, and other public areas as if this is business as usual. It is not. Every public gathering adds to the risk, at least for the next month."

I don't know how much plainer I could have been. And just as important as these specifics, I said, leaders need to set the right tone.

"All public officials, through their words and actions, must reinforce the urgency of the threat," I wrote. "When I told people in New Jersey to 'Get the hell off the beach' in preparation for a hurricane, they knew I meant it and followed my lead. Now is not a time for subtlety. We must forcefully communicate the grave nature of this threat and work together to stop it."

As soon as that column appeared, the president called again. This time, he sounded ready to listen.

"I want you to talk to me about this face-to-face," he said. "I want you to come to Washington."

By this point, most Americans had stopped traveling. People weren't flying. People weren't taking trains. I didn't know what was safe and what wasn't. That was part of the problem. No one in America was getting reliable guidance from Washington.

"Okay," I said. "When do you want me to come?"

"I want you to come now. Whenever you get here, I'll see you."

I couldn't swear it was the *Post* column that did it, even if it had been addressed to him. But something had changed. He sounded ready to listen now.

I threw on a suit. I got into my car. I drove to Washington.

When I got to the White House, he wasn't quite ready to see me.

No one was wearing face masks, including me, though the absence of masks wasn't quite as striking in March as it would be as the year of COVID rolled on. There was still a national shortage of protective gear. Doctors, nurses, and hospital techs were struggling to get what they needed. Dr. Anthony Fauci, the federal government's top infectious disease doctor, was saying that regular people shouldn't go out and buy up all the masks, leaving the medical professionals unprotected. There was a growing sense that masks might be important, but there was certainly no sense of urgency or crisis inside the White House that day.

I saw Kellyanne Conway. She was great, as usual. I saw Jared Kushner. He asked to speak with me before I met with the president. He seemed eager to know what I was going to say.

I repeated what I had said to Trump, to Mnuchin, to Azar, and to the readers of the *Washington Post*. More. More needed to be done. My views on the raging pandemic shouldn't have been a secret to anyone. Then I went into the Oval Office to see the president.

He and I spent an hour and forty-five minutes together, for the most part alone, going over everything. I tried to get him to see the bigger picture and to grasp that now was not the time for defensiveness or tepid responses.

"You're not taking this seriously enough," I told him. "What people want in a crisis like this is for you to be aggressive and to be transparent. They want to see you. They want to hear from you, and they want to know you're being honest with them, even when the news is terrible. I don't think you're doing enough."

I repeated my must-do-now list for him, the steps that had to be taken immediately or more people would die. And I said: "On top of that, I think you need to be more visible. You should go to a plant that's manufacturing PPE and encourage the people to do more and work harder to get more of this out there. Go to a plant that's building ventilators. I don't want you to go to a hospital and put yourself in harm's way, but go to these places and let people see that as president you're in charge of making sure that everything that needs to be done to deal with this crisis is being done. Invoke the Defense Production Act and make these companies convert to manufacturing this stuff. This is a national and international crisis. You don't only need to be doing things that help to solve it. You also need to look like you're doing things. Because in the end, Mr. President, this is the only thing that's gonna matter for reelection. This is the issue that will matter. Nothing else matters like this. So whether we're talking about it on a substantive or political basis, it's the same plan."

The president pushed back on me. He didn't think the problem was as serious as I did. He was convinced the outbreak was going to get better over the summer when the weather got warm. "I don't want to overreact," he said. "I don't want to scare people." More than anything, he didn't want to hurt the economy.

"The things you're talking about would destroy the economy," he told me.

"They're only temporary," I assured him. "Until everybody gets in a rhythm of how to protect themselves, and then we can slowly start to reopen. But there's got to be a period of time where we're not open."

We went back and forth like that, he and I disagreeing on the missing steps. Then, every once in a while, he'd stop and make a phone call.

He called Gavin Newsom, the Democratic governor of California. He told Newsom that California was going to get one of the Navy hospital ships to care for COVID patients.

It was funny, I thought, the way the Republican president spoke to the Democratic governor. "You've been very good to me in public," Trump said. "You've been very nice. I like that. You've said nice things."

I couldn't hear what Newsom said back to him, but I'm sure the governor was happy to get the hospital ship.

Vice President Pence came in at one point and wanted to know what we were talking about. The VP was his typical low-key and understated self, as he had been since I first met him in 2011 when he announced his candidacy for governor of Indiana. He sat with us for a little while, but he didn't say much. Then he got up and left.

I got the feeling the president was listening a little more closely this time, but he certainly never made any commitments to me. Then Trump suddenly looked at his watch. "No wonder I'm hungry," he said. "I haven't eaten dinner yet, and it's quarter to eight. Why don't you come upstairs for dinner?"

I told him I'd like to. "But I can't, Mr. President. I drove myself down here. I have to drive home. I've got a four-hour drive ahead of me."

"All right, all right," he said. "I'll call you. We'll talk more about this."

I left the Oval Office feeling like he had fought me more than he had listened. So I wasn't feeling especially optimistic as I got out of there. I thought it was unlikely that he was going to adopt a fresh tone or a different approach to this fast-moving virus. But before I left the building and got back into my car, I stopped in to see Pence.

Though he'd come in while the president and I were speaking, the vice president hadn't said much. So, I couldn't tell how he was feeling or what was on his mind. And he was, after all, now the head of the White House Coronavirus Task Force.

"I think you guys have to get more aggressive," I said.

Mike Pence isn't big on confrontation. And he avoided it with me.

"Well," he said, "you're the gold standard for handling crises, so I'll definitely take that into account."

What he really thought, I had no idea. But he was unwaveringly loyal to the president and rarely spoke a disagreeable word. He certainly wasn't sharing any sense of alarm with me. His tone was more like, "We'll get this done. No problem. We'll handle it."

But it was not handled. Far from it.

CHAPTER 3

EARLY WARNING

Donald Trump was on his way to losing the presidency.

It wasn't even July yet. I wasn't even an official part of the reelection campaign. But I could already feel the race slipping away. If I could do anything to stop that from happening, I knew I had to try.

His handling of the coronavirus had made him politically vulnerable. But it was his own ill-conceived 2020 campaign that really had the capacity to do him in. As the days got longer and spring gave way to summer, I didn't like what I was seeing at all.

Pre-COVID, I'd been confident that Trump was gliding toward a second term.

His poll numbers were as soft as ever. In a nation as divided as this one, he was never going to be universally beloved. His personality was abrasive. His mere existence instilled loathing in his enemies. And he kept causing headaches for himself and his fellow Republicans. The frequent tweet-storms made people feel uneasy in the midst of a crisis. But that was only half the story. He also had enormous political strengths. His supporters were unshakably loyal. They just loved the guy. His norm-busting behavior. His uncontrollable personality. His let-'em-squirm fearlessness. Yes, all the same things that drove his critics crazy. And the base sure was motivated to vote. They were convinced he understood them, and he certainly had a story to tell. He'd avoided new wars. He'd passed a major tax cut. The economy was roaring ahead. Unemployment was the lowest it had been in decades, including for African-Americans and Latinos. No, a better and cheaper health plan hadn't replaced Obamacare, and Mexico hadn't paid for the wall. But Trump drove the liberals nuts, and "America First" was still a concept millions of people could rally around. Plus, it wasn't like the Democratic field was all that impressive. To a lot of voters, they looked like a motley crew of lefties and wannabes and one tired old guy who used to be vice president.

In the summer of 2018, Mary Pat and I had gone to dinner in the Blue Room of the White House with the president and the First Lady. Just the four of us. Very reminiscent of our years of dinners together in New York City from 2002 to 2014. We discussed many topics that night, and one of them was the 2020 race. The president asked me at one point who I thought would be his toughest opponent. I did not hesitate.

"Joe Biden."

He laughed out loud. "There is no way I'd lose to Joe Biden!" he said. "He is too old and too tired and too boring to win!"

I disagreed with only one of those assertions—that Biden couldn't win.

"Biden will offend very few people," I said. "In the likely Democratic field, he will look moderate and reasonable. And most importantly, Joe Biden will be likeable and nonthreatening. That would not be a good contrast for us."

I was already sensing, in the run-up to the midterm elections, that the country was growing weary.

We discussed it further, and the president continued to disagree with me. He thought Biden was not much of a threat and likely wouldn't make the general election anyway. I later shared my view with other members of the president's team, hoping they could convince him not to take Biden lightly.

Once COVID showed up, the Democratic field seemed less significant, and things got worse and worse.

The virus hadn't magically disappeared with the rising temperatures. It hadn't gone from fifteen cases to none. Despite Trump's repeated assurances, the deadly virus was anything but under control. Hospitals were swamped. Schools and businesses were forced to close. Millions of people were tossed out of work. No one could say when or how the economy was coming back. People hated being so isolated and kept from their normal activities. But they were also frightened to come outside. Local and state officials, both Republicans and Democrats, kept complaining about a lack of direction from Washington.

Back in March, the president had deflected my pleas to take the virus far more seriously. In the four months since then, his rhetoric and some of his actions had been . . . *off.*

Too little. Too late. Too much denial. Not enough fact facing. Too sunny. Too disconnected from the frightening realities of people's everyday lives.

Trump's refusal to wear a face mask made him look stubborn. None of his actions gave Americans the confidence they craved in a crisis that their president was doing everything he could. And now, the reelection campaign was *off,* too.

With son-in-law Jared Kushner and digital jockey Brad Parscale in charge, the campaign had barrels of money, a massive staff, and all the other resources needed for victory. But now that former vice president Joe Biden had nailed down the Democratic nomination, I was growing increasingly convinced that the president was running exactly the wrong campaign.

He was fighting the fight of four years ago.

He was airing tired grievances, not selling a brighter day ahead.

He wasn't explaining how he would lead the country out of this terrible pandemic. He wasn't giving people a clear reason to want four more years of him.

The basic problem, it seemed to me, was that Donald Trump was campaigning like it was 2016 all over again. He was running as an outsider-disruptor—not the president of the United States.

"All right," I said to myself on June 24 as I seethed on my couch in New Jersey with the TV remote in my hand. I was angry about the way things were going, how in my view the president was missing opportunities in his reelection. I could feel it. He wasn't making the case he could be making. I hated the thought of his losing and what that would mean for America.

"What do I do here?" I asked myself. "How do I get involved in this? Do I even *want* to be involved?"

The truth is I did.

I had gone so far with the president already, even though he often frustrated me. I wouldn't bail on him now.

I had helped get him elected four years earlier, the first major officeholder in America to come out for him. I thought he'd be a better president than Hillary Clinton, the almost-certain Democratic nominee. I was sure I could help to make him a better candidate— and a better president if he actually won.

Given all that history, I told myself I had to do what I could.

No matter what happened in November 2020, I wanted to be able to say to myself, "Hey, at least I tried," even if it meant going down to the White House and shaking him by his lapels.

I couldn't just sit there and watch him lose.

I put down the TV remote and picked up my laptop. I opened a new email, and started counting backward in my mind.

The election's November 3. So October 1 is 34 days before the election. September 1 is 64 days. August 1 is 95 days. July 1 is 125 days before the election. And we have six days left in June.

In the email subject line, I wrote: *131 days to go.* Then I started a memo to the president, putting down exactly what was on my mind.

"In 2016," I began, "you were the challenger. A politically unproven but ultra-successful and famous businessman promising to drain the swamp and bring needed change to Washington.

"In 2016, you were facing the personification of establishment D.C. in the form of a former First Lady and former two-term United States Senator. In addition, polls consistently showed that she was very unlikeable.

"In 2016, you combined large rallies (which inspired a strong base) along with a very disciplined final three weeks which laid out a concise plan for the next four years: build a wall, cut taxes, cut regulation, end Obamacare and Make America Great Again. Your opponent did not—she continually attacked you as incompetent and insulted your supporters. She attempted to make the election a referendum on you as if you were the incumbent."

But, of course, it wasn't 2016 anymore. I kept typing. "In 2020," I continued,

> you are the incumbent. Your style and approach are no longer an unknown.
>
> In 2020, you are not running against an unlikeable politician.
>
> In 2020, you are running in the midst of a global pandemic, an economic crisis caused by that pandemic and a racial crisis caused by police brutality. As the incumbent, the American people want a plan to put those crises on the road to being solved. Your opponent needs only to point out your deficiencies; he is not responsible for solutions.

But instead of recognizing these differences, the president was running a time-warp campaign. I tried to explain that to him. "Despite these real and obvious differences," I went on,

> your team is taking the same approach as four years ago and expecting the same result. It will not happen. By taking the same approach, we are making this race a referendum on you rather than a binary choice between you and Vice President Biden. You will lose a referendum race that looks backward under the current circumstances; your best chance of winning is to run a forward-looking optimistic race which relies on your vision for the next four years.
>
> Incumbents who are stuck in yesterday, who insist on looking backward—they lose. Incumbents who lay out a plan for making tomorrow even better win.
>
> America has been knocked down. There is no use in denying that reality.

After such a difficult year for Americans, the president needed to convince people he was the right leader to bring the nation back. "There is no one better to lead the Great American Comeback than Donald Trump," I wrote.

The Great American Comeback. That was the slogan that encompassed what I was talking about. The 2020 campaign needed to drive that message home. Meaning what, exactly? I laid out five bullet points.

> 1. We will restore the American economy by making massive investment in American manufacturing so that America never again relies on any other country for the goods our people need.

2. We will revolutionize our health-care system by getting government out of the way, making telehealth available to every American and bringing Trump leadership to stopping insurance company rip-offs of everyday Americans who need commonsense, affordable healthcare.

3. We will use the money we have saved from ending the endless wars to rebuild every American road, bridge, tunnel and airport that needs it to leave a fabulous America for our children and grandchildren.

4. We will build on our record by appointing even more conservative judges to secure a future for our children that will not have unelected lawyers forcing a liberal agenda on them but judges who will protect our freedom and liberty.

5. We will make America even more secure by continuing to make the American military the best equipped and trained in the world and refusing to go back to the days when our power and authority was weakened and questioned around the world by terrorist organizations and rogue nations.

At every point along the way, I argued, the campaign needed to look forward, not back.

We talk about our record only as proof points for the Great American Comeback plan. Why are we better than our opponent? We have cut taxes. We have cut regulation. We built over 200 miles of the wall we promised. We have appointed more judges than anyone. We built such a strong economy that we could survive a global pandemic and comeback before any nation in the world. That is why our plans for the next four years will get done.

The huge rallies will not work now because Americans are cautious about attending while COVID-19 still lingers. I know you love doing them, but they can only resume when people feel safer. The two-hour speeches addressing every slight or grievance are not what the people want to hear; they want to hear what the next act in this great American play will be for them, not a review of the last one. The foolhardy idea that a good final three weeks will win this election again or that the same approach as 2016 will work again are born out of inexperience and nostalgia.

President Reagan certainly understood, I pointed out.

Ronald Reagan ran a fiery campaign in 1980 against an unpopular incumbent that was heavy on attacks. "Are you better off than you were four years ago?" If he had run the same playbook four years later, even though he was running against that incumbent's Vice-President (very similar to your situation), he would not have won 49 states. Instead, he ran the "Morning in America" campaign, based on the hope for tomorrow based on the accomplishments of today. That is the kind of campaign you must run to win—not the campaign of four years ago. Politically, that was a lifetime ago.

How do we get this to be a choice between your vision for the next four years v. Joe Biden's vision? We must get Biden out of the basement and onto the campaign trail again. That will not be done by attacking and insulting him on Twitter or in speeches. If you do that, he will stay hidden, let you be negative and backward looking and have you run against yourself. A referendum which you undoubtedly would lose.

We get him out by changing tactics. We bait him by being positive. We use the bully pulpit of the White House not for grievance politics but for strong, optimistic proposals like the ones we have detailed above and others. Smaller events in key states that free media will have to cover. We go on a "Thank You" tour of American factories that made ventilators and PPE to assure them that America will rebuild its manufacturing base to grow our economy. We go on a "Thank You" tour of small businesses to let them know we will keep taxes low and regulation out of their lives so they can grow again. We go on a "Thank You" tour of healthcare workers who fought off the pandemic and can spend the next four years providing available and affordable health care to all Americans. We go on a "Thank You" tour of building trades men and women to let them know that they will be on the front lines of our next big fight—the Trump fight to rebuild America.

These new tactics will so unnerve Biden that he will feel the need to leave the basement and respond. He will make mistakes. He will misspeak. He will be negative because that is what his base wants him to be because they are so angry with you. He will then move left to energize them even more. It will give us a number of counterpunching opportunities. Then we have him in a binary race with you and then victory will be in sight. THERE IS NO TIME TO WASTE.

Then, good Jersey guy that I am, I quoted a warning from New York Yankees great Yogi Berra.

As Yogi Berra said, "It is getting late early." Voting begins in some states in 100 days. If we do not change course we will lose.

•   •   •

The memo was a little longer than I'd meant it to be. It ran three full pages. Donald Trump, I knew, wasn't big on memos, especially long ones. But I also knew this was a subject he was interested in—himself and his future and his desire to win a second term. Trump, as you might have heard, likes to win. I thought I had made a strong case for steering the reelection campaign in an entirely different direction. I thought he'd probably read to the end.

As soon as I finished writing, I called his secretary at the White House.

"Molly," I said, "I'm about to email you a memo that is for the president's eyes only. If you can't promise me that you're going to give it only to the president, then I won't send it to you because I don't want to put you in a bad position. Can you do that for me?"

"I will show it to the president for his eyes only," she said.

I pressed *send*.

Molly phoned a couple of hours later. "It has been given to the president," she said.

He called me that night. "I read your memo," he said. "It's really good. It's really smart. It's really strong and it's exactly what I would expect from you. I'm gonna call you tomorrow for us to have more conversations with other people about this. But I think you're right about what we need to do. And I can't thank you enough, Chris, for doing this. Really good job."

"No problem, sir," I said. "I want you to win. I want to help. Whatever you need."

The memo didn't stay president's-eyes-only for long. I didn't expect it to. Campaigning is a team sport. I just wanted to make sure Trump saw the memo first. I didn't want any staff delays. Jared called the next day. *What about this in the memo?* he asked me. *What about that?*

One by one, he began picking apart my key suggestions. "I don't agree with this," he said. "I don't necessarily agree with that."

I wasn't going to argue with him. That seemed pointless. I just said: "Jared, I've run two races for governor and won them. I ran a race for president. I was involved in this one four years ago. I think I know what I'm talking about. You guys can take it or leave it, but that's my opinion."

It was quickly growing clear to me that Jared and his chosen campaign manager Brad Parscale did not want my suggestions. They had no intention of following my plan. I didn't really know what the president thought. He'd said nice things about my analysis, but was he willing to do anything I suggested? I couldn't tell. Was he even capable of running the kind of campaign I was talking about? That was an open question, as well.

I heard from Kellyanne Conway. I heard from Stephen Miller, the president's senior policy advisor and trusted wordsmith. They were both very flattering. Clearly, the memo was being passed around the White House. I heard from Mike Pence.

"The memo's really good," he said. "Thanks for doing it."

But no one did anything about it. Nothing changed at the campaign. Even if they'd wanted to, I'm not sure anyone on staff could have made any of this happen, not if the president didn't want it to. Which makes me believe, looking back, that Donald Trump really didn't want to change the campaign direction. His team was running the campaign he wanted them to run. It was no more complicated than that.

And after a forty-eight-hour flurry of phone calls, the back-and-forth pretty much stopped.

"My conscience is clear," I said to Mary Pat once I was certain my look-forward approach was going nowhere. "I told him exactly what to do. What to avoid. I laid it out for him. It's his life. He doesn't want to do it."

The truth is I don't think he'd given much thought to the idea of a second term, beyond that fact that he wanted one. What would he do if he won? He wasn't really sure. I don't think he was completely comfortable with the idea of basing his future on a plan that he hadn't come up with or given any great thought to. Don't forget, he'd only ever run one race in his life. I'd run three big races in my life, two for governor and one for president. All three of them were different. They had to be. Different times. Different opponents. Different objectives. He'd only run one race, and against all odds, he'd won it.

That was his whole context. He didn't know how to do it any other way. Good luck convincing him to run some other way.

I'm right, and they're wrong.

That was the prism he saw politics through. And there was another blind spot of his. He wasn't taking Joe Biden seriously. He never had.

"He's a tired, weak, old guy," Trump kept telling me as the race shaped up. "He's not even all there. I'm not gonna lose to him." I had been trying to convince him otherwise since the summer of 2018.

I kept trying. "Your vulnerability is with white, college-educated voters," I said, "and he will appeal to them without scaring them. Warren will scare them. Sanders will scare them. Harris will scare them. Biden won't. Biden looks like their uncle or their grandpa, and he's not scary. He's the guy who can flip Pennsylvania, flip Wisconsin, flip Michigan, and if he does that, he's going to be president."

From then until Election Day, he never took Joe Biden seriously, and I don't think he knew how to run any other kind of race than the one he'd run in 2016. He had won by riling up his base and tapping into some deep anxieties and frustrations that other politicians, Republicans and Democrats, failed to understand. He had run in 2016 against a very unlikeable opponent—but that wasn't the case this time.

He was not comfortable running a different kind of race. He'd won this way, and he was going to win this way again.

I continued to say to him: "You never run the same race twice. . . .

The circumstances are never identical. . . . You're different. You're the president now. You're not some long-shot challenger from New York City. You're president of the United States. People view you differently. They expect something different from you."

I never got through to him with that.

But that memo was not the last time I tried.

But that memo actually did something. For the first time since our early-COVID exchange, it put me front-of-mind with him again. He hadn't followed any of my COVID guidance. Now he was skipping my advice on the message of his campaign. But the election was getting closer, and I think he knew there was something to what I was saying about the campaign.

He called me in early July and said to me: "I want you to run debate prep again."

CHAPTER 4

DEBATE PREP

We held our first debate prep session on July 25 at the Trump National Golf Club in Bedminster, New Jersey, an easy thirty-minute drive from my house in Mendham.

We had a small but memorable group that Saturday.

It included Jared, as well as Bill Stepien. He had managed both my campaigns for governor and served as my deputy chief of staff until I fired him amid the Bridgegate scandal, saying I'd lost confidence in his judgment. Stepien had since gone to work as a political aide in the White House and had just taken over as manager of the Trump-Pence reelection campaign, replacing the freshly demoted Brad Parscale, Jared's original choice for the job. Parscale was demoted because of the horrible turnout at the president's first COVID-era rally in Tulsa and because the campaign was stubbornly lagging in the polls. He was the campaign manager. He was on line for both those things.

The group in that Saturday session also included senior campaign advisor Jason Miller, who'd been chief spokesman for the 2016 Trump campaign and, more recently, cohost of the *War Room* podcast with Steve Bannon, who'd fired me as the head of the Trump transition team days after the president won. Bannon had called me into his office that day to fire me, pretending I would just accept my fate without question. Once I told him I was going to tell the media that my sacking had been his decision, he did what most untrustworthy people in politics do—he threw the real culprit under the bus, telling me that it was Jared Kushner who had instructed him to fire me. Still, whatever baggage we all brought to the golf club in New Jersey, everyone was there for the same purpose, to prepare the president for three debates with former vice president Joe Biden. And, in fact, everyone worked together fairly well.

Everyone, that is, except for the man we were all there to help.

The four of us were sitting around a large conference table when the president bounded in after a round of golf with football legend Brett Favre. The president had on dark pants, a white, short-sleeve, knit shirt and a red ball cap with white letters that said "USA." He did not seem pleased to be joining us.

"What the fuck am I doing here?" Those were the first words out of his mouth.

"Debate prep," I reminded him. He already knew that.

"Yeah, but *why* am I doing this?"

"So you'll be ready for Biden," I said. The former vice president had clinched the Democratic nomination on June 2 when he swept the Maryland, Indiana, Rhode Island, New Mexico, Montana, South Dakota, Pennsylvania, and District of Columbia primaries.

You could say I was stating the obvious.

"I know how to do this," Trump declared. "I'm already the president."

Then, he said it again, even more emphatically. "I'm the president! I already know how to do this!"

I had expected this reaction, and I was prepared for it. I went into my briefcase and took out a stack of newspaper articles. The stack was half an inch thick. "When you go home tonight," I said, handing him the articles, "just glance at these."

"What are they?"

"Gerald Ford. Jimmy Carter. Ronald Reagan. George Bush 41. Bill Clinton. George W. Bush. Barack Obama."

Did I forget anyone? I don't think so.

"Every one of them lost the first debate in their reelects," I said. "Every one of them. And you know why? Because they all thought, 'I'm the fuckin' president. I don't need to prepare for this. I don't need to debate what it's like to be president. I *am* the president. Why am I spending time doing this?' And every last one of them lost the first debate."

At least I had his attention now. So, I pressed on. "You, Mr. President, can make history by being the first incumbent president in the modern era to win the first debate. That's what I want to do for you. I want to get you ready to win the first debate."

That seemed to make some kind of impression. "*Hmm*," he said. "All right. I'll look at it." But that still didn't mean he was ready to get down to work. For this day at least, that cause was lost. "If you don't want to be here," I said to him, "we'll give you a few weeks off."

He seemed to like the sound of that.

"Okay," I said. "You let me know when you want to start. I'll begin by reviewing Biden tape and Biden statements and all the rest of that. When you're ready, Mr. President, I will be ready."

I'd have to call our first attempt at debate prep a clear disappointment.

Except for the fact that he took the articles with him when he left and said he *might* look at them, it was an entirely unproductive session, a complete waste of time. We didn't actually do any debate prep. We just argued with him about why he needed to prepare.

We'd been down this road four years earlier, he and I, and we'd both come out smiling when we were done.

Before his first debate with Hillary Clinton, Trump had no clear strategy. Everyone and no one was in charge of preparing him. As a result, Hillary set the tone, and he lost control. Onstage at Long Island's Hofstra University, she accused him of perpetrating a "racist lie" about Barack Obama's birthplace and "stiffing thousands" of blue-collar workers by declaring bankruptcies. He got angry and defensive and looked unprepared. After the debate, he complained about a defective microphone and the "unfair" questions from moderator Lester Holt. To me, Trump sounded like someone who was making excuses because he had lost, which Rudy Giuliani only made worse when he said: "If I were Donald Trump, I wouldn't participate in another debate unless I was promised that the journalist would act like a journalist and not an incorrect, ignorant fact checker."

Thankfully, Trump ignored that Rudy advice.

But even the Fox News poll said 61 percent of Americans thought Clinton had won. Only 21 percent put Trump on top. As political strategist Doug Schoen wrote on the Fox News website, quite succinctly: "Hillary won the first debate (it helps to be prepared)."

That night, as I headed home from Long Island, I got a call from Jared Kushner, asking what I thought. I didn't hesitate. "He lost," I said. "No doubt about it."

Jared told me that Trump was convinced he had won, an assessment Jared said he did not share. "Will you call and tell him he lost?" Jared said to me. "He'll listen to you." I promised Jared I would call. I hung up the phone and thought for a moment about how I should break the news to Trump. But I knew there was only one way. I had to tell him straight out.

When I called, Trump was in his car. He didn't waste any time on pleasantries. "So how did I do?" he asked immediately.

"You lost," I told him.

But 94 percent of Drudge Report readers called him the winner, Trump told me. I said I wasn't impressed. "You should've gotten a hundred percent of those people," I shot back. "They're already voting for you." And that was pretty much the end of that call. It took another two days, but then Trump was back on the phone. I wouldn't say that this time he sounded convinced he had lost, but this was not the same Donald Trump from two days earlier.

"I wasn't as bad as you said I was, but I have to do better," he acknowledged. And he asked if I would take over his prep team for the next two debates.

I told him I'd be happy to.

Together, we really managed to turn it around.

We agreed on some basic themes for him to hammer. America needed stronger leadership. Washington should quit making bad trade deals. Illegal immigrants were taking jobs from hardworking Americans. Trump could get the economy roaring again. He showed up for the next two debates with an actual plan. He mostly executed it. The result? One loss and two wins. The real estate developer and TV host really did hold his own against the former First Lady, senator from New York, and U.S. secretary of state, who'd spent the past four decades navigating the intricacies of politics and government.

Now Hillary was the one on the defensive.

But 2020 was a whole new election and a whole new year. And now that the debate season was getting close again, Trump seemed to have entirely forgotten everything he had learned the last time.

Our debate prep team reconvened at the White House on August 11, a Tuesday. Just getting into the building was a bit of an ordeal. Five months into the COVID explosion, there was no more being waved in by the guards at the gate. This time, a security officer directed me to the Eisenhower Executive Office Building, where the medical unit is, for a rapid coronavirus test. I gave my date of birth, my Social Security number, and other personal information, and was then parked in an examining room. A nurse came in with a cotton swab, which she spun inside my nostrils. I waited fifteen minutes for the results. Only when the test came back negative was I cleared to proceed to the West Wing.

I didn't mind being tested, any more than I minded washing my hands or wearing a face mask. COVID was real, as I'd been arguing since March in the *Washington Post*. It wasn't a hoax. I knew people who'd had it. I knew people who'd died from it. Taking basic precautions seemed perfectly sensible to me, especially for anyone who'd be anywhere near the president. But other than Secret Service agents and the permanent housekeeping staff, hardly anyone inside the White House seemed to be wearing a face mask. I had an all-access security pass. Once I was cleared to go in, I could walk anywhere I wanted to. I saw very few masks.

By then, face masks had become an everyday thing for me and for most Americans. Since March, I'd been slapping one on whenever I left the house. No big deal. But Trump hated the masks. He hated the *idea* of the masks. He hated what he thought they symbolized. "This mask stuff is bullshit," he'd told me more than once. "It looks weak." I wasn't expecting him to wear one for our debate prep sessions, and he didn't.

And I didn't wear one, either.

And neither did anyone else in the room.

Everyone's being tested, I told myself. *It's gotta be safe in here.*

The lineup had grown from the group we'd had at our first session in Bedminster. Bill Stepien was back. So was Jason Miller. But Kellyanne Conway had joined the group now, as had Hope Hicks, who'd been the White House communications director. She had left to work as the corporate spokesperson for Fox and had then returned as counselor to the president, one of his most trusted aides. Stephen Miller was also there. The president's senior policy advisor and main speechwriter, Stephen was a former aide to Alabama senator Jeff Sessions, best known for his hard-line immigration views. And no Jared. We never saw Jared Kushner at a debate prep session again. But the rest of the group—Kellyanne, Hope, Stepien and the Millers, Stephen and Jason (no blood relation)—would become our core debate prep team.

We sat together in the Map Room, which is on the ground floor of the West Wing. Like almost every other inch of the White House, the Map Room exudes history. During World War II, Franklin Roosevelt used it as a situation room with maps to track the war's progress. With its English-style cabinetry and clubby feel, the room is used these days for TV interviews, small teas, and social gatherings.

I knew from our debate prep four years earlier not to bother with fat binders and briefing reports for the president. He would never look at them. And he wasn't going to study papers or memorize figures and facts. Kellyanne and I had come up with what seemed like a more promising strategy. She'd ask questions like a moderator would. I'd play Joe Biden. Everyone else would join us in analyzing the president's answers and offering suggestions. We tried that with him that day and again on August 18. I'm not saying the sessions were totally useless. But I could definitely tell his heart wasn't in it.

Yet.

We took a break for the weeks of the Democratic and Republican conventions, which started August 17 and 24. We picked up again after that. Each time, it felt like we were back at square one.

"What are you doing here?" he demanded at our last session in August. "What do you want now?"

"Um, I'm here for debate prep, and I don't want anything," I said. "You called me to come down."

I shot a glance at the others in the room. "You guys called *me*." I couldn't tell exactly what was preoccupying the president. But it certainly wasn't the upcoming debates.

"Why do I want to be bothered with this?" he said. "I've got other things to do. When is the first one?"

"September 29," I told him. "Five weeks."

"FIVE WEEKS?!" he thundered. "Five weeks is forever! I don't need five weeks to prepare for Joe Biden! I don't need anything like five weeks. I'll be fine."

Another false start.

We agreed to try again after Labor Day.

On September 2, the Commission on Presidential Debates, the bipartisan group that has organized these televised face-offs since 1988, announced that Chris Wallace, the host of *Fox News Sunday*, was going to moderate the first one. Chris was not known for his softball questions. And even though he worked at Fox, he was sure to come at Trump at least as hard as he did at Joe Biden, maybe harder. Either way, he'd be armed with facts and a willingness to drill down with probing follow-ups.

In past elections, the first meeting of the candidates was often the one that mattered most. Anticipation was high. People were curious to see how the two of them would stack up against each other. Despite the months, even years of public appearances that came first, these debates were far less scripted than a campaign rally or a TV ad, giving voters a rare chance to see the candidates live on their feet. Even in boring years—and this was no boring year—the debates always got high ratings and enormous media coverage. This year's editions, ninety minutes each, would be carried live on ABC, CBS, NBC, PBS, CNN, Fox News, MSNBC, and C-SPAN, along with assorted other TV channels, radio networks, and streaming platforms.

Because of COVID, there would be a few new wrinkles this time. For one thing, there'd be no large crowd in the auditorium, clapping and booing at the candidates' answers. The in-person audience would be severely limited—just a few aides, family, and friends. Trump and Biden would share the same stage. But because of the virus, it was agreed that the two men would skip the traditional pre-debate handshake and stand apart from each other throughout the night. The renowned Cleveland Clinic would oversee the health protocols, and the two candidates would both be tested for the virus prior to the event.

When I returned to the White House after Labor Day, the president finally seemed ready to focus. But after twenty-five minutes of Kelly-anne asking questions and me playing Biden, he was done with the question-and-answer drills in the Map Room.

"Let's go to the dining room," he said. "We'll talk in there and watch some tape of Biden."

Jason Miller had pulled together some of Biden's greatest hits. There was video of the vice presidential debates against Sarah Palin in 2008 and Paul Ryan in 2012 and some clips from the early 2020 Democratic primaries. Good Biden. Bad Biden. Times he really seemed to be connecting and times he looked meandering and confused.

Trump watched for about five minutes before he got bored. Then, out of nowhere, he turned to me: "Do you want to know who the worst member of my administration is?"

"Not really," I said.

"No," he pressed, "do you want to know who the worst member of my administration is?"

He seemed intent on telling me. "Sure," I said.

"Your guy. Your guy Chris Wray. He's the worst."

Christopher Wray was director of the FBI. Trump appointed him at my recommendation after he'd fired James Comey in the early days of the Justice Department's Russian-influence probe. I'd known Chris when I was United States attorney and he was the principal deputy attorney general and chief of the Criminal Division in the Justice Department. I had always been impressed by his intelligence, his professionalism, and his work ethic.

"He's really not, Mr. President," I said. "In fact, he's done a great job with the FBI. He's reshaping it, reclaiming it. He's fired all the people who were executive types in the Comey administration. Chris Wray is doing a great job for you."

"No, he's not," Trump said. "He's doing an awful job, and he's your pick. He was *your* pick."

Did the president really have to air this grievance *now*? Kellyanne. Hope. Stepien. Stephen Miller. Jason Miller. All of them were sitting there. All of them were waiting for debate prep to resume, as I most certainly was. "Hold on a second," I said. "He wasn't *my pick*. He was your pick. He was my recommendation. I'm not the president. I don't get to pick. And he's one of the best picks you've made in this entire four years."

"*Bullshit!*" Trump roared. "I don't want to hear it anymore. I'm done. This is over. Turn the video off. I've had enough. We're done for today."

I'd barely been there an hour. But as I followed Stepien, Hope, and Jason Miller to the Roosevelt Room, they looked every bit as frustrated as I felt. "Okay," I said, "we're gonna have to do this differently. We're obviously not getting through to him." Then something occurred to me. "Maybe," I said, "we should do lightning rounds," rapid-fire questions from Kellyanne with quick responses from him and me. Brief. Fast. Keep his attention.

"If you need to do a mock debate, you're weak," I remembered him telling me four years earlier. This might be more effective, I thought.

The difference was mostly semantic. But instead of standing behind a podium for the mock debates, he'd sit at a table for the lightning rounds. And no one was strictly timing his answers, though

Kellyanne and Jason would keep an eye on the clock to make sure he didn't go on forever.

It was worth a try.

The next time we met, when I broached the idea of lightning rounds, the president brightened up.

"When was the last time you answered a question in two minutes?" I asked him. "Do you want to know when it was? It was onstage in Las Vegas, the third debate against Hillary Clinton. You need to get back to practicing that, making a point succinctly. That's what this will help you do."

He seemed to buy it. We tried it. It worked. He wasn't exactly ready to show up in Cleveland on September 29 and debate Joe Biden. But we were making progress at last.

CHAPTER 5

SHOW TIME

It was the last full week in September. The COVID numbers were climbing again. And Joe Biden wasn't running anything like a traditional presidential campaign. Some days, it was hard to tell if he was campaigning at all. He seldom left his house in Wilmington, Delaware. He almost never sat for interviews. His aides kept posting detailed policy statements on the Biden–Harris website. But for a presidential candidate five weeks before the election, Biden was almost invisible, while Donald Trump kept doing things his own way. It struck me that Biden's invisibility strategy, while unfair to the American voters, was smart politics under the circumstances. He was winning. And when you are winning, one thing you want to avoid is any self-inflicted wounds. By not going out and campaigning traditionally, Biden, who has a deeply documented history of misstatements, was avoiding hurting himself.

That Monday, Trump held two raucous rallies in the swing state of Ohio, in Dayton and outside Toledo. On Tuesday, he had a packed rally in Pittsburgh. Asked at a White House press conference on Wednesday if he would commit to a peaceful transfer of power, he answered: "Well, we'll have to see what happens." Contrary to Biden's strategy, Trump seemed to revel in self-inflicted wounds. Not committing to a peaceful transition of power was just the latest one.

On Thursday, he and Melania paid their respects to the late justice Ruth Bader Ginsburg, who died September 18 and lay in repose in the Great Hall of the United States Supreme Court Building. Then he flew to a rally in Jacksonville, Florida, where he told supporters at Cecil Airport: "Joe Biden is weak as hell." Friday, he addressed (in person) a roundtable in Doral, Florida, and a spirited rally in the military and shipbuilding city of Newport News, Virginia.

But starting on Saturday, he was going to be ours again.

I left New Jersey that morning, which was September 26, and drove down to Washington, three days before the Tuesday night debate at Case Western Reserve University in Cleveland. I checked into the Hay-Adams Hotel across Lafayette Square from the White House. We had a packed schedule ahead, six prep sessions in all, one that afternoon, two on Sunday, two on Monday, and a final one on Tuesday, the morning of the debate. As soon as I got to the White House, I had my usual COVID test.

Negative again.

By this point, the pandemic was *the* issue in the race for president. Seven million Americans had already tested positive. The COVID death count had just passed 200,000. After a temporary let-up in the summer, people were taking extra precautions again. We had set aside three hours for our first session. We were back in the Map Room.

Before the president arrived, just to be doubly certain, I canvassed the room. It was the same group as usual. Stephen Miller and Hope Hicks were still on the White House staff. So they got tested regularly as part of their jobs. The rest of us—Kellyanne Conway, Jason Miller, Bill Stepien, and I—were all tested on the way in that day.

Negatives all around.

When the president walked in, he wasn't wearing a mask, and none of the rest of us were. But it wouldn't be correct to say that no COVID precautions were taken. The six of us were at a long table, and he didn't shake hands with anyone. No fist bumps. No back pats. No physical contact at all. He just sat at a shorter table by himself. I was the closest to him, four or five feet away. He had a glass on the table in front of him, his own ice bucket with three bottles of Diet Coke and a dispenser of hand sanitizer.

Before we got started, I said to him: "Mr. President, just so you know, all of us have been tested for COVID, and we all came back negative."

"Good," he said. "I have nothing to worry about."

"Yes, sir," I replied before we got down to the other threat at hand.

Joe Biden.

I'm happy to say we had an excellent session. This time, the president was fully engaged. He was focused. He was sharp. He didn't appear at all resentful about us being there. He answered Kellyanne's moderator questions. He mixed it up with me. We did our lightning rounds on China, immigration, the COVID lockdowns, and reviving the economy, and no one ever used the term "mock debate." He acted like a candidate for high office who wanted to be ready for anything his opponent might throw at him.

Finally.

Trump had a couple of reasons to be in a cheerful mood. That night, he was flying out to Middletown, Pennsylvania, southeast of Harrisburg, for another campaign rally. The polls in Pennsylvania seemed to be tightening, putting the state in reach for him. He loved having the rallies as a regular part of his schedule again. And before he left for Pennsylvania, he had an event in the White House Rose Garden. He was going to introduce Amy Coney Barrett, a judge on the Seventh Circuit Court of Appeals he had decided to nominate for Justice Ginsburg's Supreme Court seat. If confirmed by the Senate, she would be his third justice and would hand the Court's conservatives a solid 6-to-3 majority.

As we were wrapping up our debate prep for the day, he said to us: "Come on, everybody. Come to my Coney Barrett event. It's gonna be great."

The Rose Garden is right outside the Map Room, just across the West Wing colonnade. The six of us walked out together. The nominee and her family were already there. So were Melania Trump and a couple of hundred invited guests, sitting on white folding chairs: Mike and Karen Pence, Attorney General William Barr, Republican senators Mike Lee and Thom Tillis, White House chief of staff Mark Meadows and press secretary Kayleigh McEnaney, University of Notre Dame president John Jenkins, Pastor Greg Laurie of the Harvest Christian Fellowship, and Secretary of Labor Eugene Scalia, whose late father, Antonin Scalia, had been the intellectual powerhouse of the Court's conservative wing. Hardly any of the guests were wearing face masks. I was seated in the third row.

The president welcomed everyone and introduced his nominee. The mood was jovial all around. With less than four months to go in his term, Trump urged a "straightforward and prompt" Senate confirmation. "Should be very easy," he said jokingly. "I'm sure it will be extremely noncontroversial. We said that the last time, didn't we?" He was referring to Brett Kavanaugh's ascent to the Court nearly being derailed by an ancient claim of sexual assault.

Judge Barrett introduced her husband and seven children, who were seated in the front row. She listed some of her other important responsibilities—car pool driver, birthday party planner, and, since COVID, homeschool teacher—and joked that her family left her uniquely prepared to serve on the nation's highest court. "As it happens, I'm used to being in a group of nine."

In the days that followed, that Rose Garden event would be widely characterized as a COVID superspreader, and quite a few of the people who attended would end up testing positive. But I don't think the outdoor gathering was the real infection threat at the

White House that day. I think what happened afterward was actually far more dangerous.

No one was supposed to come inside the White House after the event, except for a small handful of guests who had special passes, primarily the judge's close friends and family. That was by order of Melania. She was concerned about COVID.

Outside was one thing, but the First Lady did *not* want a mob scene in her house.

Well, some members of the staff apparently didn't get the First Lady's directive or didn't pay attention to it, and they invited some of the guests into the Diplomatic Reception Room, which is on the first floor across from the Map Room. All of a sudden, there were a lot of people in there. Not as many as were outside but three or four dozen at least. I wasn't planning to join them. But as I walked by to retrieve my papers from the Map Room and then leave, Kellyanne waved to me.

I didn't feel like lingering. I had to get back to the hotel and change my clothes. I'd agreed to have dinner that night with Alex Azar, the secretary of health and human services, and his family. We had a full day of debate prep planned for Sunday. But when Kellyanne said, "Come here," I went into the reception room.

There were just as few masks as I'd seen outside, and now the people were shaking hands, trading hugs, standing close together, and basking in the excitement of the big nomination. In the era of COVID, of course, everything is riskier inside.

I remember interacting closely with three people.

I spoke with Father Jenkins, the Notre Dame president, whom I knew from the four years my daughter Sarah was a student there. We chatted for a few minutes. I spoke for a while with Judge Barrett, who had already had COVID and was fully recovered. She is an immensely impressive person. Smart, articulate, and very friendly. Her husband and children obviously love her, and she is clearly an involved mother. I had no doubt she'd make great contributions as a justice on the U.S. Supreme Court. My impression was that most objective Americans would really like Amy Coney Barrett. I knew I did.

And then the president called me over. We too spoke for several minutes. He was getting ready to leave for the rally in Pennsylvania. He wanted to make sure I was prepared for the next day's prep session.

"Let's keep making these sessions productive," he said. I was glad he had noticed. "You've got plenty of material," he added.

"I've got plenty of material for all our sessions between now and the debate," I told him. "Don't worry about that."

I could tell he wasn't happy that so many people from the Rose Garden had come inside. I'm not sure whether Melania had complained to him. But she was clearly upset about it when she walked over to me.

"How did all these people get in here?" she asked me. "Do you have any idea?"

I told her I didn't know. "My instructions were clear," I said. "Go back to the Map Room, get my stuff, and leave."

From what I could tell, if the president got COVID that Saturday, it was at one of two places: either in that crowded reception room or at the rally in Pennsylvania. He didn't mix with people at the outdoor reception. He didn't get it from any of us in the Map Room. We had all just been tested.

Unlike him.

The president showed up for all the remaining sessions, mentally and physically. Some were better than others, but overall, I'd say he was considerably more engaged than he'd been at the start. We'd figured out a way to open him to the process.

Whatever you do, just don't call it a mock debate!

Kellyanne put some tough questions to both of us. He and I got into it quite a bit, jabbing back and forth. We yelled at each other a few times. He got angry about stuff I said, channeling Joe Biden, who wouldn't go easy on him. ("Are you ready to apologize for the 200,000 COVID deaths? When will you admit that Mexico isn't paying for your stupid wall?") I got some good zingers in, and he came right back at me . . . as Joe Biden. ("You should take a senility test! You're not all there!")

He definitely enjoyed that one.

When a question was pending, I stayed in character as Biden. Then Kellyanne and I and the others would critique him: "Mr. President, on that last question, you might have said . . ."

One time, I came at him so aggressively, Kellyanne had to stifle a laugh as she whispered to me: "You made that argument with real conviction . . . almost as if you really do disagree."

I forget what the issue was, but she might have had a point.

As we continued working, he seemed to be feeling better about the whole thing. To me, he sounded more confident. "This is good," he said to me at one point. "It's getting me ready."

From time to time, White House chief of staff Mark Meadows wandered into the Map Room. He didn't say much. He would just sit with us for a few minutes and listen before wandering off. Jared must have been busy with other things. We never saw him again after our false start at Bedminster. And there was one other wrinkle as the process rolled on.

Rudy Giuliani.

At two of our six final sessions, Rudy made his way into the room. All Rudy wanted to talk about—all Rudy *wanted the president to debate about*—was Hunter Biden, the former vice president's troubled son who had a lucrative board seat with a Chinese energy firm. Whatever we were working on in the prep session, Rudy kept intervening: "We should be talking about Hunter Biden. We should be preparing answers about Hunter Biden."

No one else agreed that this was a central issue.

The public just didn't know enough about the story yet. Besides making a lot of money for not doing too much, it was hard to explain how exactly the man had behaved corruptly and how that implicated his father in wrongdoing. Not that we didn't think the vice president's son was a legitimate issue. But it wasn't an effective issue for the upcoming debate, a topic Trump could score points with during a thirty- or sixty-second answer. It hadn't been laid out clearly enough for the public to say, "Oh, I know about this. He was with the Chinese."

But Rudy had his teeth sunk in, and he wouldn't let go. Hunter Biden was all he wanted to talk about. To that extent, it was a problem having him there. We were trying to go over the questions that were actually going to be asked, and Rudy kept steering the president off track. It got to the point where Mark Meadows decided that he didn't want Rudy at the prep sessions anymore. The only time the former mayor returned was when the president invited him personally.

For some reason, Trump didn't want to come down to the Map Room for our final run-through on Tuesday morning. So we met in the Oval Office instead, before he left for Cleveland and I returned to the hotel, packed my stuff, and drove to New York. I had to work that night on ABC.

In that final session, we went over what we had talked about already. The importance of concise answers. The need to avoid getting mad. What a strong economy he had built before COVID and how he was itching to do it again, even bigger and better this time.

I reminded the president not to get bogged down on Hunter Biden. "You can sideswipe it," I said, "but don't spend a lot of time on it. The public doesn't understand it, and you're not going to be able to explain it in tonight's debate."

I was getting ready to leave, standing outside the office of Dan Scavino, the president's social-media guru and deputy chief of staff, talking with Dan about what was going to happen that night. I told him I was finally feeling good about the president's readiness. I thought he was in a strong frame of mind.

I also told Dan that I thought we'd done a pretty good job shutting down Rudy's Hunter obsession. "But you know how Rudy can get inside the president's head."

I know Kellyanne also left thinking, *This is going to be a good show tonight.*

As I was standing with Scavino, Molly came over and said to me: "The president would like to see you alone."

I went in, and he was with Mark Meadows.

"Governor," Meadows said to me, "thank you very much for all the hard work you put in to get us ready for tonight. I think it was really well done."

"Thank you, Mark," I said. "I appreciate that."

Mark left. Then it was the president's turn. "Okay," he said to me. "You got one last word? What is it? I'm going upstairs to get a little rest and then head out to the debate."

"Let Biden talk," I said to him. "If he talks long enough, he'll hang himself."

With that, the president gave me a smile and a big thumbs-up.

"Thank you," he said and walked out the door to the colonnade and went upstairs.

•   •   •

I felt optimistic in the car on my way to New York City. I drove directly to the ABC studio on Manhattan's West Side. The debate began in Cleveland at 9 p.m.

What a kick in the gut it turned out to be!

By any objective measure, the debate was a disaster for Donald Trump.

Just awful. Excruciating to sit through.

I sat with George Stephanopoulos and the rest of the on-air team, watching every painful moment on the giant monitors in the studio. It was a bipartisan group. Rahm Emanuel, the former Obama aide and mayor of Chicago. Tech executive Sara Fagen, who'd been a strategist for George W. Bush. Democracy for America CEO Yvette Simpson. ABC anchor Linsey Davis. *World News Tonight* anchor David Muir.

In the ninety minutes of live television, Donald Trump interrupted Joe Biden seventy-three times. What happened to my parting wisdom, "Let Biden talk"? What about, "He'll hang himself"? With Trump's constant hectoring, Biden never got the chance.

Chris Wallace tried to rein in the president. He struggled to restore some civility to the stage. That was hopeless. Wallace then got even more hostile toward the president. The president came out blazing, and he refused to cool down. It wasn't only Trump. Biden interrupted, too. But clearly, Trump did the vast majority of it, and he was the one that everyone was going to blame.

George was rolling his eyes at me like, *What the hell is this?*

Rahm was merciless. "Great job on prep," he kept saying sarcastically.

Sara threw her hands in the air: *What's going on here?*

"Please stop," I kept trying to psychically telegraph to him.

"What are you doing? This is not what we talked about. This isn't what we went over. This isn't how you're supposed to be doing this."

Mortified is probably too strong a word, but I was dumbfounded by the approach that the president was taking, given that we had spent twelve hours with him in the past four days and none of this ever displayed itself. Yes, he'd gotten angry every once in a while, but that never lasted. It came and went in a flash.

It was uncomfortable, to say the least, watching this performance and knowing I had to comment on it afterward. I didn't want to crush the president's performance when we got on the air. But I certainly wasn't going to lie and say "Great job. That's exactly what we intended to do."

As soon as the debate was over and we were live, George turned to me. "Chris Christie," he said, "you helped prepare the president for this debate. Was that the debate you prepared for?"

"No!" I said. "On the Trump side, it was a bit too hot."

I was on ABC to give my honest assessment. The viewers deserved no less, whatever my political allegiances might be.

I had some digs for Biden, too, and he deserved them. "I don't think that's a reassuring performance by the vice president," I said.

"He looked very shaky at many, many times during this debate. His numbers were way off. He would wander off in midsentence, then use lots of name calling and insulting language." But it was my Trump critique that everyone was interested in.

"You come and decide you want to be aggressive, and I think that was the right thing to be aggressive," I said. "But I think that was too hot. . . . With all the heat you lose the light."

Some people in the White House did not appreciate my comments at all, including at least one person who'd been with us all those days in the prep room. I was just off the air when Jason Miller's number showed up on my phone.

"You're killing us with this commentary," he said.

"What did you expect me to say?" I answered. "That was the kindest thing I could have possibly said. 'Too hot.' You guys need to understand. I don't work for you. The president asked me to do this.

I'm doing it for the president, but I'm not going to go on TV and lie and say 'Great debate! He won!' Because he didn't. And by the way, that's not good for Debate Two, where we're going to have to prep him to be better than he was in Debate One."

The next morning, Jared called.

"What did you think?" he asked.

"I think we lost," I told him. "We pretty clearly and decisively lost. Not because of anything Biden did, but because we kept punching ourselves in the face. You can't win that way."

His father-in-law didn't agree, Jared assured me. "He tells us everybody is telling him he won. Have you called him yet?"

"I have not," I said. "I was going to wait until after lunch."

"Call him after lunch and let me know how it goes."

By then, the reviews were really piling up.

CNN's Jake Tapper said Trump's performance was "a hot mess, inside a dumpster fire, inside a train wreck." Tapper's CNN colleague Dana Bash needed only one word: "shitshow." The *New York Times* editorial page called the debate "excruciating" and added: "After five years of conditioning, the president's ceaseless lies, insults and abuse were no less breath-taking to behold."

One line from Joe Biden was quoted almost everywhere, and it had nothing to do with the Democratic nominee's platform or plans. It was his frustrated plea to a president whose style of attack was bordering on the deranged:

"Will you shut up, man?"

In response to all this, there was even talk that the Commission on Presidential Debates would have to modify future debate rules to encourage a more civilized discussion.

I knew I couldn't wait forever. I called the president after lunch.

"Chris, you know last night was great," he said to me. "Everybody thinks I won. Everyone thinks I did a great job."

I took a breath.

"Mr. President," I said, "whoever told you today that you won is lying. They're lying to you because they're afraid of you or they're trying to curry favor with you. I don't know what. But they're lying to you. You did not win. You lost, and you lost fairly decisively because of all the interrupting."

He started to argue with me. "I had to interrupt because he was lying about my record," Trump said. "So I had to interrupt him right away and stop him from doing that."

"But it didn't stop him, did it?" I said. "You have to let him finish his lies and then very methodically you point out the lies to people in a way that, when they're listening to you exclusively, they can understand."

"No, no, no," he countered. "If he's gonna lie about me, I'm gonna hit him right back right away."

I wasn't making any progress. So I tried a less confrontational approach.

"Okay," I said. "But it didn't go well. We're going to have to try something else for the next debate."

"All right," he said. "If you say so. Thanks. Fine."

Clearly, he was disappointed I wasn't giving him rave reviews. Not happy about that at all. Then, he added: "You could have been stronger for me last night on ABC."

That I did not appreciate.

"Sir," I said, "I did the very best I could under the circumstances that you provided."

"All right, Chris," he said finally. "I'll see you at the next session."

But as the crisis of the first debate was coming into stark relief, a whole other drama was unfolding inside the Christie family. I had already been dealing with that one. What I didn't know yet was how quickly the two crises were going to collide.

CHAPTER 6

GETTING IT

Meanwhile, back in New Jersey ...

I wasn't the first member of the Christie family who came face-to-face with COVID-19. That would be Patrick, the younger of our two sons.

On Thursday, September 23, two days before I left for Washington to oversee final debate preparations for the president, Patrick called from Rhode Island, where he had just started his sophomore year at Providence College.

"Both my roommates tested positive for COVID," he said. "I'm supposed to quarantine for fourteen days."

If it was okay with us, Patrick added, he wanted to isolate at home in New Jersey.

Of course.

Though Patrick wasn't feeling any symptoms, he was right to take all this seriously. He'd been in close proximity to two people who'd tested positive for the coronavirus. The CDC recommendations were clear on that: Stay away from others for two weeks after contact.

Quarantining would be almost impossible in a college dormitory. So coming home made total sense. Plus, Patrick, like his father, had lived with asthma since he was in middle school. Both of us knew our lungs weren't the strongest, and we both used inhalers every day.

I was proud of Patrick for being so responsible about the quarantine.

"But I can't go and get him," I said to Mary Pat as soon as Patrick was off the phone. "I'm prepping the president in two days. I can't be potentially exposed to COVID. You'll have to go up there and get him. While you're gone, I'll pack enough clothes for the next week, and I'll stay at the beach house until I leave for Washington." Two years earlier, as soon as I was out of the governor's office, we'd bought a house in Bay Head on the Jersey Shore.

"I'll stay down there and isolate myself," I told Mary Pat. "I can't be exposed to Patrick and risk getting the president sick."

"That makes sense," she said.

I want to be careful about the timeline here because it's important.

Mary Pat drove up to Providence on Thursday afternoon, September 23, and I headed down to the shore. I spent Thursday and Friday by myself in Bay Head and left for Washington first thing Saturday. I had been extra careful and had never been exposed to Patrick. I was going to be around the president.

We had prep sessions on Saturday, Sunday, Monday, and Tuesday morning. I attended the Amy Coney Barrett event and dinner with Alex Azar on Saturday night. Other than that, I just went back and forth between the White House and my hotel room. And every morning before I went back to the Map Room for more debate prep, I stopped at the medical unit to get tested again for the coronavirus, negative every time.

And I felt totally fine.

The president flew out to Cleveland on Air Force One for the Tuesday night debate. I left Washington around 1 p.m. and drove to the ABC studio in Manhattan for my debate night commentary.

Trump did what he did in Cleveland, and I shared my frank assessment with George Stephanopoulos, the debate night panel, and the ABC viewers. When we were finished with our special coverage, I didn't go home to Mendham. Patrick hadn't shown any symptoms, but he was still quarantining there. I drove back to the beach house in Bay Head.

I had been in Bay Head, so I'd been totally isolated from the virus in Mendham.

I'd been at the White House, where everyone was tested.

I'd been at ABC, where the precautions were even more strict. Testing. Careful distancing. And everyone wore masks except when we were live on the set, and even there, George and the other panelists and I all sat far apart.

Other than that, I'd been living like a hermit at the beach house. Okay, a hermit with an ocean view and a backyard pool. But still a hermit.

By then, I had already decided I was going to stay in Bay Head until Patrick went back to Providence, which would be around October 7. "I'm down here," I told Mary Pat when she called on Wednesday morning asking how I was doing and if I needed anything. "I'll be okay. It's fine."

I worked from Bay Head on Wednesday. I slept there Wednesday night. I worked there on Thursday. I was eating dinner by myself on Thursday night when a text came in from Dana Bash at CNN.

"Are you feeling okay?" she asked.

"Yeah, why? Are you okay?"

"Hope Hicks has COVID," Dana said. "Didn't anybody tell you?"

Hope, who had just been with me for four days of White House prep sessions and had traveled with the president to the debate, was one of his closest aides and advisors. She was in and out of his presence constantly.

I called Dana to see what else she knew. "Yeah," she said. "They just announced Hope Hicks has COVID. She's isolating at home. Apparently, she started to feel the symptoms last night on Air Force One on the way back from the rally." After leaving Cleveland, I knew, the president and some of the staff had flown on Wednesday to Duluth, Minnesota, for a small, private, indoor fund-raiser and a large, public, outdoor campaign rally. Hope had been along for all of it.

"It was bad enough that they isolated her while they were flying back in Air Force One," Dana said. "Then they took her off the plane before anybody else and got her back to her apartment. The White House hasn't called you?"

"No," I told the CNN anchor. "Nobody called."

As soon as I said goodbye to Dana, I thought, *Oh, God. I'm gonna have to go for a COVID test now because I've been exposed to Hope.* I wasn't especially worried. *Aware* was more like it. I still felt totally fine.

I called the twenty-four-hour Hackensack Meridian Urgent Care in Brick, a ten-minute drive west of me, and asked if they gave COVID tests.

They did.

I said I'd be there at eight the next morning.

I went to sleep on Thursday night, but I wasn't out for long. Shortly after 1:30 a.m., my phone rang, waking me. It was a producer at ABC wanting me to come on the air right away to discuss the president's diagnosis.

"What are you talking about?" I asked.

"Didn't you hear? The White House just announced that the president and Melania both have COVID."

I'd been dead asleep thirty seconds earlier. I was just hearing this now. "I'm not coming on the air because I don't know anything about it," I told the producer. "It's one thirty in the morning Eastern time. I'm not dressed for TV. I'm not coming on. I've got nothing to say."

"Fine," the producer relented. "You don't have to come on." And I went right back to sleep.

I called Mary Pat as soon as I woke up the next morning. "You saw Hope Hicks has COVID," I said. "And now the president and Melania do, too. I have a test this morning at eight, but I feel fine."

"I was actually going to bring some food down for you today," Mary Pat said. "I made some stuff. I'll just leave it in the garage."

"That would be great," I said. "Thank you."

I got to the clinic at eight. I had no fever and no other symptoms. My temperature was 96.5 degrees Fahrenheit. "You're probably fine," the nurse said to me, "but we'll take the test anyway, just to be sure."

I had the PCR test, the one where they really go up your nose with the long-stemmed cotton swab. It's not the rapid exam, but it's more accurate. "We should have the results within twenty-four hours," the nurse said.

She said I could check the clinic website then.

I thanked her and drove back to Bay Head.

As word spread about Hope Hicks and then the president and the First Lady, I was already getting texts and emails and calls. From friends. From family members. From political people and business associates. All of them were expressing concern and checking on me.

I appreciated it. They all knew I had been at the White House, preparing the president to debate Joe Biden. They didn't know all the particulars. But they figured I'd been hanging around people, at least a couple of whom had now tested positive for COVID-19.

I told everyone who got in touch that I had just been in for a test, but I had no results yet, and so far I was feeling fine.

I didn't hear from anyone official at the White House.

At 9:49 a.m., I opened the Twitter app on my phone and sent out a tweet: "I want to thank all of you who called and texted in the last few hours to check on my health. I feel fine and have no symptoms. I was last tested for Covid on Tuesday, it was negative, and was tested this morning. No results until tomorrow. I'll let you know the results from here."

The TV news and digital media were now wall-to-wall with the president's diagnosis, but some of the basic facts were only trickling in. He'd sent out a tweet at 12:54 a.m., though it provided few details. "Tonight, @FLOTUS and I tested positive for COVID-19. We will begin our quarantine and recovery process immediately. We will get through this TOGETHER!"

What were the president's precise symptoms? How was he feeling now? Did it look like a mild case or one that could put him at genuine peril? Would he be treated by the medical staff at the White House or taken somewhere else? And what about Melania? How was she?

Those were just some of the questions the media were asking. But no one had any answers yet.

White House officials, the ones who were talking, didn't seem to know much. Beyond a few platitudes, no one had a clear assessment of how bad a case the president might have. No one was saying yet what treatment, if any, he would receive.

The media were quoting every imaginable outside expert. But all they seemed to know for certain was that a COVID diagnosis was nothing to mess around with for a seventy-four-year-old man.

It was sometime between one and two on Friday afternoon that I started feeling bad.

My body ached.

I never get headaches, but I could feel a whopper coming on. I gobbled a couple of Tylenols. They did no good at all.

I took my temperature. Now it was 100.4.

Crap! I said to myself. *I have it. I know I have it. I just know it. I don't have the test results yet, but I know I have it.*

Mary Pat arrived in Bay Head. I stood on one side of the garage. She stood on the other.

"Just leave whatever you have," I told her. "Don't come near me. I've got a fever. I'm feeling achy. I think I may have this thing. So stay away."

She didn't need any convincing. "All right," she said.

For the first time since Hope and the president were diagnosed, I could hear it in my wife's voice. She sounded genuinely worried about me.

"Is there anything I can do for you?" she asked.

"No," I told her. "I'll get the results tomorrow morning."

And I went back to bed. The next time I checked, my temperature was 101.5.

At 6:16 p.m., President Trump, wearing a navy blue suit and dark face mask, emerged from the White House residence for the short walk to Marine One, his waiting helicopter. It was the first time he'd been seen in public since he'd announced his positive COVID test sixteen hours earlier. He waved to the media but did not stop to speak. His chief of staff, Mark Meadows, also wearing a face mask, followed the president onto the helicopter for the short flight to Walter Reed National Military Medical Center in Bethesda.

When the helicopter landed and Trump got off, again he said nothing. He saluted his military aides before climbing into a limousine for a brief ride to the hospital's main entrance.

Late Friday night, he posted a short message on his Twitter account: "Going well, I think! Thank you to all. LOVE!!!"

By then, the president's physician, Dr. Sean Conley, had issued the first of what would be a series of upbeat reports. He said Trump arrived at the hospital with minor symptoms—a low-grade fever, chills, a stuffy nose, and a cough. "This evening I'm happy to report that the president is doing very well," Conley said. "He is not requiring any supplemental oxygen, but in consultation with specialists we have elected to initiate remdesivir therapy. He has completed his first dose and is resting comfortably."

The antiviral drug remdesivir was still two weeks away from being approved by the U.S. Food and Drug Administration for the treatment of COVID-19. So the intravenous medication was not yet widely available. But some researchers were already saying it could reduce the symptoms in patients whose COVID was serious enough to require hospitalization. Apparently, there were at least a few doses in the pharmacy at Walter Reed.

I had a rough night's sleep in Bay Head. I pulled myself out of bed on Saturday morning and checked the Hackensack Meridian Urgent Care website for my test results. Nothing yet. Then a doctor called.

"You've tested positive," he told me.

By then, I couldn't say I was surprised.

Right away, I called my own physician, Dr. Rachana Kulkarni, and told her what I had just learned.

"Let me get a consult at Morristown Medical Center," she said. "We'll figure out what we're going to do and how we're going to treat it."

I was definitely feeling worse. Now I was getting chills along with the fever. My headache was pounding even harder than it had before, despite the Tylenol. Then I noticed my quads were burning, too. When I tried to move, I felt a sharp pain in my muscles. And I was starting to sweat. My breathing wasn't terrible, but I certainly couldn't call it strong.

The doctor called me from Morristown Medical Center. Christopher Zipp was his name. I went through my symptoms with him.

I also said: "I'm asthmatic, and I'm overweight."

"Can you drive?" he asked me.

"Yeah, I think I'm okay to drive."

"Are you sure?"

"I think so."

"Are you lightheaded?"

"No."

"Listen to me," he said. There was no equivocation in his voice. "I want you to come right to the hospital. With your comorbidities, we don't want to mess around with this."

I told him I was on my way.

Not having heard anything from the White House, I called Kellyanne and told her I had tested positive. By then, Kellyanne had tested positive, too. She'd announced it on Twitter the night before and was isolating at home in Washington. I asked her how she was feeling.

"Okay, so far," she said. "Just mild symptoms."

But I knew she had to be worried, too. She sounded relieved when I told her I was on my way to the hospital and made me promise to keep her informed.

The media coverage of Kellyanne's diagnosis didn't focus so much on the many hours she and I and a handful of others had spent inside the Map Room preparing the president for the Cleveland debate. But the stories did all mention that she was the fifth person who'd attended the Amy Coney Barrett event (where masks and social distancing were rare) publicly known to have tested positive for COVID-19: That list now included the president, the First

Lady, Utah senator Mike Lee, North Carolina senator Thom Tillis, and University of Notre Dame president John Jenkins.

I knew—and now Kellyanne knew—that my name was about to be added to the list.

I also called the White House chief of staff's office. Mark Meadows was with the president at Walter Reed. But I spoke with his assistant.

"I just want to let you guys know, I just got word that I tested positive for COVID," I said.

She thanked me for calling but didn't say much more.

I got in the car. I put my phone in the charger. And before I backed out of the garage for the drive to Morristown, I thought: *I need to say something public about this.* I opened my Twitter app again.

"I just received word that I am positive for COVID-19," I typed. "I want to thank all of my friends and colleagues who have reached out to ask how I was feeling in the last day or two. I will be receiving medical attention today and will keep the necessary folks apprised of my condition."

My tweet went out Saturday at 11:37 a.m. I had no idea what I was facing next.

It's about an hour and twenty minutes from our house in Bay Head to the Morristown Medical Center.

I'd been on my way just a few minutes when my phone rang. It was our family priest, Monsignor Geno Sylva, who is the rector at the Cathedral of St. John the Baptist in Paterson. He's a longtime friend of ours. He had seen my tweet.

"Are you doing okay?" he asked me.

"I'm headed up to the hospital in Morristown," I said. "I don't feel great, but hopefully it's going to be okay."

"I want to come to the hospital and give you a blessing before you go in," he said.

"*Geno!*" I warned. "I've got COVID! Don't come to the hospital. You could get yourself sick, and I don't want you to do that."

"All right, all right," he said. "You're right. Let's just say a prayer together over the phone."

I'd never been blessed via speakerphone before. But whatever works, right? Monsignor Geno recited a prayer blessing as I cruised up the Garden State Parkway.

"May God heal you and give you strength and protect the doctors and your family. May you come out of this through the intercession of the Blessed Mother. May she watch over you, and may Christ heal you."

"Thank you," I said when he was finished. "I appreciate it." And I truly did.

After we said goodbye, I talked to Mary Pat, to my brother, Todd, to my sister, Dawn, and to my dad, just to let all of them know what was going on. "I'm okay," I told each of them. "We'll see what's going to happen. You can't come to the hospital."

As I got close, I called to let the hospital staff know I'd be there soon. The nurse I spoke to said I should come straight to the emergency room. "There's space there for you to park," she said. "Just leave your car. We'll take care of everything. We're going to bring you in that way." I made sure I had my mask on.

And when I pulled in, who was standing there but Monsignor Geno, right outside the door.

"You don't follow directions very well," I snapped as I got out of the car.

I did notice he had two masks on.

"You're not the governor anymore," he said to me. "You can't order me around."

Standing outside the busy emergency room, with patients, family members, ambulance crews, and hospital staffers streaming in and out, he made a sign of the cross with oil on my forehead and my hands and gave me a special blessing.

"Through this holy anointing, may the Lord in his love and mercy help you with the grace of the Holy Spirit," he said.

Suddenly, all this felt very serious to me.

It had been thirty-six hours since I went for my COVID test, twenty-four hours since I started feeling awful, six hours since I'd gotten my official results. But standing outside the emergency room with Monsignor Geno, this was the first time I had thought about my own mortality.

I couldn't help it.

I was thinking, *Here's this priest, and he's a friend of mine, and he's anointing me with oil and saying these somber-sounding prayers.* A dire thought occurred to me: *I may not get out of here.*

"May the Lord who frees you from sin save you and raise you up," Monsignor Geno said.

I had never been anointed like that before. It wasn't last rites, what the Church used to call *extreme unction*, the final prayers and ministrations given to someone who is just about to die. I wasn't *that bad.* A Sacred Anointing of the Sick, Monsignor Geno called it. But from half a century of Catholicism, I knew that priests don't bring out the sacred oil for every sneeze and hangnail.

All I knew was that my friend, the priest, had this oil, and he gave me a special blessing, and I needed to get inside.

Holy shit! I thought to myself as I thanked him for coming, even though I had ordered him not to. *This is very, very real!*

CHAPTER 7

INTENSIVE CARE

Two hundred and twenty-five miles southwest of me, things were sounding worse at Walter Reed. I wasn't following every fresh development in the president's COVID battle. I had my own to worry about. But I did hear a couple of updates on the radio in the car to Morristown and from the TVs in the background as the hospital staffers checked me in.

Sean Conley, the president's physician, and Kayleigh McEnany, the White House press secretary, kept issuing cheerful-sounding reports. But White House chief of staff Mark Meadows had just briefed journalists outside the hospital in Maryland in a far more dire tone.

"The president's vitals over the last twenty-four hours were very concerning, and the next forty-eight hours will be critical in terms of his care," Meadows said. "We're still not on a clear path to a full recovery."

The next two days could be "tough," the chief of staff added. The president was "not out of the woods." According to Meadows, Trump had a fever and plummeting oxygen levels when he was first brought into the hospital, raising confusion about Dr. Conley's earlier claim that the president didn't need supplemental oxygen.

"A number of us, the doctor and I, were very concerned," Meadows emphasized.

And my COVID journey had just begun.

I knew that some hospitals had struggled with persistent shortages of PPE—medical-quality face masks, latex gloves, tight-fitting goggles, sanitary gowns, and other personal-protective equipment—as the virus swamped their supplies. That didn't seem to be a problem at Morristown, from all I could tell as I was whisked inside. All the medical staffers who came near me looked like they were geared up for a walk on the moon.

I climbed into a hospital gown and turned over my wallet and regular clothes. After a few questions about my symptoms and a quick check of my vital signs, I was informed: "You're going to the ICU."

That certainly sounded ominous. But off we went to the hospital's intensive care unit on the second floor.

This wasn't an open ward like some of the intensive care units I had seen on TV medical dramas. No urgently beeping machinery. No frantic people in white coats yelling, *"CODE RED!! STAT!"* But where I was taken was hyperserious in its own way. There were individual rooms along a hallway and big, thick picture windows so the nurses and techs could look in on the patients without needing to enter the rooms.

These rooms were built for isolation.

Mine had a hospital bed, a TV on the wall, a sink, a rolling table at the bedside, two chairs that no one ever sat in, and a bathroom. I was happy to have my own bathroom. Besides a couple of rolling poles with intravenous lines hanging off of them, that was about it. I'll tell you how concerned the hospital staffers were about me and my contagious condition: Those lines I was hooked up to all snaked out of the room under the door and into the hallway, where the nurses could safely replace my fluid bags, adjust my meds, monitor my vitals, and do almost anything else they needed to without coming into the room and risking that I might sneeze, cough, or breathe on anyone. That was something I'd never seen before.

No visitors were allowed, including family members. Occasionally a nurse or a doctor would come in, covered head to toe in protective gear, maybe three times a day. But for hours on end, I just lay there by myself with only my phone and my worsening symptoms to keep me company. I had too much of a headache to read for any period of time. And watching TV just aggravated me. It wasn't relaxing. I did a lot of sleeping and staring at the ceiling and that was about it. I wasn't in any mood for chitchat, but I was also bored. I felt like total crap. You could now add a profound exhaustion to my growing list of symptoms. But at 5:52 p.m., I put an update on Twitter.

"In consultation with my doctors," I wrote, "I checked myself into Morristown Medical Center this afternoon. While I'm feeling good and only have mild symptoms, due to my history of asthma we decided this is an important precautionary measure. I am thankful for our hardworking medical professionals and look forward to coming home soon."

I didn't want to worry anyone. I knew I was in the best possible hands. But, no, I wasn't exactly feeling "good" at the time and my symptoms were a bit more than "mild." And that was the last public statement of any sort I would make for the next week.

I knew there would be some media speculation about my condition. Some of it had already begun. I didn't want to be confirming or contradicting every claim in real time. I had no idea how I was going to do or how long I was going to be in the hospital or, in my darker moments, whether I would ever go home again.

I turned the TV on and off, then on and off again. I kept looking at the clock on my phone, which was moving very slowly. People called to check on me. I tried to sound upbeat. I let Mary Pat know I'd gotten settled. I mentioned the IV lines out to the hallway and the thick isolation glass. The only reason to be here, I knew, was the prospect of getting better. Though I was in the hands of professionals, nothing seemed to be improving yet.

Then the phone rang.

It was Donald Trump.

Patient to patient. COVID to COVID. Walter Reed to Morristown. President to me.

"How ya doin'?" he said as soon as I said hello.

He did not sound well.

He was clearly having trouble breathing. His voice was raspy. He sounded tired and run-down. The way I was feeling—believe me, I could relate.

"How did two tough guys like me and you get this thing?" he asked me. "How did this thing get to us?"

"Who knows, Mr. President," I answered. "But it's obviously tough, tougher than we are right now. We've just got to fight our way through it."

Then he got to what I came to see was the real point of the call.

"How do you think you got it?" he asked me.

"I don't know," I answered.

There was a pause on the other end of the line. I thought for a second maybe the call had dropped off. But no.

"Are you gonna say you got it from me?" the president asked.

"I don't know that I got it from you, sir," I said. "So I would not say that. No."

He sounded very relieved to hear that. "Okay," he said.

And that was the last call I got in the hospital from Donald Trump.

For the first forty-eight hours I was in the hospital, from Saturday afternoon to Monday afternoon, I didn't improve at all. Actually, I felt like I was getting worse. I still had all the symptoms I'd come in with—the splitting headache, the muscle soreness, the shallow breathing, and now the exhaustion, most of it getting more severe—though I'm not sure exactly where my fever was at that point. My breathing was the thing that worried me most.

The best news so far was that I hadn't been intubated. Not yet, anyway. I knew that's what happened to many COVID patients who couldn't breathe on their own. With my history of asthma and my currently labored breathing, I was terrified the doctors would decide to intubate me. I had a general idea of what that entailed, and I didn't like the sound of any of it. They would slide a tube down my throat in a way that would incapacitate my vocal cords. The other end of that tube would be attached to a ventilator, a machine that would do my breathing for me.

You can't talk when you are intubated. You might or might not be conscious. You are alive, which definitely beats the alternative. But the plain fact of the matter is that many of the COVID patients who were being intubated and hooked up to ventilators were never coming off.

I'm sure the ventilator is a miraculous piece of medical equipment. I'm sure intubation saves lives. But just to summarize: Once you are intubated and on a ventilator, you can't talk anymore, and then you might die.

Is that overly dramatic? Maybe. But that was the scenario that was running around in my head.

I tried to stay positive with the people who called to check on me. I felt like I had an obligation to reassure them. I said I wasn't feeling great, but I was getting good care, and I was sure I'd be okay. Sometimes, as I lay there, saying that even helped me believe it. The only people I really got emotional with were Mary Pat and my friend Greg Brown.

"I'm feeling worse, and I'm worried," I told Mary Pat during the day on Sunday. "If this gets much worse, they are gonna wanna intubate me."

She knew how much I didn't want that.

I said to Mary Pat: "If the doctors want to intubate me, I need a warning before that happens. I'm gonna want to FaceTime with the kids. The tube goes right between your vocal cords. Once they intubate you, you can't talk anymore. I don't want it to happen that I never talk to them again."

That's what was in my head, and that's what I told Mary Pat. Even looking back, I don't believe I was overstating the danger at all.

When you live with asthma, you have trouble breathing anyway. As an asthmatic, you know your lungs are already damaged. There's already scar tissue down there. So if you already have asthma and the virus gets into your lungs, you just don't have the capacity that other people have. It's analogous to being a smoker. The damage has been done to your lungs, and it limits your capacity.

Add COVID into the mix, and it's hard not to worry. If I got on a ventilator, would I ever get off?

Timing was key here, I knew. I didn't want to summon my kids prematurely and alarm them. But I also didn't want to wait too long. "I don't want to do it now," I said to Mary Pat. "But if they tell me I'm close to getting intubated, you need to know I want to talk to the kids."

That was an emotional conversation. Emotional for me and emotional, I know, for Mary Pat. I was lying on my back in the hospital bed, talking to my wife about our children and the prospect of never speaking to them again. Left unsaid, hanging in the air between us, was that I might never see or speak to my wife again. I had to wipe away the tears.

Mary Pat promised that, whatever happened, she would do everything she could to make sure I got a chance to talk to our children. That was the best either of us could do. But it's no exaggeration to say I was petrified. It was Greg Brown, as much as anyone, who got me level again.

Greg's a Jersey guy. He's the CEO of Motorola Solutions.

I got to know him when I was governor. I named him chairman of the Rutgers University Board of Governors, and he's become a good friend. He was one of the people who called to check on me.

"You're too tough not to make it," he said, trying to be encouraging.

"I don't feel that right now," I answered.

"Well," he said, "I'll be praying for you every night."

I'm not sure why that particular comment of Greg's set me off, but it did. I started to well up with tears. "This is not the way I want this to end," I told him.

Greg recognized what I needed to hear.

"Nothing's ending," he said to me. "Listen to me now. You're going to be okay. This is not the way anything is going to end, I'm telling you. I know you. I know how tough you are. You're not going to give in to this. You're just not. You have to tell yourself every day you're not giving in to this. You're fighting, and you're not giving in. That's it. I know you. And when you don't give in, you don't get beat."

From all I could tell, the first order of business at the hospital was mainly about stabilizing me. Getting me isolated. Getting me hydrated. Giving the medical team a chance to gauge my condition.

The doctors would come in and say to me, "You're slightly worse in this eight-hour period, but it could get a lot worse real quick."

The truth is they didn't seem to know what I had ahead of me. "This disease doesn't only go in a gradual line," one of the doctors warned me. "It also goes in a severe line. Right now, you're going gradually, but we really don't know. It could change at any moment, in other words."

They were very careful about the expectations they shared with me and also careful not to promise too much. No one ever said to me: "Oh, don't worry about it. You're going to be fine."

As soon as I was admitted to the ICU, the doctors spoke to me about potential treatments. They wanted to come up with a plan, which I was certainly in favor of. A couple of options seemed to be in the mix, the two main ones being Eli Lilly's monoclonal antibody cocktail and an antiviral drug called remdesivir, which comes from California's Gilead Sciences.

I started on Sunday with the monoclonal antibody cocktail, which is a mix of laboratory-produced molecules that act as substitute antibodies, mimicking the body's immune system and attacking the cells that were wrecking my health. That's how the doctors explained it to me. The treatment hadn't been approved yet by the FDA, but the doctor said, "If you want it, we'll give it to you."

I signed the consent form without hesitation. Yes, I understood that no one knew for sure how effective the laboratory antibodies might be. Yes, I still wanted to take them. The doctors also put me on remdesivir, a five-day course of treatment, taken intravenously, designed to shorten the recovery time in patients hospitalized with COVID-19. That sounded good, too.

Remdesivir and the monoclonal antibody cocktail were not in wide supply at that point. But from what I was told, Morristown Medical Center was part of a trial that gave the doctors and therefore me access. Not too many people had taken the antibody cocktail yet because it was still considered an experimental drug. The trick with the cocktail, it seemed, was to get it early. I'd been in the hospital for about thirty-six hours by then. According to one study I heard about, of the people who got it right after they were diagnosed, the way I did, 75 percent survived. No one ever told me what my chances were without it, but I didn't hesitate a second in saying "Give it to me."

Part of the reason for the short supply might have been that so much money was going to the vital hunt for effective vaccines, there wasn't as much left over for treatment drugs. Clearly, when it came to this pandemic, we were all just learning as we went along: doctors, researchers, patients, family members, politicians, everyone.

I went down the path the medical experts were recommending for me. Who else was I supposed to follow?

President Trump, meanwhile, tweeted late Monday that he was leaving Walter Reed, three days after he'd been rushed there on Marine One. "Don't be afraid of Covid," he told his 88 million followers. "Don't let it dominate your life. We have developed, under the Trump administration, some really great drugs & knowledge. I feel better than I did 20 years ago!"

I had no firsthand knowledge about his current condition. I just watched the video as he walked slowly on and off Marine One and then up the stairs into the White House. His physician, Sean Conley, sounded far more somber than he had when his patient went into the military hospital. The president "may not entirely be out of the woods yet," Conley said. "We're in a bit of unchartered territory when it comes to a patient that received the therapies he has so early in the course."

The president, it turned out, had gotten much the same treatment I was getting, the monoclonal antibody cocktail (his from Regeneron) and a five-day intravenous course of remdesivir. Only now, he'd complete his treatment at the White House, where the Medical Unit can operate as a mini-hospital. Me, I wasn't going anywhere yet. We still had to see now how the treatments would work on me. By Monday night and especially by Tuesday morning, I had the sense I wasn't getting any worse. "It looks like you've plateaued," the doctors began saying to me. "Now let's see if we can get you better from here."

It wasn't a miracle reversal. I wouldn't call it that. But my plateauing, if that's what it was, was still a huge relief.

I spoke to the kids for the first time on Tuesday. It was a warm and loving checkup call. By then, the fever had broken and I was starting to feel better. Mary Pat is the eternal optimist. She would never entertain, to me at least, the possibility that I was going to be anything but better, and that's all she ever said to me.

"You'll be fine. We're good. Don't worry about us. I have everything handled here. You focus on getting better, and you'll be out of there soon. I'm talking to all the doctors. Nobody's telling me that this is going to get that bad. They're all still very hopeful."

One thing I knew was that I wasn't alone . . . in any of this. As I began to turn a corner in my recovery, I heard again from Kellyanne, checking on me. She was doing okay in her own COVID battle, all things considered, she said. But the COVID-positive list from our White House debate prep team was growing longer still.

Bill Stepien called me. He had it.

Stephen Miller called me. He had it, too.

Add their names to a lineup that, besides the president and First Lady, already included Kellyanne, Hope Hicks, and me. Now almost everybody who spent any time at all with us in the Map Room had tested positive for COVID. And all of us were convinced we got it in that room.

The only person in our debate prep group who didn't catch it was Jason Miller. Jason never tested positive. Is he a Superman? Nah, just lucky, I guess.

Though I never heard from the president again while I was in the hospital, the First Lady called or texted me every single day. She also called and texted Mary Pat.

"How's he doing?" she asked. "Is there anything we can do to help? Is there anything you need? . . . Is there anything the White

House doctors can do? . . . Do you want the White House doctors to talk to Chris's doctors?"

And she had it, too. Not hospitalized, but sick. Yet every day she was checking on me.

It reminded me, not that I needed reminding, that Melania was a genuine, caring friend. She appreciated that I had tried to help her husband. As she said to me at one point: "You got sick doing a favor for us."

I appreciated her saying that. It's hard not to like Melania Trump.

I had more flashes of improvement on Wednesday but still just flashes. By Thursday, I could tell I was actually getting better. My headaches had eased. My fever was down, which meant no more sweats and no more chills. I certainly wouldn't miss those. I wasn't as achy as I had been, though my body was definitely sore from lying in that hospital bed all day and night. I was still really, really tired, and my breathing wasn't strong. But I was finally convinced I was going to get out of there, and I was going to be okay. And, no, I wasn't going to end up on a ventilator or have that intubation tube jammed down my throat.

That might have been the biggest relief of all.

They let me out early on Saturday morning, October 10. Finally, I had some good news I could announce to the world.

I launched my first tweet in a week at 9:14 a.m. "I'm happy to let you know this morning I was released from Morristown Medical Center. I want to thank the extraordinary doctors and nurses who cared for me for the last week. Thanks to my family and friends for their prayers. I will have more to say about all of this next week."

And I headed back home.

Not to the solitude of the beach house in Bay Head. Back home to my family in Mendham.

• • •

I wanted to let it all sink in a few days before I started talking publicly about my own bout with COVID. What lessons had I learned? What message did I want to share? Then it struck me: This was a real opportunity. I could use my own hard-earned experience to help others—and to warn them.

Don't let your guard down *ever* until this pandemic is under control.

Wear a face mask. Wash your hands. Socially distance. Do all the things the medical experts said would keep us safer from this virus. Not totally safe. Nothing could do that. But safer.

Don't do like I did, in other words. Don't let your guard down, not even once.

I sat for my first post-hospital interview with George Stephanopoulos on ABC's *Good Morning America*. My decision not to wear a face mask inside the White House had been "a mistake," I said plainly. I'd felt "a false sense of security" and paid a heavy price.

"I was led to believe that, you know, all the people that I was interacting with at the White House had been tested, and it gave you a false sense of security," I said.

And I only had myself to blame.

I said: "I'd been so careful . . . for seven months because of my asthma, wearing masks, washing my hands, social distancing. Fortunately, because of the great medical care I got and I think that all the prayers that I received from a lot of people all over the country, I was able to recover. But it doesn't make it any less a mistake. I was wrong."

Not too many people in public life had spoken out like this from their experience. It was more, I thought, than getting a lecture on the topic from a medical expert. I think a lot of people, including some of my Republican friends, were surprised to hear me say that. But it was the truth, and people needed to hear it.

How many people did that help? I don't know. But I certainly felt a responsibility to try.

So how did I get COVID?

That was the question the president put to me when he called me in the hospital. It's a question I asked myself many times as the hours crept along like days.

The coronavirus doesn't leave fingerprints or DNA markers as it moves from person to person. With this virus, there is no flow-of-infection chart. But there are a few things I know for certain about the week before I started showing symptoms: Except for the time I spent inside the White House, I carefully followed every precaution the medical experts recommended, including separating myself from my family so I wouldn't risk infecting the president.

Then I spent many hours over four days in a closed room at the White House without a mask on, preparing the president to debate. Of the seven people who were in that room—Donald Trump, Kellyanne Conway, Hope Hicks, Bill Stepien, Stephen Miller, Jason Miller, and me—every one of us but Jason got COVID, as did First Lady Melania Trump, who did not participate in the debate prep.

I have discussed this with all the other people on our debate prep team at the White House. I'll let them speak for themselves. But I will say that not a single one of those who got COVID believe they got it anywhere else.

These are people, by the way, who were working around the clock. That's what you do in a presidential campaign. It's unlikely any of them got it anyplace else but in the Map Room of the White House.

And then there's the timing.

I was at the White House on Saturday, Sunday, Monday, and Tuesday. I got my first symptoms midday on Friday. Three to six days: That's almost a textbook incubation period for the coronavirus. Most likely closer to three than to six.

Could I have gotten it during the Amy Coney Barrett event? My doctors said to me that it wasn't likely. Typically, symptoms show up in three to four days. My doctors lean toward the late-in-debate-prep explanation.

The doctors say we will never know for certain, but six days from infection to symptom is longer than usual. Their best estimate is that I got it on one of the later days of debate prep.

Still ringing in my ear is the exchange we had on that Saturday before the debate just after the president sat down in the Map Room to begin our final, four-day push.

"Mr. President," I'd said, "just so you know, all of us have been tested for COVID, and we all came back negative."

"Good," he had replied. "I have nothing to worry about."

The president looked relieved. Little did we know what the seven of us in that room were about to face.

I was the only one of our group who wound up in the hospital, other than the president. Everyone else was able to recuperate at home.

I think Hope was the sickest of the others, but she was thirty-two years old. She was able to bounce back pretty quickly.

Thankfully, I have recovered. Fully. But it really was touch-and-go there for a while. "Your case could have gone either way, and it went the right way," Dr. Zipp told me after I left the hospital.

So what got me through it?

The great care from the doctors and nurses, obviously. The love and support from my family and friends. And all the prayers that were aimed my way. I do not discount that for a minute. We all need prayer, especially when we're lying on our backs in the hospital with a deadly virus no one quite understands.

The doctors said to me they think the monoclonal antibody cocktail really made a difference. The timing convinced me that it did. I began the treatment on Sunday morning, and I started to feel better by Monday night. I would not be classified as a severe case of COVID because, thank God, I was never intubated. But as far as I am concerned, my case was severe enough.

"We'll never really know why you got the outcome you did because of the randomness of this virus and how little clinical information we still have," Dr. Zipp said.

After I left the hospital, I had about four weeks of serious fatigue, serious enough that I had to take a nap in the middle of the day. I had rarely in my life taken a nap in the middle of the day, but now I had no choice. For four weeks, I took a nap every day. And I don't mean a twenty-minute catnap. I don't mean just resting my eyes. Some days, it was three or four hours.

I never lost my sense of taste or smell, the way some COVID patients do. But for months afterward, I kept getting crazy, vivid dreams.

In one dream, I'm spacewalking. Literally spacewalking. I'm in the moon suit. I have on the astronaut pack. I'm coming away from the spaceship, and I'm looking out at Earth.

The first time I had that dream, it was so vivid, it was like I was actually doing it.

I woke up, and I said to myself: "I know I wasn't just doing that . . . but *man*, that was real! Where's Elon Musk?" I felt like I was there! I remember every word of the dialogue.

I was talking to the guys in the spaceship asking them, "How do I get back?"

"Okay, hit this button on your pack," one of them said, "and it'll move you towards there."

"Can I do it backwards?" I asked. "I want to keep looking at Earth."

They were like, "Yeah. You can."

I'm backing the thing up, and I'm doing this stuff. I get back into the spaceship.

If you think you can find a less suitable candidate to be an astronaut, I dare you to try. But at least now I can say "I had the dream."

The main thing that lingers for me from all of this is that I am still mad at myself.

For seven months, I was really strict about everything. I wore my mask. I washed my hands. I stayed away from crowds. I didn't go to restaurants. Unlike a lot of people I knew, I was never in denial about COVID. Anyone who doubted could read my pieces in the *Washington Post* in the spring and summer. That was early, and I was setting the alarms off. *This is bad. Everybody get with it.* I wrote in the newspaper. I said it to the president. So I was never a denier about COVID.

But I'd let my guard down at the White House.

I put too much faith in what I was told there, and I paid a price.

So after I got to the other side I felt like I had an obligation to speak out and tell people that story. I was really good for a long time. I didn't get it. I was bad for four days and I got it. There's no place that's safe. Don't mess around. Take it seriously. I felt like I had to be even more vocal about it. Before, I'd spoken with the belief we all needed to be vigilant. Now I was proof of what can happen when you aren't, even briefly. I had a public platform, and I needed to use it and spread that message.

If people heard it from someone who'd had actually been sick, maybe that message would finally sink in.

CHAPTER 8

LOSING IT

COVID canceled the second debate, the same way it canceled so much else in America that year.

The Commission on Presidential Debates, still jumpy after Cleveland, was insisting on a virtual face-off this time, calling an in-person meeting too risky. The Trump campaign said *no way* to that. Team Biden was happy to let the memories of Cleveland linger on. In the end, neither side seemed all that disappointed about skipping round two. "It is now apparent there will be no debate on October 15," the commission announced six days out. "The CPD will turn its attention to preparations for the final presidential debate scheduled for October 22."

For three reasons, we did almost no preparation for the third debate, which was going to be in Nashville. First, the president was preoccupied. Second, he didn't think he needed to prepare. And finally, he didn't want to do it. So there was no reconvening of the original debate prep team. I did talk with the president—and this was important—about the changes he needed to make in his approach onstage, how he had to lower the volume of his attacks on Joe Biden and let the former vice president be his own worst enemy.

It worked. Trump was better, a lot better, than he'd been in Cleveland. He let Biden talk a bit, which gave the former vice president all the room he needed to drop a couple of real clunkers. Our let-Biden-talk strategy really vindicated itself at the very end of the night when the former veep blurted out, with no prodding from anyone, that he planned to "transition from the oil industry" to combat climate change.

What?!

The media jumped all over that one, as did the rapid-response team from the Trump campaign. Good luck selling that in oil-rich Texas, a state Democrats were dreaming could be theirs this time!

It proved what I'd been saying to Trump all along about the man he was running against: "He's Joe Biden. Even before he was seventy-eight, Joe Biden was likely to misspeak in a live debate. Now that he's seventy-eight and he's still Joe Biden, he'll trip himself up for certain if you give him half a chance." There were smiles and high-fives around the reelection campaign that night, as everyone, Trump included, recognized the difference from the last time. But Trump would never fundamentally change his approach to the race. He insisted on replaying his 2016 campaign, enflaming the base, forgetting suburban voters, and assuming that everyone hated his opponent. That's how he'd won against Hillary Clinton four years earlier. He wasn't running against Hillary Clinton this time, but he was still sure he could win that way again.

And there was nothing I or anyone else could say that would change his mind.

The race wasn't hopeless. He still had a strong connection with a large slice of the electorate, and the polls had always underestimated the depth of his support. But I was feeling mostly pessimistic as election day drew near.

The day before the vote, I was at the supermarket in Mendham. I saw a woman I'd known for many years. She was a Republican who had volunteered for both of my campaigns for governor. She came up to me and said, "Governor, what's going to happen tomorrow?"

This woman had been involved in politics in the county for decades. She was one of the 3.7 million New Jersey voters who'd cast their ballots early this time. "It's going to be closer than people expect based on the polling," I said, "but I think Biden wins."

She looked down at her shoes, and then she said to me: "Well, I support a lot of the president's policies, but I voted for Biden."

"Really?" I have to say I was surprised to hear her say that. "I just can't listen to that voice for another four years," she explained.

When I got home from the supermarket, I told Mary Pat, "If we lost her, we are losing a lot more like her. Trump's losing for sure."

I reported what I'd heard from our friend in the vegetable aisle. "She doesn't want to hear him anymore. She's had enough. If this white, educated, suburban woman in Morris County isn't voting for Donald Trump, he's in big trouble."

So, no, I wasn't feeling optimistic when the polls closed on November 3. I knew I'd voted for the Trump-Pence ticket, but I worried that many of my fellow suburban Republicans might have abandoned the cause.

I spent election night in the exact same place I'd been for the first Trump-Biden debate, in the high-tech ABC News studio on the west side of Manhattan. The same cast of characters was on the air with me: George Stephanopoulos, David Muir, Linsey Davis, Rahm Emanuel, Sarah Fagen, and Yvette Simpson. Because it was election night, we also had live updates from ABC correspondents across the country, reporting in from key swing states. Rahm and I sat next to each other all night, weighing, analyzing, and tossing occasional barbs back and forth. Both of us know this stuff pretty well, including which states and counties to pay the closest attention to. He's been involved in local, state, and national campaigns, as have I.

Early on, Trump looked like he might be pulling off a second win. I was legitimately surprised and then believed it when Rahm looked worried for the first time all night. But as the night wore on and I looked more closely at where the ballots were coming in from and whether they were mail-in or in-person votes, Trump's reelection prospects began to fade. "This is going to even out as the night goes on and not in a good way for Trump," I told Rahm.

He agreed, and he was happy about it. I was not.

A lot of it had to do with the order that each state's votes were being counted. All across the country, the Biden campaign had been urging supporters to vote by mail. By contrast, Trump had been warning darkly that mail-in ballots were the embodiment of election fraud. On both sides, voters seemed to be listening to their preferred candidates.

In Ohio, Biden was initially ahead by a lot. That was because, in that state, the absentee and mail-in votes were counted first. But once the election day ballots were counted, Trump won Ohio by 471,000, nearly 8.2 percent. Pennsylvania was the exact reverse. There the election day ballots were counted first. So, early on, Trump was up by three-quarters of a million votes. Then the mail-in votes were counted, and Trump lost Pennsylvania by 80,000 votes, a spread of slightly more than 1 percent.

It was all in which votes you counted first.

There wasn't anything nefarious about the way the votes were counted. If you counted the mail-in votes first, Biden was ahead. If you counted the machine votes first, Trump was ahead. But the election wouldn't be decided until all the votes were counted. As in every American election, I knew there would be some voting irregularities. But there was certainly no proof that night that any of these irregularities would change the results in any state. These were just the quirks of vote counting on an election night when COVID caused more people to vote by mail than at any time in American history. I am a traditionalist. I like the idea of voting on election day. But vote by mail continues to be an option that many Americans want to avail themselves of. As long as vote by mail is done fairly and ballots are requested by the voters themselves, I am okay with it.

Sitting in the ABC studio, commenting on the state-by-state results as they trickled in, I have to admit I felt the mixed emotions of any roller-coaster ride. Some early hope for Trump, followed by disappointment, followed by resignation, as I saw his chances slip irretrievably away. It wasn't the Biden landslide some pundits had been predicting. There were plenty of close states. It was a stressful election night no matter which side you were on because of how long it took to count the votes. The states were not prepared. The American people deserved better.

The Senate races were going well for the Republicans. The House races were going well for the Republicans. Who knew if they'd end up with a majority in either chamber, but this was no blue tsunami. Voters across the country were responding well to the Republican message and to Republican candidates.

Just not to Donald Trump.

Like my one-woman focus group in the supermarket, they had separated the message from the messenger. They still liked the message, but they were tuning out the messenger and turning out in suburbs in key swing states. The men and women who had made Donald Trump the president-elect four years earlier were decidedly sending him back to Mar-a-Lago four years later.

As I sat in the TV studio absorbing all this, the thought did occur to me. If Trump loses, which seemed to be where this was headed, it would be a particularly personal loss for him.

His party was picking up seats in the House, fifteen of them, not losing seats as almost everyone had predicted. At this point, it looked like the Republicans would remain in control of the Senate, which had also been in doubt. The two U.S. Senate seats up for grabs in Georgia wouldn't be decided until the January 5 runoff. But as midnight passed, Republicans were beating expectations everywhere you looked.

And Trump was losing to Joe Biden just as I feared he might two years earlier.

That result would be very difficult for him to accept.

The way things were looking, a big, blue wave really was crashing that night, just as the political pros had predicted. But it wasn't crashing onto the Republican Party. It was crashing onto Donald Trump alone.

When he came out to speak in front of the cameras at two thirty in the morning, I didn't know what we were going to hear from him. I tried to stay hopeful. Maybe he'd stick to what was actually known, even if he chose to give it his own personal spin. He easily could have said, "It's a very close election. It's late. I'm going to bed. All of you should go to bed. We'll get back together in the morning to see where we are. I'm still very confident we're going to win."

That's what the president could have said to the country, to his supporters and to those who'd backed his opponent. But he didn't say anything like that. Not even close. What he chose to say instead was awful, one of the most dangerous pieces of political rhetoric I have ever heard in my life, certainly from an American president standing in front of the Seal of the President in the East Room of the White House. It was simply irresponsible.

The president came out and declared himself the winner and said that the election was being stolen from him. He and his supporters, he vowed, would not accept the results.

"Millions and millions of people voted for us tonight," he declared. "And a very sad group of people is trying to disenfranchise" them. "We won't stand for it. We will not stand for it."

His speech was untrue and rambling. One grievance ran into

another. He bounced back and forth. But he straight-out called the election "a fraud on the American people."

He said: "This is an embarrassment to our country. We were getting ready to win this election. Frankly, we did win this election. We did win this election. So our goal now is to ensure the integrity for the good of this nation. This is a very big moment. This is a major fraud in our nation. We want the law to be used in a proper manner. So we'll be going to the U.S. Supreme Court. We want all voting to stop. We don't want them to find any ballots at four o'clock in the morning and add them to the list. Okay? It's a very sad moment. To me this is a very sad moment, and we will win this. And as far as I'm concerned, we already have won it."

Where to begin?

I was sitting on the set as he spoke, hanging on his every word, just feeling sick to my stomach, physically sick to my stomach with every new claim. I was thinking, *What is he doing? You can't do that! You can't say that! He'd better have evidence. Where's the evidence? What are the lawyers telling him? Where's the proof? He'd better have proof. Where is it?*

He kept talking, and I kept waiting, and he didn't offer a crumb.

His people had to be looking at the same returns we were. They had to know the votes weren't there. They had to know his reelection was doomed.

Just look at Maine. Republican senator Susan Collins, who'd been down in the polls at various points, won by 10 points while Trump lost Maine by 11. A 21-point spread! That's a lot of Republican voters in Maine who made a conscious decision to vote for Joe Biden *and* Susan Collins.

I understood why he might feel personally angry about that.

He'd been rejected by the very people he thought would save him.

From his words and his cadence, I could tell he was wrapping up his speech, wall-to-wall stolen election and voter fraud. I was still waiting for the first piece of evidence. There wasn't any, and there wouldn't be in his speech. He had decided to enflame the whole country just on his say-so.

I turned to George Stephanopoulos, and I said, "When he's done, whatever you do, you've gotta come to me first."

"What are you going to say?" George asked me.

"Don't worry," I told him. "Just come to me first."

So Trump finished talking, and our live coverage resumed. Just as I asked him to, George came first to me. I did not hold back.

"There's just no basis to make that argument tonight," I said of the president's unsupported claims of a stolen victory. "There just isn't. All these votes have to be counted that are in now. . . . I disagree with what he did tonight."

The president's eruption, I said, was factually wrong, strategically unwise, and beneath the high office that he held.

"There comes a point where you have to let the process play itself out before you judge it to have been flawed," I said. "By prematurely doing this, if there is a flaw in it later, he has undercut his own cred- ibility in calling attention to that flaw. So I think it's a bad strategic decision. It's a bad political decision. And it's not the kind of deci- sion you'd expect someone to make tonight who holds the position he holds."

Presidents just don't talk like that, certainly not without present- ing solid evidence. The damage done by that speech still reverberates across the country today.

I wasn't talking as a former governor. I wasn't talking as some- one who had run for president. I was talking as a former United States attorney who knew the difference between wild claims and fact-based evidence. I simply could not support what the president had just said.

I think the others on the panel might have been surprised to hear me talk like that. A couple of other people spoke, and we went to break.

As soon as the commercials began, my phone buzzed. It was a text from Eric Trump, the president's second son. Eric did not sound pleased.

"You know I'm a straight shooter," he wrote. "Just wait until you see what is popping up."

I wrote back immediately. "You know I'm a straight shooter, too," I said. "I've been a friend for a long time. So if we have evidence, then it should be laid out at the same time we're making the charges. That's my point. The strategic decisions that have been made here on how to communicate since the election night have been wrong. He has a different responsibility as president. If he lays out the evidence of fraud, it will outrage everyone, but you can't bring an indictment *before* you present the evidence, and that's what he did today."

I got no further with his father when we spoke.

The race was called for Biden on Saturday. I called the president, and I said to him: "You should concede the race and say there's going to be a peaceful transition. You can say, 'I'm gonna pursue the legal remedies that I have,' but you should at least commit to a peaceful transition and say if the legal remedies go nowhere, 'I will absolutely engage in a peaceful transition.' Do what Al Gore did. Al Gore fought for another month, thirty-four days. But he always committed himself, that if he didn't win—"

"Nope, nope, nope, nope." Right there, Trump cut me off angrily.

"Chris," he said sharply, "you and I disagree. I'm not going to make any commitment on that at all. This was stolen from me. It's getting worse every day. The evidence is getting bigger every day. The machines were rigged. The mail-in ballots were rigged."

There was no way I was ever going to persuade him. There was no talking to him at all.

What the president's legal team launched next was something no one should ever do in politics. They got busy deceiving the country. There was no other way to look at it. That's what Rudy Giuliani, Sidney Powell, and the president's other lawyers did. Floating the wildest allegations. Accusing people of massive criminality. Pointing the finger of blame at election technology companies. Turning on local and state officials, Democrats and Republicans, and slandering others, living and dead. They did it all without any basis in fact and were quickly dismissed by judges in every state where they challenged the results.

This was terrible.

They were backing the same candidate I had backed. A man I had given his first major endorsement in 2016. A man I had helped to elect the first time and had tried to help again. But the way they went about it was indefensible, even as he was egging them on.

So every chance I got, I kept speaking out against the president's claims in different ways.

"We cannot permit inflammation without information," I said on ABC two days after the election. "Show us the evidence. I want to know what backs up what he said so that I can analyze it. And let me tell you, if he's right, I'll be outraged, and I'm sure you would be, too. . . . And if he's wrong, then the American people are going to be able to make the judgment about this election that the results have been fair."

Speaking just before Christmas, I said the exact same thing to Breitbart News, even more personally.

"I think he's hurting himself, and I think he's hurting the country by keeping it going. . . . I'm a big supporter of the president.

I was the first one of his 2016 opponents to endorse him. We've been friends for twenty years. I prepared him for his debates in 2016, headed his transition in 2016, prepared him for his debates in 2020. But there's no evidence that I've seen that there was fraud that occurred in this election that would change the result, nor have courts all across this country found any such evidence, either. We've continued to hear from people like Sidney Powell that, any day now, we're going to hear about this evidence that's going to blow this whole thing up, and we haven't gotten it."

We never would.

Trump didn't like me talking that way, and believe me, he heard every word of it. He made that clear in our phone calls. He wanted to hear what he wanted to hear, and he didn't want to hear the negative. He brought back into his circle the people who would tell him what he wanted to hear. That included Steve Bannon, the man who'd fired me three years earlier, been fired himself, and was suddenly in Trump's good graces again, collecting a presidential pardon for crimes he had been indicted for by Bill Barr's Department of Justice. That's how small this circle was.

Which ultimately led us all to January 6.

That day, I was working in my home office in Mendham. I had calls. I had Zoom meetings. I had emails to answer and writing to do. I had a business to operate. I didn't tune in for the live TV coverage of the president's "Save America" rally at the Ellipse on the National Mall just south of the White House.

I knew about it. I figured I'd catch up later. But I didn't hear Alabama congressman Mo Brooks tell the thousands who had assembled for the rally: "Today is the day American patriots start taking down names and kicking ass." I didn't hear Donald Jr. warn Republican lawmakers who were inadequately staunch in their defense of his father's election fraud claims: "If you're gonna be the zero and not the hero, we're coming for you."

I definitely didn't hear Rudy Giuliani repeat his conspiracy theories about rigged voting machines or call for "trial by combat," an ominous-sounding term. I knew nothing about a contingent of Proud Boys who left the rally around 11 a.m. and marched toward the U.S. Capitol. I hadn't seen any of it live, but it had all played out in real time on news channels and networks across America.

I was still in my office working, not watching the news, at 11:58 when President Trump came out to the raucous cheers of his supporters and fired up the crowd even more, saying he would "never concede" the election and demanding that Vice President Mike Pence overturn the results.

To be clear: He did not explicitly call on the crowd to use violence or smash their way into the U.S. Capitol. But he did tell his supporters they had the power to keep Joe Biden from becoming president.

He said they should "walk down to the Capitol" to "cheer on our brave senators and congressmen and women, and we're probably not going to be cheering so much for some of them."

He said he'd march to the Capitol with them. He did not, but they started to march there.

Joe Biden would be an "illegitimate president," he claimed, adding, "We can't let that happen."

He quoted himself as saying, " 'Something's wrong here. Something's really wrong. It can't have happened.' And we fight. We fight like hell, and if you don't fight like hell, you're not going to have a country anymore." Then, he added: "You'll never take back our country with weakness. You have to show strength, and you have to be strong. We have come to demand that Congress do the right thing."

Before he finished, he called on the crowd to "fight much harder" against "bad people," saying his supporters were "not going to take it any longer."

Said Trump: "When you catch someone in fraud, you are allowed to go by very different rules."

By the time the president had left the podium at 1:12 p.m., an estimated eight thousand of his supporters had started moving up the National Mall toward Capitol Hill.

"Take the Capitol," some of them shouted.

"Invade the Capitol."

"Fight for Trump."

You know what happened once they got there. It was one of the worst scenes in modern American history, a deadly assault on the seat of our nation's government just as the electoral votes were being tallied to determine the next president of the United States.

I got a call from the special-events desk at ABC News, interrupting my work. They asked if I could come on to discuss the "riot" at the Capitol. I had no idea what they were talking about. I hadn't watched TV all day.

"Well, we need you to come on the air and comment on what's going on," she said.

I flipped the TV on and watched for a few minutes. This time, I could hardly believe my eyes. I was transfixed . . . and not in a good way. I sat there in absolute shock. I never thought I would see American citizens attacking our Capitol. I knew only the president could put a stop to it.

So I called Kellyanne. She sounded as agitated as I was. "Have you spoken to him?" I asked her.

"No," she said. "I'm trying to get through to him."

"We've got to talk to him," I said. "We've got to get him to stop this. He's got to go on camera right away and tell the people to leave the Capitol."

"Exactly," Kellyanne said. "I'm going to try and call him. You try and call him, too."

Kellyanne got farther than I did. She ultimately reached the president after speaking with one of his closest aides and leaving a pretty direct message about what she thought he needed to do—*now*.

Starting with a live TV address demanding that the rioters go home.

I tried to get to him four different ways, directly and indirectly. I went 0-4. I wanted to urge something similar. I also wanted to speak to him before I went on TV because I felt like I owed that to him. But he didn't take the calls. I had to assume he knew what I would tell him, and he didn't want to hear it.

"Okay, fine," I said to myself. "I tried."

I went on the air and said everything I was thinking. All of it.

That Trump had caused the insurrection, and not with his speech outside the White House that day. He started causing it weeks before election day when he kept telling people "the only way we can lose is if the election is stolen from us."

I refuted that view directly.

How it undermined American democracy and divided the nation even more.

How it was no way for a president to behave.

How Trump bore personal responsibility for what his violent supporters did.

To me, the incitement was not one speech. The incitement was also the seventy, eighty, ninety days before that. Claiming that the election was stolen without providing evidence. Promising to provide evidence and then never doing so. I had been speaking forcefully against it, and I wasn't going to stop.

I went on the air at ABC twice that night and said the same things. I knew in my heart that what had happened was avoidable. Donald Trump has been my friend for twenty years.

We've had great times together, and I have agreed with so many of the policies he pursued and achieved. But neither that friendship nor those achievements gives you the right to call a national election a fraud with no evidence.

That night, he put out a too-little-too-late video that didn't clear up anything. A day or so later, he released another video where he finally committed to a peaceful transfer of power. But that was also too late. To me, the president had jumped the shark on election night when he refused to accept the results of the race, making wild accusations about voter fraud and refusing to provide any evidence.

What he did was beneath the office the people had honored him with four years earlier. It struck me that, almost four years to the day, I had sat on those Capitol steps and watched him take the oath of office with such great hope. Now, because of his unsubstantiated claims of fraud, we had lost the White House and, with the runoffs in Georgia, had just lost the U.S. Senate, too. Even worse, the building he'd stood in front of, swearing to uphold the Constitution, was now in disarray and damaged not only physically but also spiritually.

Despite all the good things that Donald Trump had accomplished in his four years as president, his conduct from election day forward, culminating in the riot on Capitol Hill, was going to be a permanent stain on his presidential legacy.

What a disaster! And the president bore personal responsibility.

PART II

CRAZY TALK

Conspiracy theories. Far-fetched scenarios. Evidence-free narratives cooked up in someone's dark imagination or at an internet troll farm in the ancient Russian city of St. Petersburg. Whatever you want to call them, they've always been part of the human experience, purporting to explain things that some people had trouble getting their heads around.

Are hurricanes guided by cloud-seeding airplanes? Was 9/11 an inside job? Did men really walk on the moon? There's always someone peddling a shadowy explanation and always someone ready to buy it. But rarely has American politics been quite so gripped by conspiracy theories as it has been in recent years. From birtherism to Pizzagate to QAnon, these things are everywhere.

Many Republicans may wonder: Why write about this at all? Are we just giving it more attention? It's ridiculous! Other Republicans believe some or all of these. Some because they just want to. Some because they've heard it from someone they trust, admire, or want to believe. But lies left unaddressed tend to fester. The light of truth is still the best disinfectant there is. And for our party to retake leadership, we must dismiss lies (as much as we might like to believe them) and embrace the facts and the truth they lead us to.

The Republicans who firmly believe or have been convinced that some of these propaganda theories are true are almost always very smart, very involved, very passionate people. We need to share the facts with them, all the facts, unfiltered by self-interest, rhetoric, or ego. That's the only way people can potentially reach a different conclusion.

There are some Republicans who have never believed any of this and don't think we should even waste time discussing it. But according to some polls, a majority of Republicans still believe that our party won the presidential election of 2020 and that Donald Trump remains the rightful president. A Reuters survey placed the number at 53 percent in May 2021. Well, put it like this: We still have some work to do. We need to lay out the truth, all the truth, so people can make complete decisions, not ones based only on resentment, wishful thinking, or hero worship.

Of course, no one is claiming the 2020 election was perfectly executed or there were not irregularities in some of our states. That is true, however, of every election. The question for the doubters and conspiracy theorists is whether the problems observed in 2020 were sufficient to call the results of this election into question. The answer is clear to any objective observer. There is simply no proof that this election was stolen. As a former prosecutor, I was trained to focus on the facts. This book is an attempt to help you do the same.

Few people worked harder than I did to get Donald Trump elected in 2016. No one worked harder to keep him in office. But these conspiracy theories don't help him. They don't help us. And they don't put Republicans back on the path to victory.

One other reason to dispense with the conspiracy theories: We must focus on what Joe Biden and the Democrats are trying to do to our country *today*. Profligate spending. Higher taxes. Government overreach into every aspect of American life. A brutal debt burden on our grandchildren. Weakness and capitulation abroad. Crime on our streets. No enforceable border. Liberals set to take over our courts.

Aren't all of these things more important than baseless conspiracy theories?

I'm all for open-mindedness and ardent debate. Those are the foundations of human intelligence. But aligning ourselves to elaborate concoctions is no way to face the challenges ahead of us and no way for our party to start winning again.

So let's deal with some of these conspiracies and lies—one by one—*with the facts*.

CHAPTER 9

RIGHT WAY

There was plenty for me to feel sad about on January 20, 2021, as inauguration day arrived. Joe Biden was being sworn in as America's forty-sixth president and Donald Trump was already back at Mar-a-Lago, stewing about the unfairness of it all. And not just stewing. Still trying vigorously to get the election results overturned. His legal team filling his head with fantastical theories about zombie voters, corrupted machines, and the ghost of Venezuelan strongman Hugo Chávez. Bullying state and local officials, many of them Republicans. Pretending, as some were, that Rudy Giuliani and the crazy Sidney Powell were making rational legal arguments when, in fact, all they were doing was shoveling out the latest paranoid concoctions they had found on the internet or had heard from someone else who was whispering in their ears.

I couldn't imagine that any court in America would take any of this drivel seriously. The president's team was heading down a terrible path now and had been since election night. If they had real theories, I would have been happy to fight alongside them. These theories were outlandish. Hard as it was to imagine, their rantings seemed to be getting even worse.

I was sorry Donald Trump had lost the election. I'd done everything I could to help him both times he ran. Sorry for him and sorry for the country. Joe Biden had run as a fairly mainstream liberal Democrat and he had an inoffensive personality, as I had tried to warn Trump early in the campaign. But Biden was surrounded by ardent liberals, starting with his new vice president, Kamala Harris. He ran as a centrist and was now going to govern as an FDR liberal. He misled the American people. The country, I could see, was in for a very sharp left turn. Joe Biden had not been honest with the voters during the campaign. And unfortunately, the campaign was just the beginning. But, honestly, what else could I have done? I was the first major official to endorse Trump in 2016, soon after I ended my own presidential run. I campaigned energetically for him and prepared him for his debates with Hillary Clinton. I know I helped make him a better candidate and a better president. I told him hard truths when no one else would—and some of the time he even listened. I never took a full-time job in the administration, though he offered me enough of them. But I gave him advice every time he asked me to and sometimes when he didn't. Unfortunately, I never managed to convince him that he shouldn't rely so heavily on his family and, especially, his son-in-law, Jared Kushner. When Trump asked me to prepare him for the debates with Joe Biden, I immediately agreed. I wish he'd listened to more of what I told him before their disastrous first face-off.

But there were limits to what I would do for Donald Trump, and this was a big one: I wouldn't pretend he won the election. I wouldn't indulge conspiracy theories devoid of facts. And I certainly wouldn't jump on a careening crusade, run by the likes of Michael Flynn and Sidney Powell, to have the election results overturned. I said it on ABC at 2:30 a.m. on election night, and I meant it.

Where I come from, friendship is important. Very important. But like I said, there are some things you can't do even for a friend. One of those things is lying to the American people and discrediting the results of a presidential election without the facts to support the claims. Nope, no one owed that to Donald Trump.

One of Donald Trump's strengths and weaknesses as a president was his disconnection from the past. He didn't care about history. He had never read much of it. He certainly had little interest in learning from the hard-earned experiences of those who had come before him. Why should he? He was making his own history every day. That was his view, anyway.

Trump's aversion to history could certainly be a strength. It did not restrict him from doing things *his way*. Past presidents followed certain protocols. He didn't care. He did what he thought worked best for him. Party conventions were supposed to have platforms. Screw that! The Republican platform in 2020 when Trump ran the party was "Vote for Donald Trump." The political pros often shook their heads in amazement, but Trump's approach was totally refreshing to his loyal supporters, who could often be heard saying something to the effect of "Let Trump be Trump."

During the four years of the Trump presidency, it was unprecedented how often the word *unprecedented* was used by the media. Love it or hate it, no one had ever seen any like it before. But not knowing history—and not bothering to learn it—also leaves you vulnerable. You are unable to benefit from the lessons of the past.

The Trump years aren't the first time the Republican Party and its leaders have been beset by hucksters, con men, and extremists, peddling ridiculous conspiracy theories and playing to people's worst impulses, threatening to drive the party's core principles right off the deep end. Sadly, it's not the first time some of the party's so-called leaders have lacked the courage to stand up and speak the plain truth, fearing they might alienate some key supporters. Something very similar happened six decades ago, an era that carries enough similarities to this one that it could have made Trump think twice—had he paid any attention at all. Truly, here was one piece of history that could have helped him avoid some of his worst self-inflicted wounds.

Thank God for William F. Buckley and Ronald Reagan.

Those two, the editor in chief of the *National Review* magazine and the future governor of California, worked together back then to rescue the Republican Party from the looney bin. At an especially dicey time, they responded with boldness and clarity. With a few key allies, they threw the brakes on a runaway train that could easily have wrecked the party's future and doomed Republicans for decades to come. And these efforts paid enormous dividends. Buckley and Reagan sketched out a big-tent vision for the future of the party that helped Republicans elect four presidents (including Reagan), capture the House and the Senate for the first time in decades, and set the terms of American political debate for the next half century.

That's what a couple of well-grounded leaders and the right vision can do.

What the threat was and how they responded is a piece of political history that is vastly underappreciated and very much worth a deep dive now.

The year was 1962, another time the Democrats owned the nation's capital. John F. Kennedy was in the White House. His party held solid majorities in the House and the Senate. It was tough to be a Republican in Washington. Senator Barry Goldwater, a conservative Republican from Arizona, was thinking about running for president in 1964. But he hadn't made up his mind yet. Naturally, he went to see the editor of America's leading conservative magazine. People didn't use the term *thought leader* in those days. But Buckley and the *National Review* were important thought leaders on the American Right. His insights and support would be crucial if Goldwater were going to run against a president as popular as Kennedy, whose approval rating hit a high that spring, of 83 percent.

Goldwater and Buckley met in a suite at the Breakers Hotel in Palm Beach. The conservative writer Russell Kirk was also there, as were General Motors PR man Jay Hall and a couple of other prominent conservatives. They hoped to convince Goldwater that he should run as a strong conservative. But the conversation **didn't** focus on Kennedy's daunting poll numbers, the growing importance of television in politics, or the fading grip of party bosses, all hot topics of the day. Buckley used the meeting to warn Goldwater about a different kind of threat to the conservative cause.

A threat from the inside.

What Buckley referred to as "the Birch fallacy."

The growing influence of an anticommunist group called the John Birch Society.

These were not your garden variety anticommunists, appropriately suspicious about the Russian and Chinese governments the way most Americans were and still are. The Birchers could be downright paranoid, at least as wacky as the truth deniers and conspiracy propagandists of today. And they threatened the Republican Party and the cause of sane conservatism just as severely.

The organization was founded by a retired candy company vice president named Robert Welch. The homeschooled child of fundamentalist Baptists in tiny Stockton, North Carolina, Welch was undeniably bright. He graduated from the University of North Carolina at Chapel Hill when he was seventeen, the youngest and shortest in his class. After growing bored with the United States Military Academy and Harvard Law School, he went to work at a candy company owned by his younger brother, James. Bob was a natural salesman, friendly and gregarious, and he loved to travel. From a factory in Cambridge, Massachusetts, the brothers developed and marketed a popular line of sweets that included Sugar Babies, Junior Mints, and Pom Poms, forever changing the moviegoing experience for generations of Americans. In twenty years, sales at the James O. Welch Company skyrocketed from $200,000 to $20 million a year. Robert Welch retired in 1956, a multimillionaire.

So what was he going to do next? He had always been interested in politics. In 1950, he'd run as a Republican candidate for lieutenant governor of Massachusetts. Lately, he felt like the party had grown too moderate, especially when it came to the threat of communism. America, he concluded, needed a national grassroots organization to advocate against communist influence at home. At a two-day conference in Indianapolis just before Christmas of 1958, he established the John Birch Society, named for a Baptist missionary and U.S. Army Air Forces intelligence captain. Birch had been killed in a confrontation with Chinese communist soldiers while on assignment for the U.S. Office of Strategic Services, the predecessor to the CIA, ten days after the end of World War II.

Welch got busy setting up chapters across the country. Publishing pamphlets. Producing films. Building an anticommunist speaker's bureau. And there was always a strong local focus. "Join your local P.T.A. at the beginning of the school year, get your conservative friends to do likewise, and go to work to take it over," members were advised. Welch's magazine, *One Man's Opinion*, was rechristened *American Opinion*.

By the early 1960s, the John Birch Society was making real inroads and some pretty far-fetched claims. Welch alleged that "50 to 70 percent" of the U.S. government was "communist-controlled." The civil rights movement in the South, he charged, "has been fomented also entirely by the Communists." And Welch's wild theories did not stop there. By this point, he was seeing Stalinist operatives and Moscow dupes around nearly every corner of American life, up to and including the corner of Pennsylvania Avenue and Sixteenth Street in Washington, D.C. What evidence did Welch have for his crackpot theories? Not much, really. Make that *none*. But he kept repeating his claims over and over again.

Does any of this sound familiar?

The American people, Welch was widely quoted as saying, could be divided into four groups: "communists, communist dupes or sympathizers, the uninformed who have yet to be awakened to the communist danger, and the ignorant."

In an especially groundless screed derisively titled "The Politician," Welch called Dwight Eisenhower, the nation's most recent Republican president and a key architect of the Allied victory in World War II, a "dedicated, conscious *agent* of the Communist conspiracy."

President Eisenhower, a communist!? The supreme commander of the forces in World War II, a card-carrying member of the Communist Party? How could anyone believe that?

It was conservative writer Russell Kirk who quoted William F. Buckley's line: "Eisenhower's not a communist. He's a golfer."

The charge was bad enough. Even worse: Once Welch began repeating it, lots of people believed it. And not just the usual out-there characters who linger at the margins of any political movement. The John Birch Society had chapters across the country and backers who included civic leaders, academics, and prominent businesspeople. In Buckley's view, the Republican Party could easily be taken over by this delusional mob. And who knew where that might lead? It wasn't just the communist infiltrators that Welch was railing against. He also wanted to abolish the income tax, impeach Supreme Court chief justice Earl Warren, and get fluoride out of the drinking water.

To make matters worse, all this was personal. Buckley and Welch had been friends. The businessman was an early donor to the *National Review*. Both men had decried the setbacks America had suffered in the early years of the Cold War. The Soviet occupation of Eastern Europe. The frustrating stalemate in Korea. The communist victory in the Chinese civil war. The Castro revolution in Cuba. But they disagreed vehemently about the cause. Buckley blamed misguided U.S. policies and a lack of commitment in Washington. Welch saw something far more nefarious. The Soviet Union, he said, had penetrated the highest levels of the federal government.

Following the Eisenhower attack, Buckley decided he and conservatism had had enough. He was ready to take his old donor on. And he was hoping Goldwater would join him in the fight. But the Arizona senator was reluctant—for reasons that might also sound familiar today.

He didn't want to alienate the base.

Goldwater conceded that Welch's claims were ridiculous. He agreed the Birchers were sure to drive sane people away from the Republicans. *Who'd want to join a party that embraced these falsehoods?* But the Birch membership was strong and growing, Goldwater noted. "Every other person in Phoenix is a member of the John Birch Society," he told Buckley and Kirk.

"I'm not talking about commie-haunted apple pickers or cactus drunks. I'm talking about the highest cast of men of affairs." One of them, Goldwater said, was Phoenix businessman Frank Brophy, who had helped finance the publication of Goldwater's book, *The Conscience of a Conservative*. It all hit close to home.

This was a risky battle to take on. Goldwater certainly didn't want to be the Birchers' next bull's-eye. If he ran for president, wouldn't he need the members' energy and support?

The conversation was lively in Palm Beach that day. Buckley pointed out the dangers of embracing extremism, how that could make the Republican Party unpalatable to anyone in the vast middle of America, the very voters Republicans needed to win. Goldwater emphasized the tightrope he was walking. Finally, the men struck a compromise. Buckley would go first, publicly denouncing Robert Welch and his John Birch Society. Goldwater promised to speak up afterward, making a careful distinction between the group's members and Robert Welch.

Buckley published a blockbuster, five-thousand-word editorial in the *National Review*, calling on his fellow conservatives to speak out against the extremists. This was an act of true bravery. He did what he thought was right, but he had no real idea what the repercussions might be—for himself, for his magazine, or for the cause of conservatism he held so dear. But he laid it on the line.

"How can the John Birch Society be an effective political instrument while it is led by a man whose views on current affairs are . . . so far removed from common sense?" Buckley wrote. "That dilemma weighs on conservatives across America." As was his wont, Buckley opined in sweeping, historical terms. "The underlying problem is whether conservatives can continue to acquiesce quietly in a rendition of the causes of the decline of the Republic and the entire Western world which is false and, besides that, crucially different in practical emphasis from their own."

In English: Republicans must speak up or the party and the world are doomed. We don't believe garbage like this. This is not conservatism.

Once Buckley's editorial ran, Goldwater did indeed write a letter to the *National Review*, backing the editor but also carefully distinguishing between the John Birch Society and its membership. "Mr. Welch is only one man, and I do not believe his views, far removed from reality and common sense as they are, represent the feelings of most members of the John Birch Society," Goldwater wrote. "We cannot allow the emblem of irresponsibility to attach to the conservative banner."

He might have been overly generous . . . or was it overly cautious? For me, it's hard to imagine that the Birch Society members had no idea what group they had joined. And however Goldwater really felt, he pulled back as quickly as he had stepped forward. In a matter of months, he was defending the Birchers again.

"I don't consider the John Birch Society as a group to be extremist," he said. "They believe in the Constitution. They believe in God. They believe in freedom." At the 1964 Republican convention in the Cow Palace outside San Francisco, Goldwater's supporters voted down a plank denouncing the Birch Society. He famously declared in his acceptance speech: "Extremism in the defense of liberty is no vice."

The Birchers loved it, but their continuing presence in the Goldwater coalition continued to alienate open-minded conservatives, not to mention winnable moderates, just as Buckley had predicted they would. And in November when the whole country got to vote, Goldwater was trounced by Lyndon Johnson.

Ronald Reagan didn't come into Republican politics the usual way, and he understood the risks of extremism, wherever it came from. By the time he decided to enter the 1966 race for governor of California, he'd been a strong Democrat, an admirer of Franklin Delano Roosevelt ("a true hero"), an opponent of Republican-backed right-to-work laws, and a seven-term president of the Screen Actors Guild. Oh yeah, and a TV and movie star. But he'd slowly moved right over the years, and one of the main reasons was his growing revulsion for the leftward tilt of Hollywood. Among his many admirable qualities, Reagan was a very early anti-PCer. But that didn't mean he was a Bircher. He applied his skepticism to the left *and* the right. He believed in attracting new people to the conservative cause with openness and persuasion—not finger-pointing, conspiracy theories, or wild accusations. And he understood that the only way for Republicans to win was to find fresh converts.

Reagan and Buckley had met shortly before Buckley launched his campaign against Robert Welch. At the editor's request, Reagan, like Goldwater, wrote a letter backing Buckley's sharp critique, though the John Birch Society was even stronger in California than it had been in Arizona. Among the group's passionate causes: driving sex education out of the Orange County public schools, a field of study that a Birch-affiliate termed—you guessed it—a Moscow-directed plot to corrupt America's youth.

Unlike Goldwater, Reagan did not backtrack.

By the time he was ready to announce for governor, he was still warning his fellow Republicans about a "lunatic fringe" that was gaining influence inside the party, noting his "great disagreement" with John Birch Society founder Robert Welch. Asked whether he would embrace the group's extreme anticommunism, Reagan had a deceptively simple response. "It would be my intention if I seek public office," he said, "to seek the support of individuals by persuading them of my philosophy, not of accepting theirs." And he stuck with it through the campaign. "I am not a member," he said on September 11, 1966, on NBC's *Meet the Press.* "I have no intention of becoming a member. I am not going to solicit their support."

Everyone got the message. *They aren't us.*

Within a week, Reagan's words were being echoed all over Washington. The top Republicans in the House and Senate, House Minority Leader Gerald Ford and Senate Minority Leader Everett Dirksen, called a press conference that Reagan and Buckley could easily have ghostwritten.

"The John Birch Society is NOT a part of the Republican Party," Dirksen said that day. "It never was, and I don't suppose it ever will be. We do not believe in extremism. . . . That is at complete variance with the whole tradition of the Republican Party. We emphatically reject that sort of thing."

Ford seconded the Senate leader. "There is no place for that organization in the Republican Party," he said, calling Welch's group "a monolithic organization that takes its orders from the top."

Reagan's opponent in the governor's race, two-term incumbent Democrat Pat Brown, tried to hang the Birchers around the Republican's neck. "Reagan stands shoulder to shoulder with the extremists who want to halt our progress in its tracks," Brown said the night before the election as Reagan surged in the polls. "He stands for the tired, discredited voices of the past, with the voices of reaction and retreat."

It didn't work. Reagan had already inoculated himself. His rejection of Birch extremism was a help, not a hindrance, to his campaign. He attracted people who didn't usually vote Republican. He didn't let a few zealots drive the commonsense voters away. He won by nearly 1 million votes, 58 to 42 percent. His political career was just getting started. But he already understood that telling the truth, standing up to the lies, and pitching a big tent could carry him all the way to the White House.

This time is different. Of course it is. Every time is different. That's an undeniable truism of history. But my beloved party finds itself in peril now, as we come out of the Trump presidency and try to figure out what's next. We need to get some things straight, in our own minds and in our agenda. Who we are. What we stand for. Which people we want to associate with. Which people we don't. Things are more tribal now than they've been in our lifetimes. Institutions, including political parties, get less respect than they ever have before. The media was never this fractured when Buckley and Reagan were in their prime. But the best way to combat extremism then is still the best way to combat extremism, and bad ideas are still bad ideas. They have to be confronted directly with clarity, confidence, and a commitment to who we are, like Buckley and Reagan did. We have to remind ourselves what we stand for. Conservatism. Strength. Decency. Integrity. Compassion. Competence. The values that brought many of us into the Republican Party in the first place. The values we still try to live by. And we have to rebuff those who try to lure us down rabbit holes, into alliances with awful people and over to the grip of authoritarianism. Today more than ever, we need to fight left-wing extremism. But we cannot do it by embracing conspiracy theories with no facts and those who espouse them. We need to be the truth tellers, and we need to understand how we got here.

How crazy theories invaded our party.

How facts became negotiable and truth was often denied.

How too many Americans came to feel that the politicians didn't understand them.

How too many of our so-called leaders were afraid to stand up for what they knew was right.

How the long sweep of American history was, momentarily at least, pulled off course.

It's a fascinating story and a vital one. But before we can find a way out of this swamp we're in, we need to understand what delivered us here.

CHAPTER 10

HISTORY LESSON

If Donald Trump understood history, he would know this has happened before. Lots of American presidents have run for reelection and lost. He joins John Adams, John Quincy Adams, Martin Van Buren, Franklin Pierce, Andrew Johnson, Chester Arthur, Grover Cleveland, Benjamin Harrison, William Howard Taft, Herbert Hoover, Jimmy Carter, and George H. W. Bush as the unlucky thirteenth member of the "One and Done Club."

All of them won. Then, all of them lost.

You can't count Gerald Ford, who lost to Carter before Carter lost to Ronald Reagan, because Ford was never elected in the first place. He was appointed vice president by Richard Nixon after the resignation of Spiro Agnew. Ford stepped into the top job in the summer of 1974 when Nixon was forced to resign, making Ford the only person to serve as president without first being elected as either president or vice president. He's a special case.

In defeat, most ex-presidents have never sought public office again, but there are a couple of exceptions to the slink-away-quietly rule—more than a century before Trump. Neither of them contested their defeats the way Trump has, but Presidents Martin Van Buren and Grover Cleveland, both former governors of New York, returned to fight another day and got exactly opposite results.

A close ally of Andrew Jackson and one of the founders of the Democratic Party, Van Buren had also served as secretary of state and vice president when he was elected America's eighth president in 1836. But the economy quickly soured with the Panic of 1837, and Van Buren lost to the Whig Party's William Henry Harrison in 1840.

Van Buren spent the next eight years as an elder statesmen, advocating against the expansion of slavery. But in 1848, he made another run for the White House, this time as the candidate of the abolitionist Free Soil Party. He carried zero states and won a grand total of zero electoral votes. To make matters even worse, his second-place finish in New York threw the state—and perhaps the nation—to Whig nominee Zachary Taylor, a clear setback to Van Buren's anti-slavery cause.

His one claim to moral victory was that his 10 percent of the popular vote was the strongest showing by a third-party presidential nominee up to that point in history. But overall, his sequel campaign was pretty much of a disaster.

Grover Cleveland's why-not-try-again strategy was another story entirely.

The son of a Presbyterian minister, born in Caldwell, New Jersey, and raised in upstate New York, Cleveland was a probusiness Democrat, a fiscal conservative known for fighting patronage, corruption, and bossism, which were at least as common as pigeons in New York. When he ran for president in 1884, he got loads of support from like-minded members of the Republican Party. But when Cleveland ran for reelection in 1888, Benjamin Harrison just outcampaigned him. In a tight election, Cleveland won the popular vote, 48.6 percent to 47.8 percent, but Harrison easily won the Electoral College, 233–168. Yes, that happened back then, too.

But Cleveland wasn't ready for a quiet retirement. He spent the next four years burnishing his image as a fiscal reformer and came back for a rematch with Harrison in 1892. He had a better campaign manager this time, and Harrison was preoccupied at home. His wife, Caroline, was sick with tuberculosis and died two weeks before the election. Cleveland and Harrison both stopped campaigning out of respect for Harrison's ill wife. Election day was a sleepy affair. And Cleveland soared to victory, winning both the popular vote and the Electoral College.

Sweet revenge!

This made him the twenty-second and twenty-fourth presidents of the United States, the only American president (so far) to serve two nonconsecutive terms.

So, when they call Joe Biden the forty-sixth president, they are correct. But only forty-five men have served as president. New Jersey's own Grover Cleveland has done it twice.

Modern American politics is often compared to a pendulum. Swinging back and forth. Left and right. Ever self-correcting as the years roll on. It's a tired cliché, most popular with people like college professors who are far enough from the action that they can reflect on the longer trends. But like a lot of clichés, this one also has some truth in it. Nothing is forever in politics, and history teaches that the excesses of one side will eventually be reversed by a swing in the other direction. Then that side's excesses will eventually be reversed, too.

The word to watch here is *eventually*. Those swings can take decades. In fact, they've been so slow over the years, the swings are often hard to discern in real time. It's only in hindsight that they can be fully appreciated.

One of these long, slow swings started in 1933 with the inauguration of President Franklin Delano Roosevelt. Call it the Era of Big Government. The nation had been mired in a long depression. People were frustrated and broke. Washington didn't seem to have any answers. The president before Roosevelt, Herbert Hoover, had presided over the beginning of the Great Depression. Hoover couldn't seem to jump-start the economy, and FDR had something he called the New Deal.

Over the next six years, Roosevelt enacted a flurry of federal programs, public works projects, and financial reforms that created a much larger role for the federal government. The Civilian Conservation Corps. The Civil Works Administration. The Farm Security Administration. The National Industrial Recovery Act. And most consequential of all, the Social Security Administration. The New Deal also put safeguards on the banking industry to try to avoid another Great Depression. Some New Deal programs were passed by Congress. Roosevelt created others by executive order. But taken all together, they fundamentally changed what Americans were getting from Washington.

Future presidents, both Democrats and Republicans, took this idea and ran with it. Harry Truman piled on education aid and fair employment rules. His program was called the Fair Deal. Dwight Eisenhower built the Interstate Highway System. John Kennedy launched the space program. Lyndon Johnson fought a "War on Poverty" with food stamps, welfare benefits, Medicaid, Medicare, and new civil rights laws. These were all federal programs, directed from Washington. Richard Nixon created the Environmental Protection Agency to fight air and water pollution. For all these presidents, political party mattered less than you might imagine. Nixon was a hated villain for Democrats. Yet by today's standards, some of his policies would easily be labeled liberal. The EPA was certainly an example. It's hard to imagine Republican senator Ted Cruz or Rand Paul voting for anything remotely similar today.

And for nearly half a century, government grew and grew, no matter which party was in the White House, continually expanding on Roosevelt's New Deal. But eventually, you knew it had to happen: *Big* stopped sounding so good.

Jimmy Carter came to symbolize the ineptness of a bloated federal bureaucracy. Gas lines. Hostages in Iran. A failed rescue mission in the desert. Endless red tape. America in "malaise." Put on a cardigan sweater and lower your heat. All that opened the door for Ronald Reagan and the Era of Smaller Government. The pendulum was about to swing the other way.

The reversal didn't happen instantly. A new vision had to be clarified. A lot of people needed to be convinced. And there were always crosscurrents, pushing in opposite directions, and assorted other forces at play. But with his optimistic personality and commonsense conservatism, Reagan embodied how fed up many Americans felt about the excesses of Big Government. The sense of entitlement. Too many rules and regulations. The creeping involvement of Washington in everyday life. Not to mention rising crime, busted families, and continuing racial unrest despite decades of expanding civil rights. Reagan, who had helped to drive the crazies and the liars of the John Birch Society out of the Republican Party, promised a different path. Lower taxes. Fewer regulations. Less intrusion. And a more muscular foreign policy.

His smaller-government vision, the way he articulated it, didn't appeal only to hard-core right-wingers. Forty-eight years after FDR helped to swing America in one direction, Reagan would give it a firm shove the other way, attracting millions of "Reagan Democrats" and suburban moderates into the Republican Party. America was heading in a fundamentally different direction. Reagan and the passage of time were the two main reasons why.

It wasn't that complicated, really. He could sum it up in two short sentences in his 1981 inaugural address: "Government is not the solution to our problem," he declared to thunderous applause—on the steps of the U.S. Capitol, no less. "Government IS the problem." Of course, Reagan being Reagan, he couldn't resist slipping in a Reaganesque dig, a sharp point wrapped in genial humor. "It isn't so much that liberals are ignorant," he said that day. "It's just that they know so much that isn't so."

That neat articulation—and a thousand others like it—truly put America on a different trajectory, all the while helping to end the Cold War and eliminate the Soviet Union, our primary enemy for the previous four decades. As much as one generation of Americans had embraced Roosevelt, another generation defined itself in terms of Reagan.

"It's morning again in America," said a calm, confident voice. It wasn't just the most memorable TV commercial of Reagan's 1984 reelection campaign. It was one of the most memorable political commercials of all time.

A montage of images showed Americans going to work, highlighting how Reagan's policies had reinvigorated the U.S. economy in four short years. When people were asked if they preferred to return to the pre-Reagan policies of Democrat Walter Mondale, who'd been Jimmy Carter's vice president, 49 of 50 states voted to reelect Ronald Reagan.

It's no wonder so many people still hold President Reagan in such high regard. Reaganism wasn't done when Reagan left office. His vice president, George H. W. Bush, was elected behind him with his compassionately conservative Thousand Points of Light, building on Reagan's preference for private charity over government largesse. Bush 41 used this well-crafted phrase to characterize the countless private charities across the nation that he believed showed the true heart of the American people. And even when Democrats recaptured the White House in 1992, Reagan's worldview still cast a long shadow over Bill Clinton's presidency. He wasn't just another drunk-spending Democrat, Clinton told everyone. That was off-brand now. Instead of Big Government liberalism, Clinton touted a more nuanced Third Way. Though he certainly couldn't be called a Reagan conservative, not with tax hikes and Hillary-care, Clinton declared without apology in the first State of the Union address of his second term: "The era of big government is over." Working with Republican House Speaker Newt Gingrich, Clinton would actually balance the federal budget. He would pass welfare reform. Later, Republicans in Congress impeached him for lying under oath about his intimate relationship with Monica Lewinsky. Politics was growing more personal, and each new knife twist divided the country a little more. But if Clinton ever forgot that the giant pendulum was still on the smaller-government side, he could easily remind himself about what happened to his wife's grand plan to remake the nation's health-care system.

No, that didn't get too far. And it cost him Democratic majorities in Congress.

But nothing lasts forever, not even Ronald Reagan's towering influence. Just as Reagan had brought the nation together, the twelve years since his presidency had seen the nation drift apart. By 2000, America was sharply divided, and the split went right down the middle. There were red states and blue states, and they were drifting farther and farther apart, politically, culturally, and almost any other way that could be measured. Clinton's vice president, Al Gore, won the popular vote that year. But the Electoral College was won by George W. Bush when he won Florida. Gore filed suit contesting the results and, after many lawsuits in state and federal court, it took a 5–4 majority of the U.S. Supreme Court before Bush was sworn in as president in January 2001. After his thirty-seven-day court fight, Gore was ultimately gracious in defeat. The system had to be respected, he said. America had to move on. But the bitterness that lingered only exacerbated the divisions that were already there.

I sat at George W. Bush's inauguration on January 20. As Bush began to take the oath, I watched a woman strip off her trench coat to reveal her naked body. And what was painted there? "Bush stole the election," it said in bright blue letters. Al Gore had accepted defeat. But many elements of the left wing would never accept "Bush 43" as a legitimate president. It was a destructive rejection by Democrats that significantly deepened the divisions in our politics.

I don't need a stack of yellowed newspaper clippings or a pile of history books to remind myself about most of this. For as long as I can remember, I've been soaking it up. I wasn't around for Roosevelt, Truman, or Eisenhower. But Kennedy, Johnson, and Nixon were the bookends of my childhood, and I started volunteering on local Republican campaigns while I was still in high school. I've always believed that the right leaders can make things better, and I wanted to be involved. You can learn a lot by just being around, especially in a state as in-your-face as New Jersey, where politics is played in the open and almost nobody is shy. I was inspired by Reagan. I admired the first president Bush and was maddened by Clinton, whose presidency I witnessed through the eyes of a local official on the Morris County Board of Chosen Freeholders—what in any place but New Jersey would be called the county commission. I worked hard to elect George W. Bush as president, serving as counsel for his New Jersey campaign. And I was driven to make public service an even bigger part of my career—to make an even bigger difference.

It was Bush 43, the day before 9/11, who nominated me as the United States attorney, the chief federal prosecutor, for the state of New Jersey. For the next seven years, I made public corruption my top priority, second only to terrorism, winning convictions (usually by guilty plea) against 130 public officials, both Republicans and Democrats, at the state, county, and local levels. The hall of shame included Hudson County executive Robert Janiszewski (bribery),

Essex County executive James Treffinger (corruption), former New Jersey Senate president John Lynch (mail fraud and tax evasion), state senator Joe Coniglio (bribery), state assemblyman Mims Hackett (bribery), state senator and former Newark mayor Sharpe James (fraud), and state senator Wayne Bryant (bribery, mail fraud, and wire fraud). I got a reputation for being a no-nonsense prosecutor who was more concerned with right and wrong than right and left. Honestly, it wasn't too hard to find public corruption in New Jersey, whichever way you looked and whichever era you focused on. What surprised a lot of people was that the state finally had a United States attorney who wouldn't stand for it.

One case from those years would stick with me more than the others—and not because it was the most serious or the most legally impactful, though it was definitely the most sordid. Like so much else in the public life of New Jersey, the reason it lingered was personal.

The case involved Charles Kushner, a wealthy real estate developer and a generous contributor to New Jersey Democrats. As part of a business dispute with his relatives, the evidence showed that Kushner enlisted a private detective to videotape his sister's husband having sex with a prostitute, a prostitute he hired for $25,000 and sent to seduce his brother-in-law—then sent the X-rated evidence to his sister. Talk about family values! In 2005, Kushner pleaded guilty to eighteen counts of witness tampering, tax evasion, and illegal campaign contributions and was sentenced to two years in federal prison. Kushner did his time and came back home to his family.

Who knew that, more than a decade later, this one case out of thousands would career back into my life again? I certainly didn't, although I wouldn't have done anything different even if I had.

But I'm getting ahead of myself already. This all has to do with Donald Trump.

I met Trump soon after I became U.S. attorney in 2002. His older sister, Maryanne Trump Barry, was a federal judge in New Jersey, appointed to the district court by Ronald Reagan and elevated by Bill Clinton to the Third Circuit Court of Appeals. She asked if I'd have dinner with her little brother.

Trump and I became friends.

We'd meet for dinner from time to time, most of the time with our wives and sometimes just the two of us. He was a great storyteller, and he seemed to know everyone. We'd speak on the phone occasionally, kicking around some issue or sharing our impressions about the latest news. When I did something newsworthy, an article ripped from the paper would often show up in my mail, a short note scribbled in the margin in black Sharpie ink.

"Nice! DJT."

"Keep at it!"

"Can you believe these people? What idiots!"

Never more than a few quick words.

He owned casinos in Atlantic City, and maybe that's why he initially wanted to meet me. But he never asked me to do or not do anything, even when that business went south and he put his casinos into bankruptcy for the first time in 2004, the same year *The Apprentice* premiered on NBC. I enjoyed the time I spent with him. He was quickly becoming a friend.

As president, George W. Bush was no more a dogmatic conservative than Bill Clinton had been a dogmatic liberal. Some of Bush's policies were plainly conservative. Freer oil drilling. Limits on stem-cell research. Big tax cuts. But he also pushed for a comprehensive reform of the nation's immigration laws that conservatives derided as "amnesty." It fared about as well as Hillary's health plan. And Bush rang up what could only be called Democratic-size deficits. His wars in Afghanistan and Iraq were proving easier to get into than to get out of. To be fair, Bush had some bad luck when it came to timing—and I'm not just referring to 9/11 or Hurricane Katrina. His final days were sapped by a major economic collapse, just as the 2008 presidential race was coming into view. Real estate prices tumbled. Mortgages defaulted. A couple of major banks turned out the lights. Millions of people were genuinely suffering as they watched their American Dreams slip away. Whichever party had been in power when all that happened, they'd have almost certainly lost the White House, and the Republicans did exactly that. If Gore had been president for the previous eight years, the Democrats would just as surely have been sent into exile. But the Republicans were the ones who paid the price. Something new was in the air, and a first-term Democratic senator named Barack Obama benefited from it, his timing just as lucky as Bush's hadn't been.

Obama also had a unique set of gifts. He was smart and charismatic. He was new to the national scene. Though he lacked the important political currency of national name recognition that some others had, he something else on his side. He wasn't Hillary Clinton. Did I mention he wasn't Hillary Clinton? John McCain never had a chance. And so began another slow swing of the vaunted pendulum the professors had always spoken about.

Or so it seemed.

In fact, other forces were at play, unpredictable forces that no one was really prepared for. Changes in technology. Changes in the culture. Changes in the media. And a growing frustration out in America among people who felt like their futures were suddenly shrinking, their freedom was diminishing, and their most treasured opportunities were slipping away. And all this was happening so quickly, it was almost impossible to keep up.

Was the whole rhythm of American politics changing? Was the pendulum about to be replaced by a tornado?

Times were certainly becoming more volatile. People who had worked in factories were now unemployed. Jobs that built the middle class were being replaced by robots or fleeing to far-off countries. The deindustrialization of America was moving apace. And despite all the happy talk about retraining blue-collar workers as computer programmers and solar-panel installers, this rumored explosion of new-economy jobs never quite seemed to materialize, not for displaced fifty-somethings. Minority workers got the brunt of it, as they often do. But there was also a growing feeling among white Americans that the economic displacement didn't leave much room for *them*. Taken together, all this swirl seemed to push American politics off its predictable course.

On February 19, 2009, CNBC reporter Rick Santelli was standing on the floor of the Chicago Mercantile Exchange when he sent out a call for a "tea party" to oppose the Democratic policies of Barack Obama. Obama had barely unpacked his toothbrush at the White House. He was one day shy of one month in office. But several conservative activists set up a hurried conference call and scheduled a series of protests across the nation. Clearly, Santelli had struck a nerve. Soon America was dotted with local Tea Party groups, their name a nod to two things: the Boston Tea Party protests during the American Revolution and TEA as an acronym for Taxed Enough Already. These were grassroots operations mostly, though some of them did attract wealthy donors. They were mad as hell, and they weren't gonna take it anymore. They certainly didn't have much use for politicians of either party. Soon their rallies were drawing larger and larger crowds.

•   •   •

All that was just breaking into the open as I campaigned for governor of New Jersey.

The Tea Party activists were not as energized in our state as they were in some parts of the heartland. But they were making themselves heard. When I was elected in November 2009 and turned my attention to the heavy task of governing, I wasn't focused so much on these budding activists. I was aware of their existence. But I had a state to run. And the issues at the top of my agenda were not especially ideological or especially national. They were as practical as the day is long.

I was a Republican governor in a solidly Democratic state. My goal was to use the power I had, to build the coalitions I needed and to pull my state back from the brink of fiscal disaster. By and large the Tea Party supported me. In their eyes I was a big improvement from the Wall Street machine Democrat I had replaced and the ones who tried to beat me. So much needed to be done. I got busy doing it.

Keeping taxes down.

Reforming state pensions.

Demanding higher standards from local school districts.

Refusing to be bullied by the state teachers' union.

Balancing environmental concerns with business needs.

Insisting that state judges interpret the law, not invent it.

And I was just getting started.

Barely a year into my first term as governor, people pressed me to run for president against Obama. It was a heady time for me. I was proving that Republicans and Democrats could work together to make important changes. I was showing that a Republican governor could gain unprecedented levels of support from people who didn't normally back Republicans, including Black, Latino, urban, and younger voters. My poll numbers were in the stratosphere.

The pressure to run for president grew intense. Big donors were stepping forward to bankroll a presidential run. The media kept calling me the party's best shot against Obama's reelection. Even Nancy Reagan had kind words when I spoke before a packed house at the Reagan library. I decided—correctly, I still believe—that I had too much to do in New Jersey to be entertaining national ambitions. I wasn't ready. My time would come. Heck, I was still learning the ropes of being governor.

I announced my decision and moved on.

When Hurricane Sandy pummeled the Jersey Shore in October 2012, I was on the ground and in the air, personally directing the state's response and recovery. I battled with Congress for a robust aid package, and I didn't care who I offended with my demands. When the U.S. Senate approved a $60 billion aid package and the House wouldn't act on it, I blasted the delay as "selfishness and duplicity" and called out Republican House Speaker John Boehner by name. When Barack Obama came to New Jersey to survey the damage and offer aid, I was happy to meet with him and show him around. Some of my Republican friends didn't like that. They said I was consorting with the enemy. There were those who argued that photos of a Republican governor with a Democratic president in the middle of a crisis so soon before election day could sway some votes. I had an answer for people who raised that concern. I told them to shut up. They were being selfish. Our state was suffering. We needed help. It was my job to make sure the people who elected me got a chance to rebuild their lives. I didn't care where it came from.

As all this was unfolding, I didn't talk quite as often with Donald Trump. Both of us were busy. U.S. attorney had been a demanding job. Being governor, I discovered, was an even bigger responsibility. And Trump was pulled by his far-flung real estate projects and transitioning *The Apprentice* into *Celebrity Apprentice*, where he could fire famous people and extend the popular franchise for another few years. But we still talked on the phone and got together when we could.

But hold on a second.

Something was happening already, just below the surface of American politics, and it would continue to build. A new kind of extremism. A political expression of personal frustration. Bitter. Angry. Rooted in legitimate grievance but often thoroughly unhinged.

This wasn't a CNBC reporter expressing his anger and frustration in a live shot and inspiring a national movement to stand up against a return of Big Government. It was darker and more pernicious than that.

It wasn't quite conservative. It certainly wasn't liberal. It occupied a netherworld all its own. It was hospitable to all manner of conspiracies, some so far-fetched they were hard to repeat. That's how disconnected they were from evidence or fact. But these extremist concoctions were growing in popularity inside some parts of my party. First, at its fringes but slowly inching toward the middle. As Barry Goldwater had warned about the John Birch Society, you'd be surprised by some of the people who were on board.

There was nothing new about extremism in America. It's always been part of the political landscape on both left and right, rising and declining over time, often with the social pressures of the era. Sometimes violent, sometimes not. Black Panthers. Socialist Workers. Neo-Nazis. White supremacists. Islamic fundamentalists. Armed militias. The Weather Underground. Each wave is different, and each needs to be judged on its own.

This twenty-first-century extremism was fueled by cable television, talk radio, propaganda blog sites, and a new but growing force called social media, where no rules seemed to apply and anyone could say anything and it just might go viral. And it was in the family biography of President Barack Obama that these extremists found their first big claim: that Obama was not born in the United States of America and therefore it was unconstitutional for him to be president.

It started small. But it would eventually challenge the constitutional basis of the Obama presidency, shaking the soul of America and elements of my own Republican Party.

CHAPTER 11

BORN WHERE

Donald Trump isn't the father of what became known as *birtherism*, though he would eventually make himself the claim's loudest voice and most ardent advocate.

The story about Barack Obama's birthplace goes all the way back to 2004, when Barack Obama was a forty-two-year-old Illinois state senator running for the United States Senate. A perennial candidate and lawsuit pest named Andy Martin first floated the idea that Obama was a secret Muslim. Various versions of that story were passed around by Obama's political enemies, both Democrats and Republicans.

That he may have been educated in an Indonesian *madrassa*.

That he'd been indoctrinated since early childhood in a radical Islamist ideology.

That if he wasn't born in Indonesia, maybe it was Kenya or somewhere else in Africa—not Hawaii, as his official biography said.

This was all scattershot. No one offered any actual evidence for Obama's supposed foreign birth or secret religious faith. And the rumors stayed at the whisper level during the Illinois campaign, doing no obvious harm to the former community organizer from Chicago's South Side. He won the crowded Democratic primary in a landslide and beat Republican Alan Keyes in the general election with 70 percent of the vote. And nothing much was heard about the foreign-birth rumors for the next three years.

Then, on February 10, 2007, Obama stepped onto the national stage, announcing he'd be a candidate for president in the 2008 election. And slowly, the birther claims began to bubble up. Only now, the stakes were infinitely higher. If he was really born outside the country, what was he doing running for president? The U.S. Constitution doesn't leave much wiggle room: "No person except a natural born Citizen . . . shall be eligible to the Office of President."

You can look it up. It's in Article II, Section 1, right next to the rule that says presidents have to be at least thirty-five years old.

Barack Obama still wasn't exactly front-page news as the primary season began. Most of the political pros agreed that Hillary Clinton had the Democratic nomination all sewn up. But as Obama grew stronger, so too did the chatter about his citizenship. And not only on the right. In April, as Hillary's campaign began to struggle, some of her die-hard supporters circulated anonymous emails repeating the rumor about Obama's religion and birthplace. When it all blew up, a Clinton campaign volunteer was quickly fired. No one could prove that Hillary or her campaign was behind the loose talk. But when asked about the matter directly, the former First Lady dished up what can only be described as a decidedly lukewarm denial.

Obama wasn't a Muslim, she answered, "as far as I know." And the birth issue took another spin. A spin generated not by conservatives, not by Republicans, but by Senator Hillary Clinton.

A lot of this circulated through a handy new medium for conspiracy theories, the chain email. A typical one, packed with specific but completely unsupported detail, went like this: "Barack Obama's mother was living in Kenya with his Arab-African father late in her pregnancy. She was not allowed to travel by plane then, so Barack Obama was born there and his mother then took him to Hawaii to register his birth."

Clearly, the man was not a "real" American! And if he was a Muslim from some far-off country, wouldn't it also follow that he could well be a terrorist? Once the groundless conjecture got started, there was almost no cutting it off.

The Obama campaign watched all this carefully. His aides didn't want to give the story oxygen by talking about it any more than they had to. They just kept mentioning the candidate's early years in Hawaii and also his Christian faith. And the flurry of negative stories about Obama's radical pastor, Rev. Jeremiah Wright, had an unexpected upside: Wright might be a wild-eyed revolutionary American-hater. But, hey, he was undeniably Christian, wasn't he?

By the time Obama locked down the Democratic nomination on June 3, the John McCain campaign had already weighed the birther issue and decided against raising it. But talk of Obama's origins was always around, though actual evidence remained absent.

On June 9, Jim Geraghty of the *National Review Online* called on the candidate to release his birth certificate. Campaign officials scoffed at first but then requested the document from the Hawaii Department of Health. Obama's "Certificate of Live Birth," a digital copy of the so-called short form birth certificate, was posted on the campaign website under the headline "Fight the Smears." The one-page document showed that Barack Hussein Obama was born in Honolulu at 7:24 p.m. on August 4, 1961. And the campaign went one step further, directing reporters to birth notices that were published that August in two Honolulu newspapers.

All of which settled the issue for good, right?

By the summer of 2008, something was different in the way politics was played in America, something that hardly anyone had paid adequate attention to. But it was getting harder and harder to ignore. It wasn't just that Republicans and Democrats disagreed with each other. They'd always disagreed. It wasn't even that their leaders disliked each other. Those animosities had waxed and waned over the years. In modern-day Washington at least, the personal-loathing quotient had been flying high since Bill Clinton and Newt Gingrich were clashing in the 1990s and *Bush v. Gore* ended up in the U.S. Supreme Court.

These new divisions cut even deeper and in a much more damaging way.

With the economy weighing heavily against Republicans and Obama gliding toward the White House, the partisan divide had grown so bitter, a lot of people who cared about politics were having trouble seeing straight. It wasn't just the normal differences anymore. Different philosophies. Different priorities. Different life experiences. The partisan hostilities had grown to the point where people were having trouble agreeing on the most basic, provable facts.

Did someone dynamite the levees during Hurricane Katrina?

Was 9/11 an inside job?

Was Britney Spears secretly working for George W. Bush?

That depends! What does the other party say?

I had the luxury of watching most of this craziness from a distance, though the absurd 9/11 truther claims, both the left-wing and the right-wing versions, did tick me off. New Jersey lost 750 people that horrible morning, second only to New York. I didn't like their memories being soiled by crazy conspiracy theories. No! There was no dynamite inside the twin towers! Airplanes, hijacked by murderous Islamic fundamentalist terrorists from abroad, really did cause the buildings to collapse! But I had no problem ignoring most of the other silliness that had been floating around.

At that time, I was wrapping up my seventh year as U.S. attorney and thinking about entering the governor's race. Politics were hard-fought in my state. But we all knew each other, and we fought in old-fashioned ways. No one claimed that Trenton wasn't the capital. No one denied that Bruce Springsteen was the greatest rocker on earth. Facts were facts, and the debates started there.

I'd always prided myself as being someone who called 'em the way I saw 'em and let the chips fall. It was part of what most people liked about me and part of what some people didn't. I've always been big on bluntness and common sense. It seemed to me like a sign of basic intelligence—and basic honesty—to recognize what was staring me in the face, whether I liked it or not.

I wasn't alone in this. It was a skill most Americans possessed. A dog just knows whether he's being confronted by a tiger or a kitty cat, to push my animal analogy even further, and he reacts accordingly. But suddenly, it seemed, some people were sure the sky was red now . . . just as soon as the other side called it blue. People were growing so blinded by ideology, so loyal to the tribe, so adamantly convinced that all their prejudices were justified—all they could do was repeat the red or blue talking points and deny anyone else's truth. They had forgotten Senator Daniel Patrick Moynihan's famous admonition back in 1983: "Everyone is entitled to his own opinion, but not his own facts."

The release of Obama's birth certificate hadn't quieted any of the true believers. Some called it an obvious forgery. They complained the document lacked the Hawaii state seal. No one pressed the birther case harder than the conspiracy writer Jerome Corsi. The Obama campaign "has a false, fake birth certificate posted on their website," Corsi complained on Fox News. "It's been shown to have watermarks from Photoshop." Corsi didn't offer any real proof, but it all sounded ominous the way he portrayed it.

For his part, John McCain steadfastly refused to join the birther mob.

When a woman at a town-hall meeting in October told McCain

that Obama was an "Arab," the Republican nominee wasn't having it. "No, ma'am," the senator from Arizona said as he shook his head and pulled the microphone away. "He's a decent family man—citizen— that I just happen to have disagreements with on fundamental issues, and that's what this campaign is all about. He's not. Thank you."

McCain was eloquent that night, I thought. But I don't believe he convinced anyone who was unwilling to be convinced. If anything, Obama's election on November 4 only propelled the birther talk in certain circles. Most Americans still considered it far-fetched foolishness, but a small number of people were at least open to the idea.

Seven months into Obama's term, Research 2000 did a national poll. More than 70 percent of all respondents said they believed the new president was born in the United States. But doubts clearly persisted. Among the Republicans polled, 28 percent said they thought Obama wasn't born here and another 30 percent said they weren't sure. That contrasted with the whopping 93 percent of Democrats and 83 percent of independents who said they had no doubt.

Talk about two Americas! Among the many issues dividing the country, here was another one: 58 percent of my party's voters weren't at all sure the new president was a legal U.S. citizen. Clearly, this wasn't a fringe issue that could be easily ignored. And it quickly became a fixture at the Tea Party rallies that were being held across America. Speakers pounded it along with high taxes and oppressive regulations. "Go home to Kenya," one sign said. "Americans deserve an American president." These numbers show how pernicious this kind of conspiracy theory can become in the internet age. Remember, I am a former prosecutor. I never believed this because no one ever showed me any facts to prove it.

At a National Tea Party Convention in Nashville in 2010, World Net Daily founder Joseph Farah did a ten-minute riff on Obama's questionable citizenship. He told a joke about an "international medical convention" where an American doctor bragged he'd installed a guy with "no birth certificate and no brain" at the White House. Farah urged the crowd to make sure that "Where's the Birth Certificate?" signs appeared at every Obama campaign stop when he ran for reelection. And bigger names in the media were also climbing on board. Lou Dobbs, a rare anti-Obama voice on CNN, told his viewers that the birthplace doubt "hasn't been dealt with." Rush Limbaugh warned his listeners that the president "has yet to have to prove that he's a citizen." Most chilling was a YouTube video that got hundreds of thousands of hits. It showed what happened to a Republican congressman, Mike Castle, at a town-hall meeting in Delaware, where I'd gone to college. A woman stood up waving a stack of papers. It was her birth certificate, she said, demanding to see the president's.

"He's not an American citizen," she shouted over loud applause. "He's a citizen of Kenya."

Castle tried to channel John McCain, insisting that the president was indeed born an American. People started booing. As the congressman tried to change the subject, the woman suddenly demanded that everyone recite the Pledge of Allegiance. People got up from their seats, almost everyone in the room. They faced the American flag. They placed their right hands on their hearts and began:

"I pledge allegiance to the flag of the United States of America and to the Republic for which it stands. . . ."

Something was happening inside our party, and it wasn't debate club.

Opposition to Obama on his policies should have been our focus. Many did not understand that, by veering off into this unfounded conspiracy theory, we were undercutting our own very credible policy arguments. A bad move strategically, short term and long term. We needed to stand up against Obama without pursuing this unfounded birther theory.

•   •   •

Enter Donald Trump.

More than two years into Obama's first term as president, the New York real estate developer and *Apprentice* host was toying again with the idea of running for president. You have to say *again* because Trump had been talking about a White House run, on and off, since the 1980s. There he was in 1988, boasting to Oprah Winfrey: "I think I'd win." There he was in 1999, telling Larry King he'd formed a committee to explore a Reform Party candidacy. Almost every four years, it seemed, there was at least some talk about Trump for president, often fanned by Trump himself. But as Barack Obama was revving up his own reelection campaign in March 2011, the famed businessman and reality-TV star went on ABC's *Good Morning America* to say he was serious about joining the race this time.

"I have never been so serious as I am now," Trump declared during an interview on his president-sized private jet, Trump Force One, as he called it. And he tipped his hand about a weak spot he might try to exploit on the campaign trail. For the first time, Trump made clear he was ready to throw in his lot with the not-born-in-America conspiracists. As Trump put it, gently at first, he was "a little" skeptical about Obama's citizenship. Not every doubter should automatically be dismissed as "an idiot," Trump said. "Growing up, no one knew him. The whole thing is very strange."

The no-one-knew-him claim was promptly debunked by many in the media, who reported they'd interviewed people in Hawaii who clearly remembered Obama as a boy. But for the first time ever, a major public figure and potential presidential candidate had publicly embraced birtherism. In Donald Trump's hands, what had started on the fringes of Chicago politics and was fanned by Tea Party activists had been ushered onto the main stage of American media and politics.

No one did it better than Donald Trump.

In the days that followed, he said he was sending a team of private investigators to Hawaii to learn the truth. He promised to donate $5 million to charity if anyone could convince him that Obama was born on U.S. soil. There was no more evidence than there'd ever been, but the claims were getting louder and harder for the president's aides and backers to ignore. Next, he headed over to *The View*, where he tried to push the no-one-knew-him notion on Whoopi, Joy, and the other ladies at that famous table.

"If you go back to my first grade, my kindergarten, people remember me," Trump declared. "If you're going to be president of the United States, it says very profoundly you have to be born in this country." As for the birth certificate the Obama campaign released in 2008, Trump said it wasn't good enough. Only a "long form" birth certificate would do. "There's something on that birth certificate he doesn't like," Trump said.

The ladies reacted furiously, Whoopi Goldberg especially.

"It's the biggest pile of dog mess I've heard in ages!" she exploded. "It's not because he's black, is it? I've never heard of any white president who had to show his birth certificate. That's BS!"

But Trump didn't consider the uproar on *The View* any reason to back off. Quite the opposite. It only spurred him on. Next stops, Fox and NBC. "I didn't think this was such a big deal," he said in the Fox interview. "But I will tell you, it's turning out to be a very big deal because people now are calling me from all over saying please don't give up on this issue."

"I have people that have been studying it, and they cannot believe what they're finding," he teased on NBC. Clearly, the talk wasn't going away. It was having an impact. Worse for the Republican Party, it was a distraction from taking on the Obama administration directly. It continued to lead us off course. On April 27, the Obama campaign released the so-called long form birth certificate.

It showed the same thing that the short form had: Barack Hussein Obama was born in Honolulu, Hawaii, just like he had been saying all along. And the new document had exactly the same effect on America's ardent birthers, including Donald Trump, that the previous release had.

None.

All it did was give Trump something new to gloat about. "Today," he said, "I am very proud of myself because I've accomplished something that nobody else has been able to accomplish. I was just informed while on the helicopter that our president has finally released a birth certificate. I'd want to look at it, but I hope it's true so that we can get onto much more important matters, so the press can stop asking me questions. He should have done it a long time ago. Why he didn't do it when the Clintons asked for it, why he didn't do it when everybody else was asking for it, I don't know."

Again, there was no convincing people who refused to be convinced. The reason I was confident that Obama was an American citizen was that none of the conspiracy theorists showed any facts to prove otherwise. While the long-form birth certificate changed the minds of some, it didn't seem to change all minds. Here was an early glimpse of an attack strategy that was becoming too familiar in politics: Someone would make a false claim, the wilder the better. The wacky websites would pick it up and run with it. Talk radio and cable would amplify it. When the denials came in, they would propel the story even more. Through rote repetition, the claim would work its way into the national bloodstream, long before the facts would eventually have the chance to shoot it down.

Who was it? Mark Twain? Jonathan Swift? Winston Churchill? The quote has been falsely attributed to all of them, but that doesn't mean it isn't true: "A lie can travel halfway around the world by the time the truth is putting its pants on."

Suddenly, there was a lot of naked truth out there, struggling to catch up.

You knew it had to happen: the face-to-face confrontation between Barack Obama and Donald Trump. The man and his accuser. The prey and the hunter. The president and the man who, maybe, just maybe, was pushed that night to become one.

The date was April 30, 2011. The place was the Washington Hilton. The event was the annual dinner of the White House Correspondents' Association, the "nerd prom," as people in Washington like to call it. I was right there when it happened. I had a clear view of the faces of the two combatants. I witnessed every brutal knife twist and every painful grimace. It had been just three days since Obama had released his long-form birth certificate, a document Trump insisted didn't exist or contained some dreadful secret. Not only did it exist, it said exactly what Obama said it would, and that was all it said. This was Obama's victory lap.

It was a big room, but I had a prime ringside seat. This was the night Barack Obama publicly embarrassed Donald Trump.

"My . . . fellow . . . Americans," Obama began, drawing out the greeting to remind everyone that he was indeed an American, despite what some people had been saying.

For another moment, he continued toying with the crowd. "As some of you have heard, the state of Hawaii has released my official long-form birth certificate. Hopefully, this puts all doubts to rest. But just in case there are any lingering questions, tonight I am prepared to go a step further. Tonight, for the first time, I am releasing my official birth video."

The giant screens in the ballroom came alive. But rather than footage of a baby Barack being born in Hawaii, the clip was from

Disney's *The Lion King*. It was the grand unveiling of baby Simba in Africa.

"Oh, well," the president said with a shrug. "Back to square one."

Then he directed his remarks to his real target of the evening, an unsmiling Trump.

"Donald Trump is here tonight," Obama said. "And I know he has taken some flak lately. But no one is happier, no one prouder, to put this birth certificate to rest than the Donald. And that's because he can finally get back to focusing on the issues that matter like, Did we fake the moon landing? What really happened in Roswell? And where are Biggie and Tupac?"

He was mocking the baseless charge by comparing it to the most discredited conspiracy theories and pinning it on its loudest voice. The whole room, 2,600 journalists and Washington power brokers, Republicans and Democrats alike, howled in laughter. I looked at Donald Trump. He was staring straight ahead. He was rocking back and forth in his chair. He still didn't break a smile.

Obama grinned onstage until the long applause died down.

"All kidding aside," he went on, still talking straight to Trump. "We all know about your breadth of experience and your credentials. For example, just recently in an episode of *Celebrity Apprentice*, at the steakhouse, the men's cooking team did not impress the judges from Omaha Steaks. And there was a lot of blame to go around. But you, Mr. Trump, recognized that the real problem was a lack of leadership. So ultimately, you didn't blame Little John or Meat Loaf. You fired Gary Busey. And these are the kinds of decisions that would keep me up at night."

Only then did Trump finally crack a smile and give a short wave.

"Well handled, sir," Obama said. "Well handled."

It was fascinating and excruciating all at once.

What no one in the audience knew as Obama spoke and Trump squirmed was that, that evening, at the president's direction, Navy

SEALs in Pakistan were moving in to shoot and kill Osama bin Laden, the 9/11 mastermind. Obama knew. He had signed off on the mission and gave his final operational approval. But he let on about none of it. He never turned his eyes away from the man who who'd been questioning his right to be president. He showed no mercy on Donald Trump.

I can say this much: I spoke to Donald after the dinner. He was pissed off like I'd never seen him before. Just beside himself with fury.

Donald Trump skipped the 2012 election. When he threw his support behind Mitt Romney for the Republican nomination in February of that year, Romney gushed: "It means a great deal to me to have the endorsement of Mr. Trump." But once it came time for Romney to turn his fire on Obama, he never took aim at his opponent's birthplace—with one glancing exception. "No one's ever asked to see my birth certificate," Romney joked during an August campaign stop at his boyhood home in suburban Detroit. "They know that this is the place that we were born and raised."

He got some laughs from the crowd that day and also some pushback from Team Obama. The Obama campaign was not going to let Romney even make a joke about the issue without being answered. Trump, they were willing to ignore. Romney, not so much. Romney quickly backed away. "The governor has always said and has repeatedly said he believes the president was born here in the United States," a campaign spokesman said. "He was only referencing that Michigan, where he is campaigning today, is the state where he himself was born and raised."

But Trump wasn't letting up. As Democrats and some Republicans labeled the claims both racist and untrue, he continued needling Obama and kept the issue alive. Why give up an attack that seemed to work with the base? Now that Obama had released two versions of his birth certificate, Trump was demanding to see his rival's college transcript and passport application, documents that often include questions about the individual's place of birth. The week before the 2012 election, Trump was back with another $5 million offer: He would donate that sum to a charity of Obama's choice if the Democrat would release those additional documents.

Crickets.

Obama claimed victory over Romney in November 2012, and the birther conspiracy theories still didn't stop, nor the groundless questions and nor the free-floating doubts. In 2012, Trump tweeted that he had an "extremely credible source" who told him the president's birth certificate was a forgery. In 2013, he raised suspicions about the plane-crash death of Hawaiian health director Loretta Fuddy, who had verified the birth certificates' authenticity. In 2014, he asked hackers to breach Obama's college records and probe his place of birth.

Nothing came of any of it because there was no evidence to back it up.

And so it went, interview after interview, taunt after taunt. No evidence. No proof. And no retreat. The claims were thoroughly discredited, but Trump still beat the drum. He had a much larger media platform than the early birthers or the Tea Partiers ever had. Why waste the media access? Any news is good news. And if the audience responded to the story, why ever give it up?

It wouldn't be until September 16, 2016, six weeks before his own election day, that Trump as the Republican Party presidential nominee would finally concede: "President Barack Obama was born in the United States. Period." However, it wasted years of energy and credibility in corners of our party. And every time we wasted energy and credibility that way, it diminished the legitimate criticisms of the Obama administration.

Donald Trump was by far the most effective proponent of the birther conspiracy. He truly showed everyone how a lie like that can be exploited. But he definitely wasn't alone in promoting it. He got help from, among many others, former vice presidential candidate Sarah Palin ("I think it's a fair question"), Sheriff Joe Arpaio ("9 points of forgery"), Senator Richard Shelby of Alabama ("Well, his father was Kenyan and they said he was born in Hawaii, but I haven't seen any birth certificate"), Senator David Vitter of Louisiana ("I support conservative legal organizations and others who would bring that to court"), and former House Speaker Newt Gingrich (Obama can only be understood by people who "understand Kenyan, anti-colonial behavior").

And the birther campaign did one other thing. It paved the way for wave after wave of other conspiracies to come, wild fantasies, far-fetched assertions, bizarre allegations, and outright lies. It showed that personal falsehoods, even when plainly disproven, can still do political damage. Lies, even discredited lies, never really go away.

It cheapened the truth. It hurt our political and policy credibility. We are still paying the price. And for no good reason. Attacking Obama for weakening our military, caving to the Iranians, expanding the government through Obamacare and lying to the American people by telling them, "If you like your doctor, you will be able to keep your doctor"—all that would have been a much better expenditure of credibility and time.

Missteps like these and the conspiracies they promoted helped to propel the reelection of Barack Obama and, in 2020, the election of his vice president, Joe Biden.

CHAPTER 12

PIZZA TIME

You never know where one of these wild conspiracies is headed, but it's rarely anywhere good. Around 3 p.m. on December 4, 2016, a busy Sunday afternoon, a twenty-eight-year-old former firefighter named Edgar Maddison Welch walked into a pizza restaurant in northwest Washington, D.C.

He wasn't there to sample the mozzarella, and he didn't come alone.

He brought along a Colt AR-15 rifle, a Colt .38 handgun, a shotgun, and a folding knife. Police say he pointed the semiautomatic rifle at a worker, who ran for his life. Then Welch began firing inside the restaurant.

He had driven from his home in Salisbury, North Carolina, to "self-investigate" a rumor that he'd heard about on YouTube: that the Comet Ping Pong pizzeria was a front for a child-sex ring run by Hillary Clinton and her Deep State allies. Alex Jones, the conspiracy-minded host of the InfoWars media empire, had been reporting that Hillary and her cronies were sexually abusing children in satanic rituals. Welch decided someone had to do something about it. He arrived at the restaurant intent on finding the secret torture chambers and rescuing the helpless little girls.

As terrified employees and customers scattered, Welch found

no hidden tunnels, no imprisoned children, and no evidence of a pedophile ring masterminded by the failed Democratic candidate for president. There was no sign of any of that. But with Welch's armed rescue mission, the conspiracy theory known as Pizzagate had made its way from the far-off corners of the internet onto the felony-crime blotter of Washington's Metropolitan Police.

This had to be some kind of a record.

In the late 1950s and early 1960s, it took Robert Welch and the John Birch Society several *years* to whip up their anticommunist hysteria across the country. After the turn of the century, it took even longer for the Barack Obama birther conspiracy to fully take hold, even with Donald Trump leading the parade. But Pizzagate went from false rumor to flying bullets in two months flat.

All this erupted as the 2016 presidential race was entering its final month. Beginning in early October, WikiLeaks began publishing the personal emails of Clinton campaign chairman John Podesta, plucked from his Gmail account by Russian hackers. More than twenty thousand pages in all. As each new batch came to light, the emails were being carefully dissected by users of the online forum 4chan, a so-called image board that was conceived as a free-speech haven. The amateur sleuths noticed that Podesta's emails included the word *pizza* and mentioned dinner plans with his lobbyist brother, Tony Podesta. The Hillary campaign chairman also corresponded with a friend named James Alefantis, who owned the Washington pizzeria Comet Ping Pong.

And what did all that prove? That the Podestas liked pizza? Well, it certainly piqued the interest of the conspiracy sleuths.

Then, FBI director James Comey added another intriguing twist. On October 28, he announced that the bureau would be reopening its investigation into Hillary's use of a private email server while she was secretary of state, a late curveball for her presidential campaign. Data from the server had been discovered on electronic devices belonging to former New York congressman Anthony Weiner, the husband of Clinton's close aide Huma Abedin. Weiner, once a rising star in the Democratic Party, had been caught sending lewd text messages to several young women, including a jockey-shorts selfie to a fifteen-year-old girl.

This all got mashed together in some very strange ways. The next day, a claim was posted on Facebook by a user calling herself Carmen Katz. Here it is, exactly as written:

> My NYPD source said its much more vile and serious than classified material on Weiner's device. The email DETAIL the trips made by Weiner, Bill and Hillary on their pedophile billionaire friend's plane, the Lolita Express. Yup, Hillary has a well documented predilection for underage girls. . . . We're talking an international child enslavement and sex ring.

Huh?

I bow to no one in my disagreements with Hillary Clinton. Our political outlooks could hardly be any further apart. As far as I was concerned, Hillary never had half the political skills her husband did—or the ability to find common ground. But still. ". . . a well documented predilection for underage girls"? ". . . an international child enslavement and sex ring"?

The evidence for that was . . . *what, exactly?*

On its own, I guess the posting wasn't all that surprising. There were conspiracy peddlers all over Facebook, posting all kinds of crazy things. That's what happens when you have 2.5 billion users on a social media platform and God knows how many imposters, bots, and friends of Vladimir Putin. Some of them are sure to make bizarre assertions about something, which in a sane political world would be entirely ignored by the platform's 2,499,999,999 other users. But we weren't living in a sane political world anymore.

The next day, an anti-Semitic Twitter account supposedly run by a Jewish New York lawyer picked up the story there:

Rumors stirring in the NYPD that Huma's emails point to a pedophile ring and @HillaryClinton is at the center. #GoHillary #PodestaEmails23 pic.twitter.com/gkEH 5oL269

    —David Goldberg (@DavidGoldbergNY)

On closer inspection, Goldberg's name appeared to be phony, as did Carmen Katz's. But his claim was promptly retweeted more than six thousand times. From there it made its way to Alex Jones's InfoWars. "When I think about all the children Hillary Clinton has personally murdered and chopped up and raped, I have zero fear standing up against her," Jones told his audience in a video posted on November 4, four days before the election. "Yeah, you heard me right. Hillary Clinton has personally murdered children. I just can't hold back the truth anymore."

This wasn't some lonely digital ranter, pecking away at his laptop on his mama's couch. Alex Jones was the gravel-voiced superstar of the crazy conspiracy fringe. His InfoWars website launched in 1999. Since then, he'd spun off a daily radio show, a YouTube channel, documentary films, public appearances, and a mail-order operation that did a brisk business in bulletproof vests, dietary supplements, and "brain pills," all advertised on his various media platforms. The health products seemed to be the main profit center: InfoWars Life Silver Bullet Colloidal Silver. InfoWars Life Brain Force Plus. InfoWars Life Super Male Vitality. InfoWars Life Liver Shield. Jones claimed that the Oklahoma City bombing, 9/11, the Sandy Hook school shooting, and the Boston Marathon bombing were all inside jobs, "false flag" operations secretly perpetrated by a power-mad government. Let's say it plainly: Alex Jones is an opportunist, selling crazy to line his pockets with other people's money. No credible leader should associate with this character.

Donald Trump had appeared as a guest on the Alex Jones radio show in December 2015, two months before the primaries began. "Your reputation is amazing," Trump enthused. "I will not let you down." Jones later said that the two of them "formed a bond" that day. When the Republican National Convention came to Cleveland in July 2016, he headlined a "Silent Majority for Trump" rally in a park beside the Cuyahoga River. "Hillary for prison," he shouted from the stage. Once he started pounding on the alleged pedophiles at the pizza parlor, there was no turning back. Soon his digital soldiers were joining the 4chan mob in getting to the bottom of the latest Clinton scandal.

One key clue: A 4chan user suggested that the phrase "cheese pizza" might be a secret code employed by pedophiles, who on chat boards sometimes used the initials *c p* for child pornography. When Hillary's pals craved "cheese pizza," what were they *really* asking for? Those were the kinds of dots being connected to support this fast-moving and increasingly bizarre conspiracy. By this point, it wasn't much of a leap to link Hillary, Weiner, Abedin, the Podestas, and the Clinton Foundation's creepy donor Jeffrey Epstein. The hashtag #pizzagate first appeared on Twitter on November 7, the day before the election. Within a week, the term would be tweeted and retweeted thousands of times.

Trump's surprise victory didn't stop any of this. It only seemed to fuel it—and not just the social-media barrage against the popular pizza restaurant, which had always been considered kid-friendly with its Ping-Pong tables and craft rooms. Soon Hillary haters were spreading horrible slurs about other businesses on the same Connecticut Avenue block. Even the members of the local band Fugazi, who'd played a concert at the pizza restaurant, were attacked on Facebook, Twitter, and Instagram. But Comet and its owner got the worst of it. "We're onto you," said one message on the restaurant's social media. "I will kill you personally," warned another. And the purported details of the child abuse grew only more macabre. Blood drinking. Kill rooms. Cannibalism. It was anything you could imagine and a lot of things you probably can't. And according to the Pizzagate hysteria, the diabolical mastermind behind it had come *this close* to being president!

It's worth taking a moment to unpack some of this. You can see how truth, falsehood, and total lunacy can all be weaved together into an outlandish fantasy that millions of people are genuinely prepared to believe about someone they politically oppose.

First, the nuggets of truth: Bill Clinton did fly on the private plane of wealthy donor Jeffrey Epstein. Epstein would later be accused of recruiting young women and underage girls for sex and wild parties, an open enough secret that his plane did acquire the nickname *Lolita Express.* Epstein was later arrested, and he died in a Manhattan jail cell. He was a reprehensible human being who abused girls and women. But in his plane and his home, not in a Washington, D.C., pizzeria. Anthony Weiner clearly had a problem. But no one's ever shown that one had anything to do with the other. And none of this—*none of it!*—came anywhere close to Hillary Clinton performing satanic sex rituals on underage girls or an international child enslavement ring operating out of a Washington pizzeria. That part came from nowhere but out of someone's head.

And the story wasn't close to done, not with Alex Jones driving it so feverishly. On November 27, three full weeks after Clinton had lost her bid for the presidency, Jones spent half an hour firing up his audience with the latest Pizzagate claims. "Something's being covered up," he roared. "All I know is, God help us, we're in the hands of pure evil." Then he released two more videos, "Down the #Pizzagate Rabbit Hole" and "Pizzagate: The Bigger Picture."

And in Salisbury, North Carolina, Edgar Welch was lapping it all up, as were countless other people who opposed and despised Hillary Clinton and believed Alex Jones.

So, who believes this garbage? Too many people. Especially on our side of the aisle. And when they do, it minimizes our credibility on issues that really matter and allows Joe Biden and his cronies to have a freer hand bringing their left-wing agenda to every neighborhood in America.

There is no official count of people who are gullible enough or angry enough or crazy enough to accept the notion that a satanic pedophile ring is being operated by high-profile politicians in our nation's capital out of a local pizzeria. No sign-up sheets. No membership cards. But the numbers are large. When pollsters asked about Pizzagate, the self-professed believers were nowhere near a majority of the country. But there were enough to be astonishing.

The same week Edgar Maddison Welch showed up at Comet Ping Pong, Public Policy Polling asked 1,224 registered voters if they thought Hillary Clinton was "connected to a child sex ring being run out of a pizzeria in Washington, D.C." Nine percent said yes. Nineteen percent said they weren't sure. Seventy-two percent said no. That was for the nation as a whole.

At least it wasn't the other way around. But to me, the numbers weren't all that comforting. Twenty percent of my fellow Americans were open enough to the idea that they couldn't dismiss it outright or they didn't know enough to dismiss it.

Polls are never perfect. There's a little noise in all of them. Some people like messing around with pollsters. A few percentage points will say yes to damn near anything. In this same poll, 5 percent of *Clinton voters* said they believed the pizza story. Really? I'd hate to think what that might mean. But still. In a nation of 330 million, that's a lot of people who are open to a sicko fairy tale.

In fact, there's nothing new about the appeal of conspiracy theories. They've been around as long as humans have wandered the earth, and believing them wasn't entirely irrational. When people lived in small, vulnerable communities, remaining on guard for hidden plots could be a matter of life and death. Cavemen also had a lot of time to worry about potential predators. Those nights in the forest sure were long.

Scholars like Richard Hofstadter have traced unfounded conspiracy theories back to the earliest days of our nation. Americans have always been drawn to wild stories regardless of accuracy, the Columbia University historian concluded. In *The Paranoid Style in American Politics*, he recounts how clergymen in New England flew into alarm in the late 1790s over the false belief that Bavarian Illuminati were infecting American Masons with evil ideas from the French Revolution. Who knew where that might lead! And the elaborate tales have been popping up ever since, especially in times of national anxiety. The financial collapse known as the Panic of 1837. The Civil War. The Great Depression. The late 1950s and 1960s as the post–World War II boom gave way to the nuclear uncertainty of the Cold War.

Tough times always promote unhinged stories.

Hofstadter wasn't looking to blame anyone. He sought understanding for the rattled individuals swept up by these tales. "We are all sufferers from history," he wrote, "but the paranoid is a double sufferer, since he is afflicted not only by the real world, with the rest of us, but by his fantasies as well."

•   •   •

Psychologists have a view of this, and it's interesting to think about. Most people, they say, do not fall easily for falsehoods. Thankfully, most of us are armed with a powerful weapon against other people's sweeping lies. Life experience, it's called. When someone tells you something that sounds implausible, it leads naturally to doubts and questions. This isn't a sign of cynicism. It's a sign of having an active, inquisitive mind. But some people lack that. Or else their common sense is overwhelmed by their runaway curiosity or, more likely, their uncontrolled anxieties, fears, and prejudices. They quickly suspend their disbelief.

There are lots of theories about what makes some people susceptible to this and others not so much. Often, these people really do think they are saving the world. They are the smart ones, the brave ones, the truth tellers. They are sure of it. And they are equally convinced that others—the media, the opposing political party, their clueless friends from high school—are dumb or lazy or corrupt.

We all know people who think like that.

They become most susceptible, the experts say, when the divisions in society are especially intense and when the misinformation is something people *want* to believe. Because it comes from someone they already have trust in. ("Alex Jones said so.") Or because the story helps to explain something they've always wondered about. (Did one man acting alone really kill President Kennedy? Did NASA fake the moon landing? Is the government hiding Martians in Area 51? Was Princess Diana murdered? What are those chemtrails in the sky?) Or because it confirms beliefs people already hold. ("I told you that Hillary woman is up to no good!") True or false, people like having their preconceptions confirmed.

A shared conspiracy theory, even a far-fetched one, "helps restore a sense of agency and control for many people," writes Sander van der Linden of the University of Cambridge, a world-renowned expert on what people know and how they know it. And people are more likely to believe misinformation that they are exposed to over and over again, van der Linden says. "The brain mistakes familiarity for truth." That's one reason social media has proven so effective at spreading conspiracies. Once a post goes viral, it's endlessly repetitive.

The experts' final note: Be careful arguing with a true believer. Your efforts could easily backfire. And pushing may only harden the person's views. The believers feel pressured. The repetition kicks in. The debunking is taken as further proof that the forces of evil are hiding the truth again.

The Pizzagate story played out pretty much as I expected, far beyond the hothouse world of politics. Thankfully, no one was hurt during Edgar Welch's armed assault. Forty-five minutes after he arrived at the pizzeria, he was in police custody. "What happened today demonstrates that promoting false and reckless conspiracy theories comes with consequences," the restaurant owner said. "I hope that those involved in fanning these flames will take a moment to contemplate what happened here today, and stop promoting these falsehoods right away."

In February 2017, lawyers for the owner sent Alex Jones a letter, demanding he retract his claims and apologize. Under threat of a slander suit, the influential media conspiracist did apologize, though he tried to spread the blame around. "To my knowledge," Jones said that March, "neither Mr. Alefantis, nor his restaurant Comet Ping Pong, were involved in any human trafficking as was part of the theories about Pizzagate that were being written about in many media outlets and which we commented upon."

Alex Jones and others spread these lies to line their pockets, become famous, or both. They almost always back away when their wealth could become debt or their fame could become infamy due to their lies, regardless of what damage they've done in the process to our party and our country.

If it wasn't so sad, it would be ridiculous. But many in our society use these wild, untrue conspiracy theories to advance their political agendas. When that happens, it does damage to whichever political party members have spread the tales. That's what needs to stop . . . and we need to stop it.

CHAPTER 13

Q AMOK

Here's the thing about QAnon: It's huge.

Most of the conspiracy theories that have taken off, they try to explain one thing. Where was Barack Obama born? What caused the twin towers of the World Trade Center to collapse? Why are those black helicopters flying over my house?

QAnon offers an explanation for *everything*.

It's the big-tent conspiracy theory for people ready to dive into a fantasy world of evil villains, cryptic clues, bold predictions, surprising plot twists, and an unstoppable superhero named Donald Trump. That's QAnon. As elaborate as *Harry Potter*. As fantastical as Dungeons and Dragons. As frantic as Grand Theft Auto. "The Storm is coming," and the patriots are racing to save us all.

I won't try to review every aspect of this vast, imaginary terrain. There are rabbit holes here that people just don't ever climb out of. This far in, the QAnon story is so convoluted and self-contradictory, there is no linear narrative anymore. Just a bunch of inexplicable adventures colliding with each other, sharing a paranoid worldview and a biblical sense of the Apocalypse. QAnon has to keep changing. How else can it keep up with all the predictions that haven't come true?

The QAnon seed was planted eleven months after Donald

Trump was elected president, ten months after Edgar Welch burst into the Comet Ping Pong pizzeria. The evening of October 5, 2017, the president was at the White House in the State Dining Room. The First Lady, Melania, was there. So were twenty or so high-ranking U.S. military officers and their spouses. The pool reporters were called in for a photo op.

"You guys know what this represents?" the president said to no one in particular, tracing a circle in the air with his right index finger.

"Tell us, sir," someone said.

"Maybe it's the calm before the storm."

"What's the storm?" one of the reporters called out.

"Could be the calm—the calm before the storm," Trump said again.

"What storm, Mr. President?"

"You'll find out," was all Trump said.

What did he mean by that? Did he mean anything at all? Was he just saying *Here's a bunch of our military leaders. They look relaxed right now, but don't you worry. They'll be ready to fight when the time arrives*? Who knows what the president was thinking? He never explained. His passing comment barely caused a ripple at first, but millions of people would eventually read an amazing amount of meaning into those thirty-seven seconds.

Three weeks later, an anonymous user now widely known as Q appeared for the first time on 4chan, a so-called image board that was conceived as a haven for free speech and also hosted gross-out pho-tos and shocking memes. In an urgent tone, Q predicted imminent trouble for the woman who had run for president against Trump, Hillary Rodham Clinton.

HRC extradition already in motion effective yesterday with several countries in case of cross border run. Passport approved to be flagged effective 10/30 @ 12:01am. Expect massive riots organized in defiance and others fleeing the US to occur. US M's [Marines] will conduct the operation while NG [National Guard] activated. Proof check: Locate a NG member and ask if activated for duty 10/30 across most major cities.

In a second message, Q added this detail: "Hillary Clinton will be arrested between 7:45 AM - 8:30 AM EST on Monday - the morning on Oct 30."

None of that happened, of course. October 30 came and went, and Hillary still wasn't in handcuffs. But the provocative "Q drops," as these messages came to be known, had only begun. There were thousands to come. The anonymous poster portrayed himself as a well-placed U.S. military official or intelligence officer whose "Q-level clearance" gave him access to highly classified information. He was now ready to share some of the shocking details of a truly sinister plot, a massive conspiracy perpetrated by Democratic politicians, anti-Trump movie stars, tech titans, international bankers, One World Order diplomats, and the Mexican cement giant Cemex. All the liberal "villains" were in the mix: both Clintons, Joe Biden, Barack Obama, Nancy Pelosi, George Soros, Bill Gates, Mark Zuckerberg, Ellen DeGeneres, Tom Hanks, Oprah Winfrey, Stormy Daniels lawyer Michael Avenatti—if you'd heard of them and they were suspected of leaning left, chances are they were part of this global cabal.

As in Pizzagate, many of the cabal members were said to be part of an organized ring of Satan-worshipping pedophiles who cannibalized children after sexually abusing them. Only now, the crimes weren't limited to a single pizzeria. Q claimed to have proof that corrupt leaders were secretly torturing children all over the world.

"These people need to ALL be ELIMINATED," Q declared in one early post. And the Q drops were often peppered with other spy-novel conspiracy clichés.

"Follow the money."

"I've said too much."

"Where we go one, we go all."

"Some things must remain classified to the very end."

And don't forget "the Storm," when America will experience a Great Awakening and the Deep State actors will finally get what's coming to them.

Was that the storm Trump was referring to in the State Dining Room when he warned obliquely about "the calm before the storm"? As ridiculous as that sounds, the QAnon faithful were sure of it as the all-encompassing conspiracy theory migrated from 4chan to successor boards 8tran and 8kun and onto mainstream platforms like Twitter, Instagram, and Facebook.

Once the Storm arrives, Hillary, Obama, Biden, Pelosi, and their co-conspirators will all be rounded up. Many will be shipped off to the super-secure prison camp at Guantanamo Bay. Others will face military tribunals and almost certain execution. And then, with righteous brutality, Donald Trump and the U.S. military will deliver peace and salvation across the land.

Got it?

In the universe of QAnon, Trump isn't just a New York businessman and media figure who was elected president. He's a comic-book superhero. With no factual support, Q asserts that America's military leaders recruited him to run for president so he could vanquish the nefarious Deep State plotters before they destroyed everything. Trump may face temporary setbacks here and there (such as Hillary slipping through the previously mentioned "dragnet" or his having his reelection victory temporarily "stolen" from him). But he's still all-knowing and all-powerful, and he will certainly prevail in the end. But only if QAnon believers and other America-loving patriots do their part. Here, the audience isn't just an audience. In this way, QAnon is more like a multiplayer video game. People are expected to join in. By deciphering the cryptic clues. By publicizing Q's insights. By recruiting new followers and spreading the message around. So with each new Q-drop, there is another mad scramble to make sense of the latest acronyms, the confident-sounding predictions, and the relentless spy-speak.

Q's not perfect. That's an understatement. He's made all kinds of claims that haven't stood up well to the light of day. That the CIA installed North Korean's Kim Jong-un to be an agency puppet. That former Democratic National Committee chairwoman Debbie Wasserman Schultz hired gang members from El Salvador to murder DNC staffer Seth Rich. That German chancellor Angela Merkel is Adolf Hitler's granddaughter. That Barack Obama, Hillary Clinton, and George Soros organized a coup against Donald Trump. Not one of those assertions is true. Q's been even worse at predicting the future. He's often wrong—but never in doubt.

The Storm would come on November 3, 2017, he promised. No Storm. Something major would happen at the Defense Department on February 1, 2018. Nope. President Trump's enemies would die in a mass suicide on February 10, 2018. No prominent suicides that day. John McCain would resign from the U.S. Senate. McCain was still a senator when he died. Mark Zuckerberg would quit Facebook and flee the country. Zuckerberg did neither. Pope Francis would be arrested on a felony charge. The pope wasn't. And the one that Q was really, really, really sure of, so sure he repeated it many times: Donald Trump would be re-inaugurated on January 20, 2021.

Obviously, that did not happen.

Underlying all of Q's conspiracy talk is a basic, timeless question: When governments are controlled by despots, don't the people have a duty to revolt?

It's a fair question . . . in the abstract. Sentiments like that one inspired the American colonists to break away from England. But our forefathers were not conspiracy theorists. They lived in reality. They were guided by facts. They didn't convince themselves that King George was a Satan-loving pedophile atop a nefarious global cabal. For them, life, liberty, and the pursuit of happiness was a powerful enough cause.

Our forefathers stayed focused on core issues that affect every American's freedom, issues that Republicans should always stay focused on: oppressive taxation. Ridiculous regulation. Haughty rulers. Entrenched bureaucrats. And an abiding love for the country. That's what we believe in. It's still the best route to victory that we have.

Because QAnon is so over-the-top, it's easy to dismiss the conspiracy imaginings with a quick, "Who could possibly believe this stuff?" That would be a big mistake. Clearly, something about this explain-it-all conspiracy theory has connected with a lot of people. There has to be a reason QAnon keeps drawing fresh recruits.

Is it the fun of clue solving? Is it the sense of secret community that comes from associating with an out-of-the-mainstream club? Is QAnon just the latest iteration of Americans' long fascination with conspiracies?

Yes, yes, and yes. And it's also doing real damage to QAnon's purported allies.

As always, the exact numbers are hard to pin down. And since QAnon can be so encompassing, those who show up fall into several different categories. Some are total cultists. Others are merely curious, there to poke around and explore. They may find the theory interesting or thought-provoking or totally bonkers. Regardless, they aren't ready to abandon themselves to the dark fantasies. But here's what we do know: More and more, people identify with one side, hate the other, and can never admit fault with the side they're on. It's *Go, Red! Go, Blue!* Like high school football. That tribal mindset has allowed both parties to tolerate some people they never would have tolerated before. And today's narrowly segmented media makes it even worse. People who watch some cable channels hear pro-Democratic propaganda around the clock. People who watch other channels hear very nearly the reverse. Opposing voices—even the point-counterpoint segments that used to be such a staple of the news channels—are seldom heard anymore. The talking heads have been replaced by nodding heads.

"Good point, good point," they keep telling each other. No one's ideas are tested, and no one tries to change anybody else's mind.

How will anyone learn anything from that?

In the general election of November 2020, at least twenty-five QAnon candidates ran for Congress, including two in Delaware and one in my home state of New Jersey. Though most of them were long shots, QAnon supporter Marjorie Taylor Greene was anything but.

Greene had left her job as chief financial officer of a family-owned construction company in Alpharetta, Georgia. She cofounded a CrossFit gym and started posting political content on social media. Soon she was making videos, recording podcasts, and writing articles for the conspiracy-news site American Truth Seekers. Calling the deadly white supremacist rally in Charlottesville, Virginia, an "inside job" to "further the agenda of the elites." Questioning the mass shooting at Florida's Marjory Stoneman Douglas High School as a "massive false flag" and bullying student survivor David Hogg, whom she labeled #littleHitler. As Pizzagate and QAnon got hot, Greene was all over social media expressing support for the various conspiracy claims, especially the anti-Hillary kind.

"Have you guys been following 4chan, Q—any of that stuff?" she asked at the start of a November 2017 video. "I don't know who Q is, but I'm just going to tell you about it because I think it's something worth listening to and paying attention to." For the next thirty minutes, she lays out several tenets of the QAnon conspiracy.

Hillary Clinton, she argued elsewhere, had murdered her enemies, including John F. Kennedy Jr., who died in a 1999 plane crash and, according to Greene, was a Hillary rival for U.S. Senate from New York. And Greene was all in for President Trump, saying in one video: "There's a once-in-a-lifetime opportunity to take this global cabal of Satan-worshiping pedophiles out, and I think we have the president to do it."

As for Q, she said: "He is someone that is very much—loves his country, and he's on the same page as us and he is very pro-Trump, Okay? Now, he appears to have connections at the highest level. . . . It's not just someone poking in the dark, messing with people. He seems to be very high up. He seems to be very close to President Trump."

The northwest Georgia congressional district that Greene ran in is one of the state's reddest and one of the most pro-Trump in the country. Her campaign slogan was "Save America, Stop Socialism!" She called herself "the Squad's worst nightmare." "I'm 100% pro-life, 100% pro-gun, and I'm the strongest supporter of President Trump," she stressed.

Greene didn't feature QAnon in her campaign literature, and she told Fox News at one point that the group no longer represented her priorities. But she continued to include QAnon conspiracies in her campaign. It wasn't the easiest line to walk, but there was no arguing with the results. On June 10, Greene led the nine-candidate Republican primary field. In the July 15 runoff, she easily defeated a local neurosurgeon and toy store owner who ran a conventional conservative campaign.

"The GOP establishment, the media, & the radical left, spent months & millions of dollars attacking me," Greene tweeted once the votes were in. "Tonight the people of Georgia stood up & said that we will not be intimidated or believe those lies. I'm excited to be the next Congresswoman of GA 14. God bless America."

And Donald Trump agreed.

In a tweet following her runoff victory, he added his voice to the congratulations pouring in, calling the QAnon stalwart a "future Republican Star."

"Marjorie is strong on everything and never gives up—a real WINNER!" the president enthused.

That sparked an instant uproar, the president of the United States speaking so glowingly about a candidate connected to a highly publicized conspiracy cult. But when the issue came up during a White House media briefing, Trump spoke as if he'd barely heard of QAnon.

"Well," he said, "I don't know much about the movement, other than I understand they like me very much, which I appreciate."

When pressed, he mentioned that QAnon members had spoken out against the violence at some Black Lives Matter protests. "These are people that don't like seeing what's going on in places like Portland and places like Chicago and New York and other cities and states," Trump said. "And I've heard these are people that love our country."

When one of the reporters noted that QAnon followers believe "that you are secretly saving the world from this Satanic cult of pedophiles and cannibals," Trump sounded surprised and also pleased. "I haven't heard that," he said. "But is that supposed to be a bad thing or a good thing? You know. If I can help save the world from problems, I'm willing to do it. I'm willing to put myself out there."

Some people in the media have tried to use these comments by President Trump as proof that he believes in these outlandish QAnon conspiracies. I disagree. President Trump likes—and will say nice things about—anyone who says nice things about him. No more complicated than that—no other nefarious or insane explanation.

As the November election grew closer, some national Republicans kept their distance, but others joined Trump in backing Greene's candidacy: Ohio congressman Jim Jordan, House Minority Leader Kevin McCarthy, and White House chief of staff Mark Meadows. That was more than enough in Georgia 14. Marjorie Taylor Greene sailed to victory, and the headlines declared that America had its first "QAnon congresswoman."

Why am I writing about QAnon and its outlandish conspiracy theories? Isn't it too ridiculous to merit a chapter in a serious book about the future of the GOP?

No, it is not. Someone who identifies herself with the Republican Party also identifies herself with QAnon. Do the people of Georgia have the right to vote for her? Of course they do. But it does not mean that by calling ourselves Republicans, the rest of us must be associated with her views. We must speak the truth. QAnon theories are baseless, factless, absurd, and dangerous. Most Republicans in this country believe in the truth, and we need to say it out loud. Both things can and must exist. Georgia 14 can vote for Marjorie Taylor Green as a Republican, *and* most Republicans can reject the QAnon philosophy she adopts. But if we don't openly reject it, we diminish our party on other very important national issues. There will be some who say that by talking about this, we lend credence. I disagree. We must remember that Democrats will not use this ethically. They will say our failure to speak out is acquiescence by silence. I for one do not believe anyone in our party should give them the chance to unethically smear us.

Why single out Congresswoman Greene? It's not just her association and adherence to QAnon. Here are just a few of her statements: In 2018, after California wildfires, she suggested that "lasers or blue beams of light" started the fires at the urging of Governor Brown and his solar-energy allies. In November 2018, she claimed "there's never been any evidence" that a plane flew into the Pentagon on 9/11. In 2021, she compared wearing masks during COVID-19 to the treatment of Jews by Nazi Germany. This is not just political rhetoric we disagree with. These are reprehensible, crazy statements that diminish our ability as a party to be taken seriously on major policy issues with the Democrats. We have to speak clearly that we reject these statements and the public officeholders who make them. For my part, I do.

Our party has core values that matter. They are why we have come together, and we can't sell them out, even for momentary advantage. We believe in honesty and integrity, facts and fair play. We don't smear innocent people. We don't make wild accusations. And we can't tolerate people who do. Just like we can't align ourselves with violence, corruption, abuse, or racism.

That's not who we are. That's not what we believe in. That's not how we win.

There's a practical part to this, as well.

Republicans win when we make a case that people find persuasive. That's why Reagan still looms so large for so many of us. He made the party welcoming. He brought new people in. Not just the true believers. Not just the rigid ideologues. People with open hearts and open minds who never before imagined they'd be Republicans.

Yet here they were. And he did it in part by distancing himself and the party from the extremists of his day.

I'm not equating the John Birchers and QAnon conspiracists. They are creatures of different eras. They represent different kinds of threats. But they both embraced ideas that are fundamentally incompatible with the core of what our party stands for. In both cases, they are not us.

We need younger voters. We need women in the suburbs. We need diversity of many sorts. We need Democrats who've grown disillusioned with the socialist ideas of the hard left of their party. We need fresh recruits every day.

The way we will get them is to be for things that people want to be part of. Truth. Not conspiracies. Facts. Not fantasies.

QAnon is nothing if not resilient. With each new false prediction, with each new date that passed, Q climbed back onto his keyboard and delivered a new one.

If the Storm didn't come this week as promised, it's definitely coming later. If Hillary's not in custody now, she must have been slapped with an ankle bracelet before being sent home.

It takes a lot to rattle a true believer, no matter what the evidence says. When Marjorie Taylor Greene got to Congress, things unfolded about like you'd expect them to.

She'd barely arrived at the Capitol when Democrat Debbie Wasserman Schultz introduced a motion to remove the new member from her committee assignments, saying she'd "helped fuel domestic terrorism, endangered lives of her colleagues and brought shame on the entire House of Representatives." Minority Leader McCarthy admitted that some of Greene's comments were "deeply disturbing." When Senate Republican leader Mitch McConnell denounced "loony lies and conspiracy theories" as a "cancer for the Republican Party," he didn't mention Greene by name. But there was little doubt who was on his mind.

On February 4, the full House voted to remove Greene from her spots on the Education and Labor Committee and the Budget Committee. Eleven Republicans joined all the Democrats. And Greene, no longer saddled with doing the committee work she'd been elected to do, got busy just being Marjorie Taylor Greene.

She showed up for work her first day in a COVID face mask that said "Trump Won." When the presidential electoral votes were being tallied, she objected to the count from Michigan. But no one in the Senate would join her objection. (To proceed to a vote in a situation like that, someone must object in both houses of Congress.) So it went nowhere. During the January 6 insurrection at the Capitol, other members complained that Greene refused to wear a face mask while sheltering in place.

In June, the freshman from Georgia was one of twenty-one House Republicans to vote against giving the Congressional Gold Medal to the police officers who had defended the U.S. Capitol.

From reading this chapter, I hope you have concluded (as I have) that QAnon and its theories are untrue, ridiculous, and bad for this country. Our country is founded in part, however, to allow views like this and their expression to be protected. As much as I disagree with these opinions, it would scare me even more if government were allowed to suppress them. But as a party and as a political movement, we must reject those views and those who espouse them. If we do not, we diminish our ability to do big things for America.

CHAPTER 14

LIES PLURAL

If the requirement for getting your support is to say a bunch of things that aren't true, *no, thank you.* That's not who I am, and that's not who we are as Republicans, no matter who's demanding we tie our futures to a pile of lies.

We are better than that.

Leave the lying to the cynics and the extremists, in and out of the party, and to the far-left Democrats. We as Republicans need to keep being the party of reason, decency, integrity, and truth, regardless of who's counseling otherwise. Believe me, the truth will win in the end.

I really do believe that, despite all the wild claims that are swirling around us now. And I'm convinced that most of my fellow Republicans believe it, too.

Telling the truth isn't just the moral thing to do, though morality has to be part of the equation—even in politics. Truth-telling is also the smart thing. It's what makes other people believe us. It's what shows them we have something valuable to say. It's what convinces the voters to follow us and join our movement. In practical terms, telling the truth clears the decks and lets us get on to the issues that really matter, pulling the nation back from the wrongheaded direction it's now heading in. Telling the truth, even when it's difficult, is what shows the American people they're in better hands with Republicans than with Democrats.

All this lying is doing harm to our nation, to our party, and to us.

You already know what some professional political operatives are telling Republican politicians, don't you? *Pander to the lies and the liars,* they say. *The lies are crazy, but just nod and pretend to agree. Say as little as you can get away with and duck when the reporters come around. Whatever you do, don't upset the truth deniers, the conspiracy propagandists, the QAnoners, the white supremacists, and the wild extremists who are making so much noise these days. They could easily come for you next.*

And then the cynics warn: *Look at Mike Pence.*

Mike Pence is a conservative. He was a loyal vice president to Donald Trump, standing at the president's side on easy days and hard ones. But Mike had also read the U.S. Constitution, and he knew that a vice president had no legal authority to overturn the choice of the American people or the vote of the Electoral College. The moment of truth came on January 6, 2021, when it came time to record the Electoral College results. Following the Constitution and the law, Mike refused to pretend that someone who had lost had really won.

There is no doubt that Mike Pence wanted Donald Trump to win reelection. It would have advanced the causes the vice president had spent a lifetime fighting for. A Trump-Pence victory would have given Mike another four years as vice president and set him up to run for president in 2024. But in politics as in life, we don't always get what we hope for, try as we might. And when Mike refused to join the liars and enablers who were telling Donald Trump he had won, an angry mob stormed the Capitol and many of the angriest thought they knew who was most to blame.

"Hang Mike Pence!" they shouted. "Hang Mike Pence!"

Mike was inside the Capitol as the mob broke in. He'd just read a letter to the joint session of Congress that said in part: "My oath to support and defend the Constitution constrains me from claiming unilateral authority to determine which electoral votes should be counted and which should not." His family was there with him to witness history being made. This wasn't the kind of history they expected. The threat from the mob was so imminent, the vice president's Secret Service detail had to spring into action without a moment's delay, hustling the Pence family out of harm's way. What the Pences didn't know yet but would soon find out was this: Outside the Capitol, someone had already constructed crude wooden gallows, assembled symbolically for Mike Pence.

If a future in the Republican Party requires silence in the face of that, count me out. If timid acceptance is the price of admission, we're not the party we have always been. Mike Pence is a friend. Mike Pence is a patriot. On January 6, he did the only thing he legally could do. Simple as that. We Republicans are used to having truth on our side.

It was Republicans, you'll recall, who told the truth about the Soviet Union during the Cold War while people on the left called for a nuclear freeze and accepted the permanency of the "Evil Empire." We said *no*. The communists in Moscow are thugs. They oppress their people. They dominate their neighbors. They'll come for us if we give them a half a chance. It was Ronald Reagan who said: "Mr. Gorbachev, tear down this wall." And history has proven that Reagan was right. Joe Biden and liberal Democrats wanted the nuclear freeze and capitulation. Where would we be if that had prevailed?

A hard truth, well told.

It's Republicans, not Democrats, who've spoken up reliably for freedom at home and abroad. Freedom from communist dictatorships. The freedom to travel and trade. Freedom from the oppression of high taxes, union abuses, and excessive government regulation.

The freedom of faith and belief. Freedom of opportunity, which so many of these other freedoms depend on. Those freedoms have helped America become what it is at its best, a strong, compassionate nation where individuals are allowed to make their own decisions and to succeed. Over and over, it's been Republicans who've spoken up.

A hard truth, well told.

It's Republicans who've told the truth about fiscal responsibility, not always a cheery topic, while Democrats sought political advantage from spending more and more. We've been the ones who've said, "Someone is going to pay for this, and it's hardworking Americans. They're already overburdened." We've been the party to show mercy on *them*. We've been the ones to call the profligate spending what it is. Unsustainable. Irresponsible. Undermining to American energy and ambition. Unfair to future generations who will be buried in debt and expected to pay all these overdue bills.

A hard truth, well told.

From the riots of the 1960s to "Defund the Police," it's the Republicans who've told the truth about public safety while Democrats were repeatedly swept up in liberal guilt. We said crime was wrecking our cities and creeping into our suburbs and small towns. One need only look at the latest rioting and looting in our nation's cities that Democrats have rationalized and supported, even bailing out some of the criminals. After the summer, there can be no doubt which party is the party of law and order. We said the border must be secured. We stood up for our police even when it wasn't popular. We said, "We can have a fair justice system and still keep the streets safe." Criminal justice reform done with the police and the community— not done *to* the police and the community. It's all about the balance. Those goals are not in conflict.

A hard truth, well told.

It's Republicans, not Democrats, who have turned the courts back toward what our forefathers envisioned—interpreters, not makers of the law. This job is far from done, but we've made tremendous progress. Rescuing the courts from judicial activists. Appointing judges who understand their role. Giving civil parties and criminal defendants what they deserve, a fair hearing guided by the rule of law. Not some appointee's political preferences. Not the legal fad of the moment. The law.

Another hard truth, well told.

Notice a pattern? Republicans keep telling hard truths, and America benefits mightily. The question going forward: Will the truth set us free again?

The Big Lie.

That's what the critics call it, Donald Trump's adamant assertion that he'd have easily won the 2020 election if only it hadn't been stolen from him. It's a loaded phrase, of course. The term is designed to highlight the toxic nature of Trump's never-say-die victory claims. It indicates the high stakes of presidential elections and the media's intense distrust of and dislike for Donald Trump.

Trump being Trump, he grabbed the phrase and turned it back on his enemies. The Big Lie, when Trump uses those words, is anyone's claim that he *didn't* win.

The truth, however, is that the phrase is wrong, whichever side is using it. There is no one big lie about the 2020 election. There are dozens and dozens of them. Small and medium ones. In varying shapes and sizes. Haphazardly documented, thinly sourced, and thrown at the wall. Designed not so much to convince anyone as to give the die-hards something to cling to and feel aggrieved about as reality slowly settles in.

An election for president was held on November 3, 2020. Joe Biden won. Donald Trump did not. That is the truth. Any claim to the contrary is untrue.

I'm sorry the election turned out the way it did, but that's what happened. It wasn't the result I was hoping for, but it's the result we got. There's only one thing to do in a situation like this: Come back and win the next one and the one after that. No amount of wishful thinking is ever going to change the past.

This is not to say that some irregularities did not happen. Too many mail-in ballots were sent to people who didn't ask for one. Too many rules were haphazardly changed due to COVID, causing confusion and delays in counting. But none of that would have changed the results. None of it. All the yelling and wishing in the world won't change that fact.

No defiant rally speeches. No bamboo ballot investigations or preposterous accusations against voting machine companies. No seances with Hugo Chávez. What worries me now amid all the noise and anger is that a lot of decent people, including some friends of mine, still actually believe the election was stolen.

As the 2020 election grew closer, I grew more concerned for Donald Trump. He retained his usual bravado, boasting about how easily he was going to beat the hapless Joe Biden. From time to time, however, he did float what sounded like preemptive excuses, hinting that maybe he wasn't so confident of victory, after all.

He raised alarm about the security of mail-in ballots. He highlighted the historic corruption in cities where Democrats were in charge. He warned about dead people voting. And he brought up a dark possibility. "The only way we're going to lose this election," he said in August, "is if the election is rigged. Remember that."

And he kept using the word *rigged*, joking about the special pressure he was under facing an opponent as inept as he said Biden was.

"If I lose, can you imagine?" Trump said on October 17. "I will have lost to the worst candidate, the worst candidate in the history of presidential politics. If I lose, what do I do? I'd rather run against somebody who's extraordinarily talented. At least, this way I can go and lead my life."

I tried to warn him about Biden. He didn't want to hear it.

The next day, he blamed Democratic governors for purposely harming their own states' economies with unnecessary COVID shutdowns. "We have like five or six of these Democrats keeping their states closed because they're trying to hurt us on November third," Trump told supporters in Carson City, Nevada. "New York should be open. Michigan now has to open because of the court case. North Carolina should be open. They should be open. You guys, you want to open. Yeah, you want to open. Pennsylvania has to open. I mean, you know." He was right that those states should have opened sooner. But conflating that with the election made no sense.

The only conclusion I can come to is that, by then, he was having real doubts that he was going to win reelection. But that didn't mean he was anywhere near ready to accept defeat.

So, how do we know all the election fraud stories aren't true?

Well, we just have to look at the facts and the glaring absence of evidence. Taken together, they're a devastating combination. Despite the endless claims and swirling allegations, no one has ever come up with solid proof of voter fraud on a scale that could possibly overturn the results. Not Donald Trump. Not his clown car of a legal team. Not the breathless media. Not the 74,216,154 honest American citizens who voted Trump-Pence on November 3, 2020, myself included. No one.

By now, more than sixty courts have weighed these voting fraud claims. State and federal judges, all across the country, including quite a few appointed by Donald Trump. Exactly zero of these cases have gone the president's way, including the handful that have made their way to the conservative majority on the United States Supreme Court. No credible attorneys remain on the Trump legal team. The ex-president's rally speeches are scraping up nothing new. And he keeps turning against more and more of his former allies. By late June 2021, when Bill Barr, the president's staunchly supportive attorney general, told ABC's Jonathan Karl that the voter fraud claims were "bullshit"—well, it was hard to imagine they would gain much traction anywhere.

Of the many, many voter fraud claims that have been floated by now, there are what I would call the Big Five, the ones that garnered the most attention from the president's backers and from the media:

- That corrupt political operatives in heavily Democratic Detroit and Philadelphia stuffed the ballot boxes for Joe Biden, costing Trump two key swing states he'd won four years earlier.

- That hacked Dominion voting machines counted Trump votes as Biden votes.

- That some states had more votes than voters.

- That the proliferation of mail-in ballots in response to COVID led to rampant voter fraud.

- And that routine, minor election screwups were in fact something more.

There are scores of others, far too many to wade through at this late date. But let's address the Big Five straight on. Facts are facts. We should follow them. If there's any truth out there, this is where it should lie.

"BIG CITY BALLOT DUMPS"

We might as well start in Detroit and Philly. Trump pushed his big-city-Democrats-stole-the-election theory. Unfortunately, there are no facts in the 2020 election to support it.

It was in Detroit that Trump supporters howled the loudest about mysterious "ballot dumps," boxes of paper ballots arriving at the downtown TCF Center after the polls had closed on election night. The corruption was even caught on videotape, Team Trump said. And soon enough, the video "evidence" was popping up all over YouTube. But there was a major problem with this supposed *gotcha*. It proved nothing of the kind. In Wayne County, Michigan, home of Detroit, ballots aren't counted at the 662 local precincts. They are all brought to the downtown convention center to be counted and tabulated in that central location. Just as expected, the ballot boxes arrived through the night.

All that videotape wasn't proof of voter fraud. It was proof of the system working exactly as it was designed to work in Wayne County. Also, one of the alleged "ballot dumps" was, in fact, an image of a local TV photographer carrying in his equipment—not a case of ballots. That's according to a report from a Michigan GOP Senate oversight committee. Again, hardly part of an inner-city Democratic vote-stealing cover-up.

And look at the totals. Voter turnout was up in Michigan over 2016 by 15.4 percent, but only up 11.4 percent in Wayne County, debunking the ballot-dump theory. Also, Trump actually did *better* in the city in 2020 than he'd done in 2016 and better than any other Republican presidential candidate had done there in recent years. His 12,654 votes in the city were almost 5,000 *more* than he'd gotten against Hillary Clinton. He also surpassed the 8,881 votes McCain received in 2008 and the 6,019 votes Mitt Romney (who was born in Detroit) pulled in 2012, when the city had tens of thousands more voters. More important, in 2020 Donald Trump received 5.02 percent of the Detroit vote, more than 2 percent *more* than in 2016. In 2020, Joe Biden got 1 percent *less* than Hillary Clinton in 2016. A very ineffective steal by the Democrats.

Unlike the conspiracy theories, these numbers don't lie.

So where's the fraud? Trump did better this time! Better in the number of votes and better in the percentage of votes—and Biden did worse. Instead of trying to use Detroit as proof that he was robbed, Trump should probably be sending a fat bonus check to whoever ran his Wayne County campaign. The numbers say "pretty good showing there for a Republican, all things considered." Sorry, the only thing the numbers don't say is "massive voter fraud against Republicans."

Something similar happened in heavily Democratic Philadelphia, where Trump got 18 percent to Biden's 81 percent, a slightly *better* Trump showing than in 2016. Trump was up 24,000 votes in Philadelphia from four years earlier. Trump did 3 percent *better* than he did in 2016. Biden did one and a half percent *worse* than Clinton. Net gain, Trump.

The problem in both places was the same, and it reflected a problem Trump faced in other metropolitan areas, as well. He did far *worse* in the suburbs than he needed to do to win, especially with suburban women. To win these states, Republicans need to do well in the suburbs. In the four collar counties that make up suburban Philadelphia, Donald Trump lost to Joe Biden by 104,741 more votes than he lost to Hillary Clinton. Fraud in Philadelphia didn't cost him Pennsylvania. Suburban voters did. The numbers don't lie. He lost all of Pennsylvania by a total of 80,555. If he had done as well in the Philly suburbs in 2020 as he did in 2016, along with his better total in the city of Philadelphia, he would have won Pennsylvania.

Trump knew he had a problem there. In the weeks before the

election, while he was railing against mail-in ballots and Democratic governors, he also pleaded at a rally in Pennsylvania: "Suburban women, will you please like me!" He got his answer on election day.

As the *Philadelphia Inquirer* put it: "Biden's victory in Pennsylvania was fueled in large part by winning an overwhelming majority of votes in Philadelphia's four collar counties, along with strong performances in the suburbs of Pittsburgh and Harrisburg."

But in those same Philadelphia collar counties, Republicans held on well in down-ballot races. Biden didn't have strong coattails. It wasn't Republicans who got beat in the suburbs. It was Trump. And Pennsylvania was a loss that really stung. Once the Associated Press called the state for Biden on Saturday morning, it gave the Democrats 284 Electoral College votes, easily putting him over the 270 needed to win the presidency.

"DOMINION OVER THE EARTH"

And then there were the Dominion voting machines.

The alleged conspiracies involving them are so outlandish, so bizarre, it's hard to recount them without an incredulous head shake and a knowing smile. Did anyone really believe this stuff? A lot of it originally bubbled out of the swamp of QAnon, which I wouldn't call surprising, and was quickly seized on by the Trump legal team and amplified on the president's own Twitter feed. The basic idea: that the Dominion Voting Systems' software caused millions of Trump votes to be deleted or assigned to Joe Biden.

That would be terrible . . . if it were true.

The alleged Dominion vote switching became a favorite theory in large part because of its scale. The company's voting technology was just about everywhere. If the software or the hardware was truly corrupted, that could have a profound impact on the election results.

So where was the proof? Actually, it was nowhere.

Trump lawyers Rudy Giuliani and Sidney Powell were all over this one, as was MyPillow CEO Mike Lindell. They claimed (falsely) that Dominion used software developed by a competing firm, Smartmatic, which the lawyers (falsely) said Dominion owned and (falsely) said was founded by Hugo Chávez, the late socialist dictator of Venezuela who had died in 2013. Yes, when you're talking about these conspiracy theories, the word *falsely* comes up a lot. The Trump lawyers also falsely said Dominion sent their voting data to Smartmatic at foreign locations around the world and that Smartmatic was a "radical-left" company with connections to Antifa. False, false, and false. The company was actually founded in Toronto, has its co-headquarters in Denver, and is now owned by a private-equity fund in New York, with no history of nefarious behavior or evil political ties. These people just want to make money, as far as anyone can tell.

Among the many other voting technology falsehoods:

That the Dominion machines had backdoor connections to the internet, allowing Democratic hackers to slip in. That the machines would print a paper receipt accurately showing the voter's selection but change the vote inside. That Edison Research, a respected political data company, had uncovered massive Dominion fraud.

None of that was true. And that couldn't possibly have come as a surprise to anyone.

On November 12, 2020, barely a week after the election, CISA, the Cybersecurity and Infrastructure Security Agency, a tech-savvy unit of Trump's own Department of Homeland Security, released a formal statement debunking the supposed Dominion conspiracies: "There is no evidence that any voting system deleted or lost votes, changed votes or was in any way compromised." The statement was endorsed by government and voting industry experts, including the presidents of the National Association of State Election Directors and the National Association of Secretaries of State. But the conspiracy claims were already in the political bloodstream, and they wouldn't easily be flushed out.

Dominion employees were stalked and threatened. Doctored videos appeared, claiming to show Dominion workers manipulating election results. Employee addresses and other personal information popped up online. The company had to hire security teams. Eventually, this all devolved into lawsuits—against the Trump lawyers, against some of the media outlets that parroted the claims, and against the MyPillow guy, Mike Lindell. Dominion sued for $1.3 billion, claiming defamation. Lindell returned with a $1.6 billion suit against the company, although Akiva Cohen, a popular attorney on Twitter, did seriously call the pillow guy's lawsuit a "craptastic legal job."

And still, no one has ever been able to produce any reliable evidence showing Dominion and its software did anything wrong. In fact, Attorney General Bill Barr put it most succinctly: The voting machine is a counting machine, and it saves everything that was counted. So, you just reconcile the two. There has been no discrepancy anywhere. Even President Trump's lawyer Sidney Powell said in a court filing defending herself against the Dominion lawsuit that no reasonable person could have taken the claim seriously. Yet she advocated it all over the mainstream media. She advocated it to the president of the United States and got him to repeat it. When sued, she then said that no reasonable person could believe what she had said publicly, over and over, as a lawyer for the president. All I can say is: Wow.

Case closed on Dominion.

"MORE VOTES THAN VOTERS"

The message sounded urgent when it landed in the president's Twitter feed at 11:37 p.m. on November 22, not quite three weeks after the election: "In certain swing states, there were more votes than people who voted, and in big numbers. Does that not really matter?"

Of course, it would matter . . . if it were true. If the evidence supported the claim, it could be a voting fraud smoking gun! But the evidence said no such thing.

Trump, it seemed, was recycling an inaccurate claim that in some key states, the vote totals exceeded the number of people who were registered to vote. That talk had been circulating on social media since shortly after election day. On closer inspection, every cited example was wrong, including the six states Trump was vigorously contesting—Arizona, Georgia, Michigan, Nevada, Pennsylvania, and Wisconsin. Each of those states had far more registered voters than votes cast, and the numbers of people who voted precisely mirrored the number of votes cast. Stick with me. The math isn't hard to follow. In Georgia, Michigan, and Pennsylvania, the difference between registered and actual voters was more than 2 million people in each state. To be clear, that's over 2 million more registered voters per state who could have voted than *did* vote. Bad for America perhaps but not an obvious legal problem. Wisconsin reported the narrowest margin at 387,612 voters, and that number didn't include same-day registrants. So the true cushion was even larger.

Nowhere did the votes surpass the voters. But that didn't quiet anyone.

In Pennsylvania, state representative Frank Ryan came out blazing on this one. He had such precise detail, his allegation sounded like it must have some truth to it: "A comparison of official county election results to the total number of voters who voted on Nov. 3,

2020, as recorded by the Department of State shows that 6,962,607 total ballots were reported as being cast, while DoS/SURE system records indicate that only 6,760,230 total voters actually voted," Ryan announced.

The claim immediately rocketed across social media. Trump's retweet was itself retweeted 117,000 times. But hold on. According to the Pennsylvania Department of State, the agency that maintains voter records, Ryan's allegation was based on "obvious misinformation." In fact, a shade under 7 million voted for president in Pennsylvania, the same number of votes that were counted, out of just over 9 million registered voters. And despite various court challenges, no one in any state could ever provide evidence to back up these too-many-voters claims.

And another claim is defeated by the facts.

"MAIL-IN CATASTROPHE"

Once it became clear that the COVID-19 pandemic would not be over in time for a normal presidential election day in 2020, governors across the country and some state legislatures began to enact drastic changes in their voting laws, including making mail-in voting easier and more available. From state to state, the changes in law varied from the small (allowing voters to receive excuse-free mail-in ballots) to the significant (sending mail-in ballots to all registered voters whether they asked for the ballots or not).

From the beginning, President Trump was spooked by this. He told his supporters that mail-in ballots were rigged, that they wouldn't be counted if the votes were for him, and that his backers should vote only on election day. Mail-in ballots, he warned, would be one of the ways that Democrats would steal the election from him. These statements caused real strategic strife within his own campaign. Bill Stepien, the president's campaign manager, was concerned about the impact this could have on traditionally Trump-loyal senior citizen voters, since seniors were among the most vulnerable to the coronavirus. Stepien feared that many seniors would not want to go to the polls on election day because they feared the virus and would not vote by mail because their leader said those votes wouldn't count. Those were votes in key swing states that the president could be driving out of his vote total with his own words.

Other senior members of the campaign, including Jason Miller, Hope Hicks, Kellyanne Conway, and I, shared Stepien's concern. At one time or another, individually and collectively, we all urged the president to lower his rhetoric on mail-in ballots. He would hear nothing of it. Unfortunately, the president may very well have driven many of his own voters not to vote for him over their fear of the virus and his fear of rigged mail-in ballots. We will never know for sure. But that was a real danger identified by the president's closest and most experienced strategists.

Many Republicans were worried about the proliferation of mail-in ballots. Stories circulated across the internet about people receiving multiple ballots in the same name at their homes. I am confident that many of those stories were true. However, when you looked at the number of votes cast in each state and the percentage change in that vote from 2016 to 2020, none of the totals indicated a massive, illegal, election-changing ballot dump in any particular state. Further, there was no evidence that this voter fraud theory ever became a reality.

Some people have pointed out that the mail-in ballots went overwhelmingly to Joe Biden. Skeptics contended that the wide margin for Biden on the mail-in votes was the result of fraud. But two readily apparent explanations prove that was highly unlikely. First, Trump's words themselves. It was President Trump who directly told his voters not to vote by mail. He was the one who told them they should all vote on election day when they "knew" their votes would be counted. And what did we learn on election night as a result? The states that counted the machine votes first, like Pennsylvania, showed a huge lead for Trump early in the evening. But when the mail-in votes were counted, Biden roared back, overtaking Trump in Pennsylvania by 80,000 votes. On the other hand, in Ohio, where the mail-in ballots were counted first, Biden had an early, unexpected lead. Then, when the machine votes were counted later that night and early the next morning, Trump won Ohio by a convincing 9 percentage points.

Second, Democrats were always more reluctant to go out in public during the pandemic than Republicans were. Biden barely left his basement in Wilmington for most of the campaign. When he did, he and his supporters held small rallies, socially distanced with everyone wearing masks. Republicans followed their leader's example. Donald Trump began big rallies again over the summer. He did not wear a mask during those rallies, nor did most of the people in his crowd. Almost none of the participants in those rallies were socially distanced. Given those facts, should it surprise anyone that more Democrats voted by mail from the safety of their kitchens and more Republicans voted in the traditional method on voting machines in their school cafeterias on election day?

Yes, mail-in ballots led to a higher voter turnout in 2020, more votes for both presidential candidates than ever before. But that doesn't prove that there was fraud. With more than 74 million votes, Donald Trump got the second-most votes of any presidential candidate in U.S. history—second only to his 2020 opponent, Joe Biden.

We should not permit the Democrats to turn our country into a mail-in voting society. There is something admirably communal about election day, in-person voting. That is why you see so many red states now tightening their election laws to make sure that there will never again be a large number of mail-in ballots sent to people who did not request them. That will not only reduce the chance of fraud. It will also shorten the election night wait in 2024 for the results. These laws are not, as Joe Biden likes to describe them, designed to prevent people from voting. They are designed to make sure that everyone who has the right to vote gets to vote and not one person more.

To say that mail-in ballots created a fraud that determined the winner in the 2020 election is simply not supported by the facts. But if mail-in votes won the election for Joe Biden, Donald Trump may have only himself to blame.

"MINOR MISHAPS, MAJOR CONCLUSIONS"

People want to hear what people want to hear, and a lot of Republicans wanted to hear that Donald Trump won reelection. I get that. So, it was no big surprise, through the spring and summer and into the fall, that so many people in our party were at least open to Trump's stolen-election claims. A national poll from Reuters/Ipsos in late May found that 53 percent of Republicans were prepared to call Donald Trump the "true" president while 47 percent said that description belonged to Joe Biden. Another 56 percent of Republicans said that Biden's victory was "the result of illegal voting or election rigging."

And those numbers stayed fairly steady through 2021.

It's hard to say how much of that was wishful thinking and how much was genuine belief, but there's no denying that Trump's daily, incessant claims found an audience among disappointed Republicans. The problem is that we are doing ourselves no favors as a party and as national leaders when we refuse to accept facts that lead to a different conclusion than the conclusion we favor and worked for in the election. It distracts us. It exhausts us. It saps our credibility. And the truth will assert itself eventually.

There were problems in the last presidential election. There always are. Elections are human endeavors. They are never perfect. Something always goes wrong. But the evidence is clear this time: There were no irregularities that could have possibly changed the result in any one state, let alone four. That's how many the Trump campaign would have needed to change the results.

I am not naïve. I am from New Jersey, after all. One of my predecessors, the late Democratic governor Brendan Byrne, would often say, "When I die, I want my wife to bury me in Hudson County—so I can stay active in politics." He was joking, kind of.

Election fraud happens and has happened in this country. That is why we always need to improve our laws and voting systems to make sure people trust the results. That's why the new Georgia law is not "Jim Crow 2," as Joe Biden (falsely) states. It will lead to more people voting who have the right to vote and to a more trustworthy result. Democrats in Congress are trying to rig elections in their favor by having the federal government take over every state election. The feds in charge? What could possibly go wrong?

But there is no credible evidence that the 2020 election was stolen. I say this as a former prosecutor. I say it as a disappointed Trump voter and supporter. I say it because it is true. It's just that simple.

PART III

WINNING AGAIN

It's a truism of politics that you can't beat something with nothing.

That's true about candidates, and it's true about the ideas that candidates discuss. Many of us, we look at what Joe Biden and the Democrats are trying to do in office and think, purely on the merits, that they should lose because their ideas are so awful. In my experience, that's not the way politics works. The way politics works is that your opponents may have bad ideas. But when they're in charge, you can unseat them only if the ideas you present are better than the ones they're pushing on the voters.

Well, Joe Biden and Kamala Harris are testing that theory. Look at what they've already wrought in just their first year in power. A completely porous southern border where not only Mexicans and people from Central America are crossing illegally but people from all over the globe are traveling to Mexico to take advantage of Biden's open-border policy. How does he deal with this problem? By putting Kamala Harris in charge, then watching her do nothing. We've seen how ineptly these two have handled the vaccine roll-out by being heavy-handed with Americans who wanted to learn more before rolling up their sleeves, leaving far too many people still unvaccinated long after the vaccines became widely available. Huge federal subsidies to state governments without budget deficits. Enormous grants designed to force electric cars on every American. Large unemployment insurance checks that have caused a serious labor shortage for American business. Profligate federal spending that is causing inflation not seen since the 1970s. Tax increases both here and around the world to penalize success and diminish the capitalist system. Congressional attempts to take over the election laws in every state. Actions every day that undercut our police officers on the street, leading to a record spree in violent crime across the country. Surrendering every classroom in America to radical teachers' union leaders who want to feed critical race theory to our next generation of children. Joe Biden, the moderate uniter who campaigned to bring Americans together, is gone. He has been replaced by a Joe Biden beholden to socialist Bernie Sanders, his sidekick Elizabeth Warren, and the out-of-touch Nancy Pelosi.

It is that straightforward and that scary. Only a renewed, truth-telling Republican Party can stop these policies and restore freedom and protect capitalism.

So, there's no use writing the first two parts of this book if I'm not going to write the third part. Learning how we got here and learning the truth about some of the conspiracy theories—that's worthless if it doesn't give us a platform to present alternative ideas, ideas that are superior to the ones the Democrats are foisting on the American people. This only works if we have a better course to offer than the one the country is currently on.

That's what's coming next.

In the pages ahead, we'll confront issues domestic and foreign. Challenges that are both near and long term. Problems that need specific solutions, not just platitudes. That's how we start a larger conversation inside our party and with all of the American people about the destructive course we're on.

We have a better alternative.

Look, here it is.

Underlying each of these proposals is a foundation of powerful, time-tested ideas.

That capitalism is better than government control of the economy.

That a strong America only remains strong if we provide leadership, not just at home but also around the world, because part of our strength comes from our alliances, an international advantage the Russians and the Chinese only wish they had.

That a public education system must give our children the opportunity to succeed by teaching them the truth about our country and the world, not indoctrinating them with union-generated garbage meant to make them hate being Americans and distrust the children next to them because of the color of their skin or where they come from.

That the American military must rebuild to deal with the challenges of tomorrow, not yesterday—led by a Navy second to none on the oceans of the world.

That while the American military remains a key source of strength for us, the integrity and goodness of our ideas and our people also needs to be something that others want to emulate everywhere.

That every American is entitled to law, order, and justice regardless of zip code or skin color or political philosophy. That we don't defund our police. We work with them to solve the problems in our streets, whether those problems are caused by criminals looting or by the actions of ill-trained officers. Communities and police can work as one to restore order and justice, once we lead the way and show them how.

And that the strength of America still lies in the founding principles of our nation. Protection of life. Protection of liberty. And the freedom to pursue happiness.

All these ideas provide a foundation for the American people to do as they choose to, not as the government dictates what must be done. This, inevitably, means taking on the various elites who have gained far too much power in our country. Big Tech. Big Media. Public-Sector Labor. And Big Government. Unless we can tame those runaway forces, we and America don't have a chance. The fight to win the future needs to start immediately—and it won't succeed if all we do is to keep looking backward and litigating the grievances of the past. America is at stake *right now*.

CHAPTER 15

ON EDUCATION

I have quite a history with the teachers' union.

When I became governor of New Jersey, I inherited an $11 billion budget deficit. That was the welcome-to-Trenton gift my Democratic predecessor left for me. I was looking everywhere for ways to share the sacrifice, committed to closing the gap without increasing taxes on the people of the state. One of the places I went looking was the teachers' union.

My suggestion at the time: Freeze teacher pay for a year and cover a small portion of health-care premiums. That would have prevented any reduction in aid to the classrooms. The union wouldn't even discuss it. They laughed at the very idea. By then, the teachers' union had become the most powerful force in modern Democratic politics, not just in my state but all across America. I was getting an early taste.

In New Jersey, when I became governor, membership in the teachers' union was mandatory if you work in the public school system. The only way out it is to *pay* your way out. Instead of paying your full annual union dues, you paid 70 percent. But if you only paid the 70 percent, you lost your right to vote in the union. It was just like the Eagles' "Hotel California": "You can check out anytime you like, but you can never leave."

How much money did all that produce for the New Jersey Education Association, as the teachers' union is called? Well, they had 200,000 members at $700 a year. If you can't multiply that, ask a unionized math teacher. It's a lot of money. I know that. They were paying the union leaders seven-figure salaries. Those dues also didn't contribute anything to teacher pensions, teacher salaries, or teacher health-care costs, and the rest of the money was used to reward their friends and attack their enemies with aggressive TV commercials, billboards, and digital advertising.

I was high on their enemies list, but I never backed down.

I fought to bring teachers in line with other public employees, who helped to pay their own pension and health-care costs. When I got started, teachers paid nothing toward their health care. Zero. Those health-care benefits cost the state a fortune. In the long run, teacher pensions probably cost the state even more. After a year and a half of retirement, the average New Jersey teacher had already exhausted all of the money he or she had put into the system, based on the formula at the time. Everything after that had to be generated by investment returns or covered by the taxpayers.

In April 2010, while we were in the middle of fighting over all this, the head of one of the county teachers' unions sent out an email containing a prayer for my death. "Dear Lord," the prayer began, "this year you have taken away my favorite actor, Patrick Swayze; my favorite actress, Farrah Fawcett; my favorite singer, Michael Jackson, and my favorite salesman, Billy Mays. . . . I just wanted to let you know that Chris Christie is my favorite governor."

What do you say after that? "Amen"?

I didn't consider it a threat. I think it was more of a wish. In some ways, a wish is even creepier. But that was the tenor of the relationship. And the nastier the teachers' union got, the more the public turned against them. I urged everyone to send a message to the teachers' union, and they sent one loud and clear. The people of

New Jersey voted down 65 percent of the local school budgets that year.

Nothing like that had ever happened before.

The lesson I took from it was that people overwhelmingly liked their teachers. But they understood the difference between their teachers and the teachers' union. And if you spoke up honestly about this reality, people would act on it. Here's something else I learned eventually: Though we tamed the New Jersey teachers' union for the next eight years, that was just one state, and there's been some real backsliding under my uber-progressive successor since I left office in 2018. This goes to show: Absent changes in law, which I couldn't do with the Democratic-controlled legislature, much as I would have liked to, your successor can often reverse the tone and tenor of your reforms and accomplishments. It's maddening.

Meanwhile, all across America, things have been getting worse. The National Education Association, the country's largest teachers' union, and their like minded cousins at the American Federation of Teachers have never been more out of control than they are right now. Our children are already paying the price.

Look at some of the latest agenda items the union delegates have been pushing.

That students in all fifty states be indoctrinated with *critical race theory*, which says that a person is defined above all else by race, gender, and sexual orientation and that American institutions are designed to ensure white supremacy and patriarchy.

That all teachers in all public school systems be taught *cultural responsiveness*, *implicit bias*, *trauma-informed practices*, and *restorative justice practices*.

That similar indoctrination be imposed on students in grades K to 12. Just what we need today! Second graders being taught how to distrust kids just because they're a different color! Dr. Martin Luther King would be appalled.

That the union issue a study to union members nationwide criticizing *empire, white supremacy, anti-blackness, anti-indigeneity, racism, patriarchy, capitalism, ableism, anthropocentrism,* and *other forms of power and oppression at the intersections of our society.* I know what most of those words mean, though I had to look up *anthropocentrism.* I'm still trying to decide if I'm for it or against it. I think I'm for it, and I also think that's not the answer the union wants to hear. Look it up yourself. You'll be stunned.

That the union join forces with Black Lives Matter and the Zinn Education Project (promoters of "the people's history") to organize national and local rallies on George Floyd's birthday. Also to advocate for a national day of action to teach about structural racism and oppression. Incredible but true.

Lastly, the union delegates want to "share resources to decolonize the curriculum." Are they kidding? Tragically, they are not, and they are coming for our children and grandchildren with this radical agenda. And they have the support of Joe and Jill Biden.

Now, most of this stuff is so ridiculous on its face, you'd think most Americans could dismiss it out of hand. And they will. But here's the problem: The National Education Association represents three million educators across the country. The American Federation of Teachers has another 1.7 million. And the leaders of both unions appear equally dedicated to all this American self-flagellation. As teachers, principals, and administrators, they are pushing the message in school districts everywhere and spending hundreds of millions of dollars in union dues to spread this left-wing version of intolerance, rigidity, and hate. Clearly, the union leaders are ready for a fight. Are we?

Any parents who oppose any of this will be quickly attacked as bigots, people who trade in racial hatred and enemies of free speech. This is where my "good friend" Randi Weingarten comes in. As president of the American Federation of Teachers, she seems to have concluded that the best defense is a highly aggressive offense. It's the critics, she says, not the hard-driving union activists, who are trying to stifle debate. Let me quote her stirring words: "Culture warriors are labeling any discussion of race, racism or discrimination as critical race theory to try and make it toxic and bullying teachers to try and stop us from teaching students accurate history."

Nothing could be farther from the truth.

I thought the teachers' union was bad when they were fighting for disproportionate pensions and out-of-line free health benefits at the expense of New Jersey taxpayers. Boy, those were the good ol' days!

The two big teachers' unions have now become the leaders and the muscle behind progressive politics in America. They are the most important players in the Democratic Party's progressive wing. And they've never had a stronger ally in the White House than Joe Biden and his teachers' union wife, Jill Biden. Sorry. *Doctor* Jill Biden. What's really going on here is not an attempt to correct the erroneous teaching of history but a fierce ideological campaign to turn history on its head. To teach our children that America is irredeemably racist and inherently evil. And all this needs to be done, according to the revved-up union leadership, because we haven't made any progress in this country on the issue of race.

President Biden contributes to this skewed view of America every time he calls the Georgia election law "Jim Crow 2.0" or makes a similarly ungrounded comment. He really needs to stop. He is lying to the American people and trying to divide the American people along racial lines for his own political benefit. Shame on him.

To say that we haven't made progress on racial matters in this country from the time of our founding to today is to fundamentally bastardize our history. It's to mischaracterize America for political purposes. How many examples would you like?

Slavery was abolished in the mid-1800s.

Poll taxes and voting tests were eliminated a century later.

As recently as sixty years ago, we still had segregated lunch counters, segregated water fountains, and segregated bathrooms, all part of the public domain and generally accepted in the country. Those are all long gone. We've even had folks like Bill Maher, who could hardly be tagged a conservative, calling out this nonsense for exactly what it is.

"Progressophobia" is Maher's term.

"It's a brain disorder that strikes liberals and makes them incapable of recognizing progress. It's like situational blindness, only what you can't see is your dorm [today] is better than the South before the Civil War." If you're thinking Americans are now more racist than ever, which is exactly what the union leaders want us to believe, then you have Maher's "progressophobia." And before this, I thought Bill Maher's best trait was that he is a fan of the New York Mets!

Just look at how much we've actually changed. In 1958, only 4 percent of Americans approved of interracial marriage, according to the Gallup poll. No one would even think to ask that question in a poll today. In the 1960s, we were putting children on buses to integrate public schools. Now parents actively seek diverse schools for their children. It's preposterous to say white power and privilege are at an all-time high. Higher than when the Ku Klux Klan rode horses and lynched African-Americans? Higher than when the National Guard had to help integrate colleges and schools? That's ridiculous. But it's what the union enforcers want to teach our children.

In the predominantly Republican, white suburb of New Jersey where I live, students were recently given a project called "American Dream: Myth or Reality?" They were asked to write whichever one they believed, but they were told they had to write from the written material the teacher handed out. However, the fix was in.

All the material the teacher provided supported only myth.

My niece in the fifth grade wrote an essay saying the American Dream is a reality. She was admonished by her teacher because her essay didn't conform with the written materials. All of this is rooted in the teachers' unions' adherence to the most progressive policies in the Democratic Party and the unions' role as enforcers. The best way to destroy the great American institutions you hate is to lie to the next generation about them. And the teachers' unions are using their power to do just that.

Just because racism still exists in certain forms does not mean we are an inherently racist country. And just because we've made significant progress over the past decades doesn't mean we don't still have farther to go.

We need to keep making the country better.

But rewriting history according to the playbook of the teachers' union is the most certain way to make our children stop feeling proud of being Americans and believing that our democracy is worth fighting for and saving. This is the Republican Party's most important fight today. It's more important than taxes. It's more important than trade. It's more important for the survival of our country than any other issue you can name.

That's why we can no longer *require* teachers anywhere in the country to be members of unions. The United States Supreme Court has already ruled that such requirements are unconstitutional. But state laws have been passed to continue the practice. They say that teachers aren't required to be in the union but make it nearly impossible for anyone to leave. Even after the Supreme Court decision, as new teachers enter the profession, they often face unbearable peer pressure to join the union, even if they disagree with the union politics. It's not only a fight to free the minds of our students. It's a fight to free teachers who are not a part of the woke, progressive mindset and simply want to teach the truth. There is no more important issue for the country's future than this one.

It's the fight over how our children will be taught about who they are, who their neighbors are, what our country has been in the past, and what our country can be in the future. That's why every parent who believes in this cause should be standing up at their school board meetings and speaking out against critical race theory and whatever else the teachers' unions have in store next. And our party is the only one left to lead this fight. The Democrats are bought and paid for by the teachers' unions. We need to focus on this issue, not the grievances and conspiracies of the past. The very survival of our democracy is dependent on getting this right.

CHAPTER 16

ON CRIME

Suddenly, crime is roaring back again. We need to get on top of it . . . *immediately*.

In cities across America—and not just big ones—violent crime is shooting up like it hasn't for twenty or thirty years, and it's making people feel unsafe again. We're starting to see the kind of pessimism that New York City felt in the late 1980s and early 1990s, when Times Square was a battle zone, gangs ran wild, and crack cocaine was king. New York is not a timid city. But people were scared to ride the subway and walk home at night. This led to some thoughtless overreaction in Washington. Super-long mandatory minimum sentences. Packing the prisons with some people who didn't need to be there. Too many one-size-fits-all solutions. It also led to some appropriately aggressive policing. Two strong Republican mayors with very different personalities, Rudy Giuliani and Mike Bloomberg, showed that crime could be drastically reduced if leaders were prepared to act. And that produced a stunning turnaround in New York City. Rapidly falling crime rates. Unprecedented safety in rich and poor neighborhoods alike. A much-improved quality of life for everyone.

Crime isn't an unsolvable problem. Someone just needs to take responsibility for solving it. In Joe Biden's Washington right now, they are doing the opposite. Not only do we have everyday crime rising, but the summer of 2020 gave us the rioting and looting of the Black Lives Matter protests. Democrats did not just support the peaceful protestors. They also openly supported rioters burning our cities and looters destroying small businesses. They urged defunding of police and, worse, demoralized police officers all across America. So demoralized in Seattle that the police allowed radicals to establish an "autonomous zone" that seceded from the United States. Crime is out of control under Democratic influence and Joe Biden's leadership.

Well, things in politics often come in waves, and now we're confronted with some of the consequences of all that aggressive policing. Was it overly aggressive? A lot of people in minority communities thought so, and that provoked a reaction. The reaction was named Bill de Blasio. When he ran to replace Bloomberg in 2013, de Blasio was propelled to victory by a single TV ad. It featured his eighteen-year-old biracial son, Dante, talking straight to the camera about his father.

"He's the only one that will end a stop-and-frisk era that unfairly targets people of color," Dante said. "Bill de Blasio will be a mayor for every New Yorker, no matter where they live or what they look like, and I'd say that even if he weren't my dad."

The ad did its job. What happened over the next eight years has been a diminution in funding for the police and, more important, a diminution in their morale. Instead of honoring the police as New York did during the Giuliani and Bloomberg years, especially after 9/11, City Hall kept making the police the enemy, culminating in the summer of 2020 after George Floyd's murder in Minneapolis. Democratic politicians demanded: "Defund the police!" One candidate in the 2021 New York mayor's race, Maya Wiley, even suggested disarming the police.

To me, all those extremes are just ridiculous.

People protested in New York, Portland, and other places across the country, which is appropriate. But some of those peaceful protests devolved into mayhem, which is not. And too many political leaders on the Democrat side of the aisle began to say: "The violence is okay. The rioters deserve to burn things down. They are justified in looting stores and homes of people who had nothing to do with the problems being protested. They'd earned their rage." That led to a sense in the country that these elected enablers didn't care any longer about providing public safety. They cared more about catering to the political whim of the moment.

Bad call.

Now politicians are learning the hard way: Public safety is too important to the public to give in to the whim of the moment.

So how do we deal with this? We can start by learning the lessons of Camden, New Jersey.

When I became governor in 2010, Camden was rated the most dangerous city in America. Huge murder rate. Shocking levels of armed robbery, rape, assault, and other violent felonies. And the city had a police department that was highly compensated, thoroughly ineffective, and poorly engaged with the community, which was 95 percent nonwhite. The police in Camden just weren't delivering the services they were sworn to provide. After exploring potential reforms, I concluded that there was no way to fix the disaster that was the Camden City Police Department. It was too far gone. With support from the city's African-American female mayor, Dana Redd, and the city's state legislators, we fired the entire Camden City Police Department.

We reconstituted a police department under the leadership of the county, creating the Camden County Police Department Metro Division, and we got busy hiring an entirely new police force without the toxic attitudes and outrageous wages and perks that had defined the previous crowd. That allowed us, at the same cost, to increase the number of police officers in Camden by 33 percent.

That was prescription number one: "More police on the street is better than fewer police on the street," assuming they are properly trained. That's where prescription number two comes in. "Train them to be *community* police officers for the 21st Century." Some of the hires in Camden were brand-new police officers. Some had experience but needed to be retrained. All of them had to learn modern community policing. That meant truly engaging with the community. Face-to-face. Hand-to-hand. We put dozens of police officers on bicycles. No longer were all Camden cops behind smoked windows in police cars. On bikes and on foot, the newly trained officers were a physical presence in the neighborhoods like they'd never been before, interacting with the people of Camden on a human level every day. As a result, these police officers weren't doing something *to* the community. They were working *with* the community. They were hearing people's concerns. They were interacting with human beings, not only enforcing the law. Showing up at school meetings. Attending picnics and other community events. Coaching teams of young people at the Police Athletic League. Gradually, the police stopped being seen as occupiers in Camden. They became neighbors, friends, and protectors of the law-abiding citizens of Camden.

Prescription number three: "Teach the police to de-escalate." That was never done before in Camden, just as it's never been done in most cities and towns.

There's a video on YouTube that shows well-trained Camden police officers subduing a knife-wielding man. The officers are talking to him, calmly, working to lower the emotional temperature and thereby keep everybody safe. The agitated man. The bystanders. And the police. As a result, no one was shot. Nobody pulled out a gun. No chokeholds were employed. In a few short minutes, the man with the knife was disarmed and arrested. A crisis was averted. Lives were saved. The officers knew how to use the techniques of de-escalation to make the city safer and also to avoid the things that have led to real discontent in too many of our communities.

It made me so proud to see that video. Check it out if you can. Compare it to the George Floyd video that everyone found so heartbreaking. De-escalation isn't soft on crime. It's smart on crime. It keeps everyone safer. And Camden is proof.

Officers from the Camden County Police Department are now training police officers statewide on the proper use of force and the techniques of de-escalation. Camden teaching the rest of New Jersey? Imagine that. Now Camden should teach the rest of the country. When George Floyd was murdered, what happened in this overwhelmingly minority community? The white police chief of Camden, Joseph Wysocki, joined with African-American community leaders at the front of Camden's Black Lives Matter protest. They didn't march separately. They marched as one. People in the community no longer felt their police were an occupying army. They were neighbors and friends. The police were part of them. Camden didn't have the kind of violence that a lot of cities suffered that summer. Effective changes had already been made.

But what about violent crime in Camden? Is the famously dangerous city any safer than before? You bet it is. For the third year in a row, violent crime in Camden has stayed at a fifty-year low. Twelve hundred violent crimes, compared to 2,000 in 2012. The per capita rate of crime has also declined: 42 percent of what it was in 2012 and 22 percent of what it was at its peak. Murders dropped 66 percent, compared to before we fired the entire police department. Robberies, down 17 percent. Burglaries, down 77 percent. Fatal shootings, down 68 percent. Nonfatal shootings, down 50 percent. The people of Camden deserve huge credit for this. They embraced the reforms and made them work. In Camden today, you can see a city coming back to life with less crime and more social justice. People are comfortable on the street like they haven't been in years. New businesses are opening, again.

None of this, by the way, is an argument for disarming or defunding the police. Police need their guns for when guns are needed—to keep themselves and the people they're protecting safe. These aren't either/or choices. Police can be strong and fair at the same time.

Republicans should embrace the lessons of Camden. We don't have to be on the defensive. We can say: "Absolutely, there are problems with social justice in certain police departments. We know how to solve them. It's by working with the police and the community, not by supporting the criminals as Democrats keep doing all across America." And for police departments that need to be disbanded and start over? It can be done. It's been done before.

One, two, three.

More police, not fewer police.

Trained and funded to be part of the community.

Practicing the laudable act of de-escalation.

Crime reduction and social justice aren't a zero-sum equation. They can both happen at once.

While these policing issues are being confronted on the streets of America, there is also a place for broader criminal justice reforms. That's part of what we did when I was governor of New Jersey. It's what gives people a sense that the system is working *for them*. We did it in an entirely bipartisan manner, Republicans and Democrats working together, in a way that helped everyone.

Violent criminals need to be locked up for a good, long time. There is no doubt about that. But our state's prisons, like so many others across the country, were overcrowded with nonviolent offenders who didn't always need to be there. This time, we took some positive lessons from the federal system. As a Republican governor, I agreed to a more rational system for deciding which defendants were held on bail. We used monitoring bracelets and other techniques to make sure people came back to court. But it made no sense to turn our jails into debtors' prisons, holding nonviolent defendants just because they couldn't make five-hundred-dollar bail. That was also hugely expensive for the state.

In exchange for the policy shift, I got the Democrats to agree to tougher bail standards for the truly violent criminals. It used to be that New Jersey had a mandate for bail. A risk of flight was the only reason a judge could use to deny a defendant bail. I thought judges should also be able to consider a defendant's history of violence. To me, that was logical and fair. And a judge should be able to deny bail entirely if that's what it took to keep a dangerous criminal off the street. After some heavy negotiation, the Democrats in Trenton agreed. Then we put it on the ballot and the people of "blue" New Jersey overwhelmingly agreed. Good ideas bring us together.

This was crucial in helping us combat gang violence, a constant threat to our cities. Our strategy can be just as helpful across America. We can't keep plaguing our communities with these gang members and their long, violent rap sheets. We can't have them wandering around their neighborhoods while awaiting trial on violent felonies, intimidating or killing the witnesses who will testify against them.

That was the deal: Common sense on the nonviolent offenders, tougher on the violent ones. We ended up with a far more realistic standard in New Jersey. Other states could definitely benefit from that. And just look at the results. By doing the criminal justice reforms we did, the crime rate on my watch went *down*. And we had enough of a change in the prison population that we were able to close two state prisons. From overcrowding to excess capacity: To me, that had "public safety" and "taxpayer savings" written all over it.

As Republicans, we should be advocating for reforms that promote public safety and also show fairness to everyone. Lock up the violent criminals. Hold nonviolent criminals responsible for their own conduct. And don't create a system of debtors' prisons for people who only have to stay in jail because they're poor. That's rational criminal justice reform. It'll produce safer streets, a greater sense of social justice, and a system that people can have confidence in.

Defund the police? Ridiculous.

Disarm the police? Even more ridiculous.

But commonsense reforms are necessary. They've shown a history of working in the most densely populated state in the country, which is what New Jersey is. By all rights, we should have it even tougher than other states do. But we met our challenges and overcame them.

The New Jersey approach beats the New York City under de Blasio approach any day, anywhere. His approach produced less safety, more crime, and greater fear, and it never delivered the grand social justice improvements it was supposed to. Our way added safety, cut crime, and reduced public fear while reconnecting the police and the courts with the communities they serve.

Take your pick.

I think most people will prefer the smart Republican version of criminal justice reform.

CHAPTER 17

ON BUSINESS

It started as the summer of Black Lives Matter, but that's not where it ended.

When Minneapolis police officer Derek Chauvin murdered George Floyd and a YouTube video made the sheer brutality of it impossible to ignore, a modern movement was given new life. Yes, the phrase had already been around awhile. Other police killings of African-Americans were protested under the same banner, *Black Lives Matter*. But Floyd's "I can't breathe" video was so excruciating to watch, it brought a huge burst of attention to the cause and millions of supporters who otherwise might never have shown up. Outrage is a powerful recruiting tool, and this was a potent one. But what started as a demand to improve policing soon morphed into something much more radical than that, a media-savvy campaign to change almost every aspect of American society.

A political sleight of hand from the radical left, this is called, and here was an especially far-reaching one.

Initially, most people didn't understand the real agenda of the group's leaders, including a lot of well-meaning people who showed up at the large-scale protests in hundreds of cities and towns. Black and white. Young and old. Liberal, conservative, and in between. They came together to share in the moment and add their voices to the chorus. But soon, the deeper agenda of the organizers became clear. It wasn't only, "We see injustice in policing in some places across the country." The true aim was to change the entire way that business and society dealt with America's minority citizens and how much influence they would have across all the different levers of social power. Even more important to the Black Lives Matter organizers, it was a vehicle to promote a radical, left-wing agenda and personally enrich themselves and their organization. That's not what brought all those folks to the streets—or what most of them were agitating for.

As many of them soon came to realize, they were truly being used.

Though Floyd was the flashpoint, pressure had been building from at least a dozen high-profile police killings, many of them caught on cell phone video, going back to Eric Garner in New York City in 2014. "Say his name!" the protest leaders demanded. "Say her name!" And the crowds roared back: "Michael Brown!" "Walter Scott!" "Freddie Gray!" "Alton Sterling!" "Ahmaud Arbery!" "Breonna Taylor!" But it was Floyd's murder that gave the movement its critical mass. I have no trouble, by the way, calling it a murder. Officer Chauvin was tried and convicted in open court. The evidence was there for everyone to see. And his lawyers never got anywhere close to justifying the nine minutes and twenty-nine seconds the veteran officer spent kneeling on the unarmed man's neck.

Here's what I do object to, *strenuously*: Racial activists and hyper-progressive Democrats using this case to seek cynical political advantage and to push radical social changes they've been promoting for decades, changes that the vast majority of Americans have made clear they absolutely do not want. This is especially ironic, given the silence of most Democrats as cities across the United States were stricken with violence initiated by Black Lives Matter organizers. The street protests were the visible part, along with the eruptions of looting, shooting, arson, and other riotous violence. But just out of view, the movement organizers were pushing a parallel campaign, pressuring American business and American media, demanding wholesale changes in how race was reported and acted on. Then several things happened quickly that pushed the American societal fabric to a real stress point.

There was the presidential election and its angrily contested result, which fired up nearly everyone. And that was followed almost immediately by the uproar over changes in the Georgia voting law. As you recall, Georgia passed a voter integrity law that was falsely characterized by President Biden as "Jim Crow 2.0," when in fact it expanded early voting, vote by mail, and the ability of folks to register. No need to relitigate that fight here, except to note some of its echoes. Because of pressure from the Black Lives Matter movement and the very progressive wing of the Democratic Party, the 2021 Major League Baseball All-Star Game was pulled out of Truist Park in Atlanta. The game was supposed to be a hometown tribute to the Braves' beloved Hank Aaron, who had died that January. Instead it was played in Denver.

Normally, an institution like Major League Baseball would not give in so timidly to pressure from a band of activists and one wing of a political party. What made the difference this time was the rise of corporate cancel culture: jittery companies allowing themselves to be cowed by political activists, often in ways that make no sense at all for the shareholders, employees, customers, or communities those companies would usually feel responsible to. But here we had Delta Air Lines and Coca-Cola, the two biggest corporate citizens in the state of Georgia. Both companies, it turned out, were consulted throughout the discussions over the new election law to avoid any last-minute surprises. Even though both companies had been active participants in the negotiations and appeared at peace with the final bill, when the pressure came on, they folded immediately. They put their considerable corporate clout behind the calls that the All-Star

Game be moved out of the state where Delta and Coke were the largest corporate citizens. Completely contrary to the interests of the city of Atlanta. Completely contrary to the companies' own interest as leading corporate citizens of the state of Georgia. Completely contrary to the interests of ordinary working people in Atlanta who would have benefited from economic activity brought by the All-Star Game.

Just a cheap fold.

And it didn't go unnoticed.

This debacle awoke millions of people to the idea that corporate America was playing a new kind of politics, ignoring the companies' own self-interest, ignoring the views and values of many of their customers, aligning these corporations instead with a band of political shakedown artists.

Then came the aftermath of the January 6 riots on Capitol Hill, when some Republicans in Congress decided to vote against certifying certain states' results. That was a position I disagreed with. But the members of Congress certainly had the right to vote that way. And another wave of progressive pressure poured down on corporate America, aimed not just at one or two major companies but at the full Fortune 500 and beyond:

You must not donate to the campaigns of the 147 members of Congress who objected to certifying some aspect of Joe Biden's win! In fact, you'd better not make donations to the campaigns of any Republicans because of the actions of some Republicans!

Or else?

Or else you could be called some very bad names or, worse, get fired from your job or have your business targeted by a devastating boycott.

That was the threat, and it proved to be effective. Across the corporate world, companies began folding immediately. In the finance industry. In consumer goods. Microsoft announced its PAC would "suspend contributions for the duration of the 2022 election cycle to all members of Congress who voted to object to the certification of electors." Wall Street titans Citigroup, JPMorgan Chase, and Goldman Sachs said they were pausing, too. The Business Roundtable, an industry group that represents the CEOs of corporations like Amazon and General Motors, deplored the "inexcusable violence" and called for "the nation and lawmakers to unite around President-elect Biden and Vice President–elect Harris." Soon it seemed like half of corporate America was issuing chest-beating statements. Some said they were taking six months off from making campaign donations. Others suspended their political action committees or eliminated their PACS entirely.

Soon progressive activists like the so-called Citizens for Responsibility and Ethics in Washington were taking a victory lap. "By our count," the group said, "nearly 190 companies pledged to halt donations from their political action committees in direct response to the violence, thus cutting lawmakers off from the lifeblood of their political existence." There was no denying real money was at stake. By that group's count, business PACs gave more than $377 million in contributions, nearly double the combined total from all other PACs, including labor and ideological groups.

And this happened because of Democratic pressure from the party's progressive wing, working in concert with the Black Lives Matter movement. For the progressive Dems, it was a twofer. They not only got to play to a part of their party that they wanted to keep energized. They also got the enormous political advantage of intimidating corporate America, while at the same time disarming Republican politicians as everyone was beginning to prepare for the drive to the 2022 midterm elections, where Democrats held a tiny, five-seat majority in the House.

Not a bad deal if you can get it. In an environment like this one, a handful of races can make all the difference in the world.

No, nothing is ever purely about the issue in Washington. Not in the 2020s. The calculations are always partly cynical, another naked attempt to gain some political advantage, whatever the purported underlying policy justification might be. So what are we seeing now? What's the result of corporate America's shifting allegiances? Well, one thing's certain: It's produced a sharp diminution in the respect that many Americans, especially Republicans, now feel for big companies.

It used to be that, by and large, successful corporations were held in high regard by the Republican Party and Republican Party supporters. That is fading fast. And it's mostly because so many corporations have fallen out of touch with where everyday Americans are.

These companies are so worried about not being criticized, not offending anyone, not being called racist, sexist, ageist, homophobic, or a long list of other nasty names, they've become putty in the hands of cynical activists, who've learned to manipulate them into silence, paralysis, and fear.

It's an extraordinary transformation, and it will have a huge impact on the business lives of these companies—unless they change course. They've gone from selling products that Americans want to buy to selling beliefs that a majority of Americans have absolutely no interest in. One need only look at the declining TV ratings for the NFL during the National Anthem controversy to see where a majority of Americans stand on this type of political correctness. It isn't just that people didn't ask for all this progressive ideology. When confronted with it, people have consistently opposed it and will continue to do so. In most instances, they won't oppose it as loudly as Black Lives Matter and the progressive wing of the Democratic Party will advocate for it. But these everyday Americans know what they believe in. They are pushing back now, and these woke corporations are beginning to feel it.

The tide could soon be turning again. We Republican leaders need to make sure of it.

The All-Star Game had already been moved. But by opening pitch at Coors Field in Denver, Delta and Coca-Cola had both noticeably backed off their staunch opposition to the Georgia voting law. They weren't exactly cheering it. But neither company was pushing the Georgia legislature to repeal or revise anything. And I'm convinced that's because they'd gotten so much pushback from so many of their (former?) customers.

Everyday Americans are saying to these companies, "Wait a second! This isn't your function! That's not your role! That's what we have elections for. It's not the job of corporations to come in and try to change past election results."

And frankly, why should they even try? It's a dangerous game for corporations to be playing. Companies do best when they remember what their purpose is: building great products. Providing excellent service. Creating good jobs. Making money for their shareholders. Selling interesting new products. Surpassing the competition. But when they start inserting themselves into the divisive social and political issues of the moment, believe me, that's a loser from the start.

This corporate cancel culture manifests itself in many different ways. How companies deal with their own employees. What people can and can't say in the workplace, even in private conversations with their colleagues and friends. How so many things are interpreted in the most negative possible way. Then people see all these stories about these woke corporations second-guessing the American people on matters of politics.

You wonder why the Republican Party has had such a populist feel lately? It's not just Donald Trump. This corporate cancel culture is a big part of the reason why. A reaction to the heavy-handed conduct of so many American companies. Everyday Americans standing up to this "woke" culture and standing up for traditional American values. This is our sweet spot as Republicans. All of us should be supporting the grassroots uprising. And on the winding path that politics often follows, it all goes back to George Floyd.

So here's what the Republican Party specifically needs to do: We need to stand up and say very clearly: We are against intolerance everywhere. But we are also against having progressive politics foisted upon us by corporate America. When it comes to our own values, we can make decisions on our own—without these corporate overlords constantly scolding us. Given their recent performance, it's no wonder so many Republicans don't trust them anymore.

CHAPTER 18

ON MEDIA

People used to love tech companies. Really, it wasn't that hard.

Facebook. Google. Apple. Twitter. All the stars of Big Tech started as quirky, entrepreneurial points of pride for the American people. We even knew their founders by their first names: Mark. Larry and Sergey. Steve and Jack. This was American innovation at its best. Not only did we innovate technology, we innovated an entirely new category of distraction that became central to many aspects of people's lives. Their social lives. Their political lives. Their personal lives. And not just in America. The lives of people all around the world.

The platforms these companies created and the technologies they launched came together in a seamless fashion and became, among other things, a central place to advertise, causing huge disruption for the powerhouses of traditional media. The TV networks. The cable companies. The newspaper and magazine industry, which was just about demolished. But in those exciting early years, these homegrown technology companies and the people who started them were seen as enormous heroes, regardless of anyone's political ideology. People everywhere thought, *Wow! This is great! Smart, young Americans who are dreaming up big ideas and turning them into major influences on our society and the whole world.*

Washington knew exactly how to show its appreciation and protect this entrepreneurial business that was still in its infancy. Section 230 of the Communications Decency Act of 1996, it was called.
Congress passed it. President Clinton signed it into law. It was written in the usual federal legalese: "No provider or user of an interac-
tive computer service shall be treated as the publisher or speaker of
any information provided by another information content provider."

They might sound obtuse, but those were some very potent
words.

What they meant in practice was that Facebook, Twitter, You-
Tube, and their various social-media cousins couldn't be sued no
matter what lies, deceptions, or lunacy that users might post there.
That's because, essentially, these companies were not exercising editorial control.

Section 230 said they should be treated more like a bulletin board
or a telephone company than a traditional media outlet. You can't sue
a bulletin board for the things people post there any more than you
can sue the phone company if someone talks trash about you—or
even takes out a hit against you—in a telephone call. The bulletin
board and the phone company are just providing the platforms. They
don't control the content of what is being presented there. If something offensive or illegal pops up, they'll say: "Hey, you can't blame
us. Go after the people who said it. We are just providing the cork
board or the fiber-optic lines."

This gave the tech companies an unprecedented level of protection that newspapers, magazines, and TV stations never had. Section 230 was meant to make sure that the new industry would allow
for free expression and wouldn't get buried with lawsuits that would
quash them before they could ever reach their full potential.

And everything was fine until the tech companies started becoming editorialists and started using their newfound power for their
own politics.

Until they began deciding what could and couldn't be posted on their sites.

Who could post and who couldn't.

Who was in and who was out.

And that's exactly what they are doing now.

That editorial control, combined with the monopoly these giants have on this hugely profitable marketplace, has led to an arrogance that has empowered them to act in ways that are completely contrary to the promise they made a quarter century ago.

They still want the legal immunity. They just don't want to be fair in return.

The most prominent example, of course, is the social-media censoring of Donald Trump. You can agree or disagree with the things that Trump has said on Twitter, his former favorite platform. You can even think his messages are untrue, divisive, destructive, or dumb. The real question is, *Why just him?*

Ayatollah Khamenei, the tyrannical leader of Iran, has a Twitter account. Donald Trump does not. That's the decision that Twitter has made. Does any American—right, left, or center—really think this is fair?

If you didn't like some of the things that Trump posted before the January 6 Capitol riot, you should see what the despotic Khamenei is still putting on his account. It's breathtaking how inciting and untrue some of the ayatollah's rantings are.

Twitter's decision is clearly based on its proprietors' own politics, not the type of content being posted or its potential impact.

So now, these Big Tech companies are dominating the marketplace in ways that have made Facebook, for instance, the world's second trillion-dollar corporation, after Apple. And some of the other companies aren't that far behind. Their wealth gives them power. Their monopolies give them power. And it's a dangerous combination when they start deciding which views can be expressed and which views will be silenced. Our forefathers would be appalled at that misuse of the First Amendment.

Why do you think Republicans are so upset about this, other than the broken promises, the legal overstepping, and the maddening arrogance? Well, because they have eyes and ears and brains. Most Republicans recognize that the politics in Silicon Valley lean heavily to the left. It can't be an accident that the people Big Tech chooses to censor—and not only Trump—are almost always figures on the right.

As Republicans, we've spent decades dealing with a Big Media culture that is almost always stacked against us. For good reason, we've grown highly suspect of their biases. And those biases have never been more pronounced than in recent years. The Trump era brought a new crescendo of this, the way certain media outlets became passionate advocates for the president and even more became his equally passionate adversaries. All that choosing up sides exploited divisions that were already present in our politics—then proceeded to severely exacerbate them.

Look at NBC and MSNBC and the people hosting programs there, programs that used to be places of equal-opportunity scrutiny, programs like the grandfather of all the Sunday shows, *Meet the Press*. When Tim Russert was hosting, both Democrats and Republicans got his tough interrogations, despite his Democratic pedigree. The same was true of most of the show's previous hosts going all the way back to 1947. Well, no more. Not with Chuck Todd in the chair. He is a complete liberal advocate each and every Sunday, a reflexive booster of Democratic progressive causes and a relentless opponent to whichever conservative Republican happens to appear. It's much the same equation at CNN, which used to brand itself as the place for down-the-middle news, planted in the ground between right-leaning Fox and left-leaning MSNBC.

No one makes that claim about CNN anymore, including the people who work there. It's not just the bias of Big Media. It's also the cynicism. And there's no better case study than CNN. In 2015 and 2016, no network gave more airtime to Donald Trump than CNN did. The reason was simple. It was super-profitable programming. In 2016, CNN had one of its best years ever, and Trump got more airtime than any of the network's full-time hosts. They'd carry Trump's speeches uninterrupted for an hour or two at a time and spend the next six hours analyzing every "lock her up" and "build that wall."

And the ratings shot up some more.

Then, Trump won, and CNN spent the next four years attacking everything about him. His policies. His family. His character. His appointments. His ethics. His Twitter posts. His hair. If they ever missed an opportunity to air a negative Trump story, it was only because those minutes were filled with another negative Trump story.

So many ways to smear the president, and only twenty-four hours in the day!

The American people saw more than liberal bias. They saw breathtaking cynicism. As long as Trump was good for network profits, he was lavished with unimpeded airtime. But the network programmers never thought he would actually win! They were in the corner of the candidate they were confident was the inevitable next president, Hillary Clinton. When that proved to be a major miscalculation, the media had to change their approach to Trump. He had to remain a source of massive profits, but he also had to be destroyed. In the end, he proved to be even more profitable as a target than he'd been as a hero, as the networks turned right around and used the same platform to try to destroy him.

So, what's the answer for Republicans? It isn't simply to seek out right-leaning media that's equally biased in the opposite direction and accept those distortions unquestioningly. Our job isn't to swallow whatever slant any of them dish up. That would leave us just as sorry as our narrow-minded adversaries. In fact, we can do much better than that.

We have to stand up and speak the truth about *everything*. When we see things that are wrong, when people on our side behave in ways that are problematic, when our TV talking heads spew unsupported trash, Republicans need to speak up loudly. We need to call the distortions what they are—*distortions*. We have to stay loyal to the truth. When Fox News airs coverage that's plainly biased, when NewsMax pretends some falsehood is true, when OAN goes down another rabbit hole, we have to say loudly and clearly, "Hold on a second . . . This is wrong . . . What's the evidence for that?" The truth also requires that we call out the bias and lies of CNN, MSNBC, the *New York Times*, and other traditional liberal media outlets.

We can never be afraid of reality. That's where our credibility comes from. That's one of the reasons forty-nine states voted to reelect Ronald Reagan. He fought for our principles and always stood up for the truth.

Freedom of speech and the principles in the Constitution and the Declaration of Independence are the things that our party should stand up for, not the latest distortions from our friends that mirror the distortions on the other side.

When it comes to Big Tech, it's time to get Section 230 off the books, along with the unjustified immunity it brings. The tech titans are big boys and girls now. Their companies are well established and mega-rich. They should be able to stand on their own two feet, including in an American courtroom. If they want to start banning people from their platforms, if they're picking and choosing whose speech is acceptable and whose is not, if they want to play all those political games, then it's time for them to be held legally accountable the same way other companies are.

Whenever an American company is accused of wrongdoing—producing a dangerous product, bringing harm to the environment, mistreating employees—the issue is adjudicated in a state or federal court. Big Tech should also step up to the bar and defend its editorial slant there.

Both political parties bear the responsibility and share the guilt here.

Republicans had complete control for two years, and they didn't eliminate Section 230 and hold Big Tech accountable. At that time, they saw the social-media outlets as a political plus for them. Democrats are in control now. They've done nothing about the partisan bias, either. And why would they? They see the recent conduct of the social-media companies in banning Donald Trump, and they like it. They're convinced it's a political plus for them. We need to say, "Both those approaches are wrong. Big Tech and Big Media have created these problems, and it's their job to solve them."

We all must hold them accountable—or, next, they will ban your beloved, strongly held beliefs.

We can take legal steps in Congress to strip Big Tech of its Section 230 protection. Big Media? The only way to confront their imbalance is by speaking up and speaking out. And we maintain our credibility to do it by speaking the truth no matter who we're speaking to. When our friends are spreading falsehoods for political purposes, we need to stand up against that, too. Republicans must stand for the truth—and not just sometimes.

We must call out Joe Biden for characterizing legitimate election integrity laws as "Jim Crow 2.0." We must stand up and call out Marjorie Taylor Greene for equating COVID-19 restrictions with Nazi atrocities. We must hold Nancy Pelosi's feet to the fire of truth when she lies about Republicans being the party of "defund the police." We must say it's wrong to undermine our democracy by claiming the 2020 election was stolen when no evidence exists to prove it. How do Republicans win elections again and regain the power to get America off the disastrously wrong track of Joe Biden? By standing up to all media—social and mainstream—the only way we credibly can. By telling the truth. By telling it like it is. All the time.

CHAPTER 19

ON THREATS

It's time to get personal with North Korea and even tougher on Iran.

These are the two biggest near-term threats to American national security and peace in the world. *Near*-term threats. And the challenges the two nations present for us have some surprising points in common. In both cases, what we've been doing hasn't been working. We need to recognize why and adjust our strategies in some carefully thought-out ways.

Begin by recognizing that the Iranian nuclear deal was fatally flawed from the start.

The 159-page Joint Comprehensive Plan of Action, as the agreement was officially called, was negotiated in Vienna in the summer of 2015 by Iran and six other nations: China, France, Germany, Russia, the United Kingdom, and the United States. The JCPOA is a complex document, as multilateral nuclear agreements tend to be. But the essence of this one is that Iran agreed to certain limits on its nuclear program in exchange for the lifting of certain international sanctions against Iran.

This particular version was missing three key points that need to be part of any such agreement with Iran. Otherwise, it's not something the United States should ever embrace.

First, the Iranians can never have a nuclear weapon under any circumstances. That would be incredibly destabilizing to the Middle East and the rest of the world. This understanding needs to be explicitly spelled out in any deal. Despite some valuable limits on the Iranian nuclear program, the previous agreement, signed by Barack Obama, never precluded that chilling prospect.

Second, the Iranians' ballistic missile technology has to be included in any agreement—and sharply limited. It makes no sense to address Tehran's nuclear program and overlook the missiles that can deliver nukes around the world. If the Iranians keep rushing ahead with the development of these long-range delivery systems, how can we be confident they won't develop something truly scary to strap on board? It's just too tempting for an interventionist regime like Iran's.

And finally, there has to be anytime, anywhere inspections of Iran's nuclear facilities. No limits. No warnings. No running to the United Nations for sign-off. Inspectors, *independent* inspectors, need full access. It's just a fact that Iran has a long history of evasion, deception, and cover-up. As part of any agreement, we need to know exactly what they are doing in the nuclear realm. If they have nothing to hide, this won't be a problem. If they consider unfettered inspections a problem, maybe they don't intend to live up to the deal.

Obama's 2015 Iran deal, which Trump pulled America out of, failed to achieve any of that, and the Biden administration was wrong in trying to drag us back in. Lengthening it, straightening it, tweaking it, crossing our fingers, and hoping for the best: None of that can ever rescue that poorly crafted, inadequately comprehensive deal. And it shouldn't be used as a framework for the future without getting up-front agreement on those three key points.

We have to pay close attention to the intentions of the Iranians. Take a moment, and look at the world through their eyes. Their motivation is twofold. They want to become a nuclear power, and they want to get out from under the punishing sanctions that have been crushing their economy.

The Iranian leaders hate not having nukes. India has them. Pakistan has them. Their sworn enemy, Israel, is widely believed to have them. Even the lunatics in North Korea have them. *Why not us?* The Iranians want to know. It's about bragging rights. It's about international leverage. It's about their enemies thinking, "We'd better not mess with Iran. They have *the bomb.*"

And the Iranian government desperately wants sanctions lifted. Undeniably, they are making life in the country hard.

Obama lifted some of them after the international deal was signed. Trump reimposed them once he pulled the United States out of it. And the prospect that Joe Biden will lift the sanctions again in response to anything that doesn't include those three, key conditions—well, that's absolutely unacceptable.

Imagine if Iran had *more* money to keep spreading upheaval around the world. The ramifications of that should give anyone pause. All you have to do is look at the terrorist group Hamas and their repeated, egregious attacks against Israel, our longest and closest ally in the region. It's all been done with Iranian sponsorship, Iranian funding, and Iranian encouragement.

Do we really want more of that? If we stand for that, Hezbollah will be next and much worse than anything Hamas is capable of doing.

If we are going to have a reasonable relationship with Iran, its leaders need to understand that all sanctions will stay in place unless and until those three criteria are met. And if the Iranians can't or won't meet those conditions, then the sanctions will stay in place and get even tougher.

Over time, I am convinced, that really might begin to destabilize the theocratic regime in Tehran.

Not getting tougher on Iran is also destabilizing to our relationships with Israel. How could it not be? The zealous leaders in Iran have said repeatedly they will only stand for the complete destruction of Israel. They now have a "countdown-to-Israel's-annihilation clock," set for the year 2040. And all this is happening just as things in some parts of the Middle East had started looking up.

The Abraham Accords of 2020 were, in part, an effort to combat Iran. That agreement between Israel, the United Arab Emirates, and Bahrain, brokered by the Trump administration, marked the first public normalization of relations between an Arab country and Israel since Egypt in 1979 and Jordan in 1994. It's been encouraging to see some progress there.

This clearly wasn't what Iran was hoping to achieve with its aggressive intransigence, but I'll take it: bringing the rest of the neighborhood closer together. Because of Iran's adventurism, Saudi Arabia has been drawn into combat in Yemen and elsewhere, inevitably fighting surrogates of Iran. There's almost no difficult situation the Iranians can't make worse.

What we need to do now is make sure we keep the pressure on. It's no time to be lifting painful sanctions, as Joe Biden seems intent on doing while walking America back into a flawed deal with Iran. It's destabilizing for a region that is already a powder keg. And try as we might, we won't be able to control what Israel or the smaller Arab states do next when they believe their very existence is threatened by Iran.

Remember what Robert Gates, defense secretary for both Bush 43 and Obama, said about Biden: "He has been wrong on nearly every major foreign policy and national security issue over the past four decades." Be scared, America. Very, very scared about Joe Biden deciding on Iran. We need to get back in charge of these decisions.

• • •

Our problem in North Korea is that American presidents from both parties keep believing the hype: that—*somehow, somewhere, someday*—they will be able to negotiate with a North Korean dictator and convince him to voluntarily give up his nation's nuclear program.

It didn't work with Kim Jong-il.

It hasn't worked with Kim Jong-un.

It won't work with Kim Jong Whoever's-Coming-Next.

We have to face facts. That is *never* going to occur.

The economic sanctions we've placed on North Korea are the most aggressive in the world. These sanctions are without a doubt harming the people of North Korea. But it doesn't matter. That's not enough to destabilize the Kim regime. He simply doesn't care about the suffering of his people. As a result, we're going to see no change in North Korea's nuclear ambitions, which are far more advanced than those of the Iranians and just as destabilizing, if not more so.

North Korea's nuclear program obviously threatens South Korea, their neighbor on the peninsula. But the threat doesn't stop there. It certainly extends to Japan, just a quick missile ride away. Given the continuing development of North Korea's missile technology, there's certainly a threat to Hawaii and Guam and, potentially, to the American West Coast. Once that's for certain, the North Korea government will be in a position to blackmail the United States with impunity.

It's not hard to imagine the shakedown scenarios.

"If you don't remove your troops from South Korea, we'll hit Hawaii."

"If you don't withdraw support for Japan, we'll target California."

"If you don't lift the sanctions against us"—well, you get the idea.

That's a situation we can't wait around for. We need to act before that day arrives.

So, how should America respond to the hair-trigger threat? What should our North Korean policy be? There's only one answer. It's time to get personal.

We need to ratchet up our sanctions but not against the people of North Korea. Between the international sanctions and the cruelty of their government in Pyongyang, they are already suffering mightily. We need to impose harsh sanctions against Kim Jong-un. Personally. Even more so. We know the North Korean dictator has tens of millions, if not hundreds of millions, of dollars, secreted around the world. We already know where much of it is. With our intelligence capability, we should be able to find even more of it. That's the money we should be freezing, not just the hard-currency imports that used to arrive at the ports of Hungnam and Haeju Hang.

We should freeze the personal bank accounts Kim controls or that are maintained for his benefit. Using international money-laundering laws, we should seize his overseas investments. Wherever we can find them and in whatever forms they exist, we need to bust open his various piggy banks. He's shown that he and his family and his military cronies don't care a bit whether the people of North Korea eat or have heated homes or have vehicles besides bicycles. The ruling Kims don't care as long as they're well fed, well warmed, and well transported. And no number of promises, whether to George W. Bush or Barack Obama or Donald Trump, is ever going to change that.

No exchanges of love letters. No overwrought bouquets of flattery.

Evil people keep doing evil things until they become too scared that their own personal futures and fortunes are at real risk. They need to face the right kind of threats.

Kim Jong-un can clearly live with the suffering of his people. But I strongly suspect that he believes he cannot live without his money and all that his money buys—money, by the way, that he has stolen from the people of North Korea and others around the world. Only when we credibly threaten to separate him and his family from that will he ever consider changing his ways.

It is time—*past time*—in both these countries, Iran and North Korea, for American foreign policy to get tougher and more personal. We have to personally go after these evil leaders.

Not with assassination but by taking the money and resources that they steal from their own people. The money that's made them wealthy and comfortable. The money they use to disrupt the world. Only then will we get their attention, because that's the way you get the attention of evil people.

The Iranian sanctions have been more effective than the ones in North Korea, and they should stay in place. Iran's society is more developed and evolved and more subject to political uprisings, many of which began stirring in 2019. And not just in the major cities. It was in the countryside that these uprisings began. COVID quieted that for a while. But the dissatisfaction remains. If we can maintain our tough sanctions, the internal uprisings will rise again. But that's a false hope in North Korea. That society is too backward, too non-evolved, and too closed for sanctions alone to change much.

We need to get personal there. And there is not a moment to waste. As Republicans, every time we are looking backward toward 2020, arguing about 2020, we are wasting the time and credibility we need to solve the big problems heading our way.

Is it worth it?

CHAPTER 20

ON ENEMIES

George W. Bush started by making a fundamental mistake.

It was June 2001, five months after Bush took office. He'd flown to Slovenia to meet with Vladimir Putin. The Cold War was over, but the United States and Russia were still divided on many issues, including America's missile defense system and whether Russia should be invited to join NATO.

At the summit's closing press conference, a reporter asked Bush how he could trust the former KGB officer who was now the Russian president. "I looked the man in the eye," Bush said. "I found him very straightforward and trustworthy. I was able to get a sense of his soul."

Well, not so much.

To state what should be obvious, former KGB officers do not have pure souls. And this one has spent the years since then proving it. His heavy-handed maneuvers in Syria, Ukraine, and Crimea. His vicious treatment of Alexei Navalny and anyone else who dares to speak out against the regime. Putin's philosophy and his tactics come right out of the Russian spy handbook. He's an immoral, corrupt thug. George W. Bush misspoke, and his words set exactly the wrong tone. As Condoleezza Rice, Bush's national security advisor, put it later: "We were never able to escape the perception that the president had naïvely trusted Putin and then been betrayed."

Barack Obama came to office during the four-year period when Vladimir Putin wasn't the Russian president. Obama's first-term counterpart was Putin lackey Dmitry Medvedev.

May 2012. Obama and Medvedev were in Seoul, South Korea, where the Russian president had raised objections to America's plans for a missile defense system in Europe. As a small pool of TV journalists set up nearby, Obama leaned in to offer Medvedev a quiet assurance, which was caught on a hot mic.

"After my election, I have more flexibility."

Again? Are you kidding me?

Like Bush, Barack Obama was too trusting of those at the top of the Russian government. His error in judgment was on full display during that fall's presidential debates when Obama pounced on Mitt Romney for calling Russia "without question, our No. 1 geopolitical foe."

"The 1980s are now calling to ask for their foreign policy back," Obama scoffed. "The Cold War has been over for twenty years. But Governor, when it comes to our foreign policy, you seem to want to import the foreign policies of the 1980s, just like the social policy of the 1950s, and the economic policies of the 1920s."

Snappy debate line . . . but a totally wrongheaded view of the world, as I hope even Obama would recognize now. If he doesn't, he should ask the people of Crimea whether they believe Russia is no longer a threat. Or the people of Ukraine. Or those opposing the Assad regime in Syria, who keep being pounded with Russian missiles. Obama could even ask his former secretary of state, Hillary Clinton, or his former vice president, Joe Biden, whether Russia attempted to influence the U.S. presidential elections in 2016 and 2020. No, the threat from Russia is not laughable and shouldn't be reduced to a debate punch line.

Donald Trump thought Vladimir Putin was just like him. That if he complimented Putin enthusiastically enough, the Russian president would behave. That turned out to be wrong. Trump's flattery never ceased and neither did Putin's ruthlessness. And so far, Joe Biden seems to think that rhetoric is the way to tame the bully in the Kremlin. But where's the action against Russia? Biden's willing to kill the Keystone Pipeline in America for domestic political consumption while at the same time approving a Russian pipeline for Western Europe. What happened to global warming and the evils of fossils fuels, Mr. President? Do European fossil fuels not contribute to global warming? Too afraid or too cynical to say no to Putin? Certainly, Putin is reading this for what it is, more weakness from an American president. Putin believes that the United States is in decline and that now is the time for him to put even more pressure on us. The flurry of cyberattacks from Russia, without any serious retaliation by the United States, continues to send the wrong message to Putin. As with North Korea and Kim Jong-un, broad sanctions against Russia have no impact on Putin personally or on the oligarchs who surround him and further empower him. Intelligence reports in the media put Putin's net worth somewhere between $90 billion and $300 billion. However we may try to squeeze the Russian people, believe me, Putin's doing just fine.

As with Kim and his mob, the only thing Putin and his oligarch friends will understand is when we make this personal and start to freeze *their* assets. And it can't be Putin alone. It's those oligarchs who are holding many of his assets overseas. We should seize their huge holdings and the fortunes of their families in the West. We should quit welcoming their children at our Ivy League and other elite universities and let them get their educations at all these world-class schools in Russia. Oh, right. Too bad that's a very short list. If Putin's cyber jockeys want to keep interfering in U.S. presidential elections and with U.S. companies, then they have no business taking advantage of the many benefits of American success. Their money and children and lavish vacation dreams have no place here.

It's all part of getting personal.

Direct, personal action against Putin and his friends, that's something they will understand. It'll be far more effective than squeezing the Russian people another few degrees harder or Joe Biden wagging his finger at the latest abuse from Moscow.

Putin's Russia remains a strategic military threat to the United States, a nuclear threat to the United States, and a cyber threat to the United States. But his country is no economic threat. The Russians have a second-rate economy, and Putin has done almost nothing to strengthen it. He's invested in foreign military adventures and cyber-attacks on Western democracies, not the economic future of his own people. That's why he's been so eager to team up with China. He wants to work with Chinese president Xi Jinping and his world-class economic strength to create problems for the United States around the world.

Talk about a match made in despot hell. There can't be any doubt any longer that China will be America's number one adversary for the next fifty years.

The Chinese have the second-largest economy in the world, after ours. That instantly makes them a potent force everywhere. And they've been busy exploiting that fact with their Belt and Road global infrastructure initiative and a rash of new military alliances on several continents. They're working hard to buy friends around the world, while they keep messing with the U.S. economy. Despite all that, we keep failing to treat the Chinese like the profound threat they so obviously are. President Trump made a big error when COVID first exploded around the world, lavishing praise on the leader of the country where the deadly virus was born, most likely inside a Chinese lab. As early as January 2020, Trump was buttering up Xi and the secretive government in Beijing.

"China has been working very hard to contain the Coronavirus," Trump tweeted, most likely on a phone assembled in China. "The United States greatly appreciates their efforts and transparency. In particular, on behalf of the American people, I want to thank President Xi."

Really? Thank that murdering, lying thug?

Two weeks later, Trump had more. "I just spoke to President Xi last night and you know we're working on the problem, the virus. It's a very tough situation, but I think he's going to handle it. I think he's handled it really well. He is strong, sharp, and powerfully focused to lead a counterattack on the Coronavirus. Great discipline is taking place in China as President Xi strongly leads what will be a very successful operation." A week later, it was this: "I think they've handled it professionally. I think they're extremely capable and I think President Xi is extremely capable and I hope that it's going to be resolved."

It was only in the fall, after China's lying and mishandling of the virus had become impossible to ignore, that President Trump started saying negative things about President Xi. If COVID-19 was the only example of Chinese lying and treachery, perhaps his approach could be forgiven. But Xi is the same leader who restricts the number of children his citizens can have and enforces policies that lead to forced abortions. He is the same leader who rounds up political dissidents and sentences them to forced labor camps. He is the same leader who has engaged in genocide in his own country. He is the same leader who regularly steals American intellectual property and converts it for Chinese profit. He is the same leader who has built artificial islands in the South China Sea to use as military bases in violation of international agreements. On behalf of the American people, I want to thank President Xi? Why would we ever thank such a treacherous, untrustworthy adversary to freedom and liberty?

Huge flattery . . . huge mistake.

United States policy toward China needs to change dramatically. First, we have to vastly increase the size and capability of our surface Navy so we can have a much larger presence to protect our interests in the South China Sea and elsewhere. That's the best way to discourage Chinese adventurism and trade restrictions that would choke that region. We need to insist that China respect the copyright and trademarks laws and quit stealing American intellectual property. They have to stop dumping illegally subsidized products on foreign shores. The global economy depends on all nations following the trade laws—and being sternly punished when they don't.

This looking-the-other-way approach is not a good strategy for America, not with the rampant abuses by the Chinese. Because of their constant outlaw behavior, we need to seriously question whether China has earned its place in the World Trade Organization and other international bodies.

The personal sanctions I propose for Russian leaders can be just as effective when they are deployed against President Xi and his enablers. If their nation is going to keep plundering the American economy, why should they own New York penthouse apartments, vacation in Miami, or send their sons and daughters to Yale? Those are privileges they have not earned.

America First is exactly the right policy for America to pursue. One of the things that have kept America first for the past eighty years is our alliances and friendships around the world, which are based on a shared love of freedom and liberty. These alliances need to be strengthened. These relationships haven't always gotten the love they deserve. And we have to do a much better job of blowing our own horn. Believe me, the Chinese are constantly bragging about the "good deeds" they do in other countries. We need to do a far better job highlighting our amazing generosity around the world. And let's start with the invention of the vaccines that are saving the world from a global pandemic. No one is begging for Chinese vaccines.

We are not going to win the fight against the Chinese with just one approach. It can't be purely military or purely economic or purely cyber based. We have to use the entire menu of options to let the Chinese know we mean business and we always expect to be treated fairly. And that starts with leveling the economic playing field. We should ban TikTok and other Chinese-owned apps that are used to gather intelligence in this country. We should continue to stop Huawei from being involved with any 5G networks that we create. We should urge our allies to do the same. If the Chinese want to dominate the technological marketplace, they'll just have to get better at dreaming up their own ideas—and quit stealing ours.

We need to make it absolutely clear that any type of Chinese intervention, direct or indirect, in Taiwan will be met with a devastating American response. We can't have another Hong Kong. Not only do we have a moral obligation to protect the Taiwanese people but a majority of the world's microchips are now manufactured in Taiwan. That gives us powerful moral and economic reasons to draw that line.

It is important to remember that during the Cold War, many Democrats were for appeasement of the Soviet Union through the nuclear freeze movement. In the same way, many Democrats today have a much-too-cozy relationship with the Chinese and refuse to condemn their conduct. This is why Republicans must speak out strongly and consistently on these topics. It was Ronald Reagan and the Republicans who stood up to the Evil Empire of the Soviet Union. We must now do the same to China.

Some people used to argue that if we would only introduce American-style capitalism into China, they'd respond with American-style democracy. Well, today China is flooded with

McDonald's, Coca-Cola, Nike, and just about every American brand you can name, in their legitimate and bootleg manifestations. And what has the West gotten in return? A China that oppresses and kills its people, steals from the rest of us, and seeks to dominate the world.

This doesn't mean we need to pursue regime change in Beijing or start a land war with China. But it does mean we need a clear-eyed toughness as we deal with China in the years ahead. President Xi will not be won over with unearned, flowery compliments. He is a hardened communist dictator. Only strength and clarity will give us a chance to clinch the twenty-first century as the second American century. It is only the Chinese who stand in the way of that worthy goal for us and the rest of humanity. Will dwelling on the mistakes of the past or the grievances of 2020 get us there? No chance. Only strong, honest Republican leadership can get this done. And we need to get to it.

CHAPTER 21

ON COVID

In Part I, I pointed out the mistakes the Trump administration made in the early handling of COVID-19. Not taking the beginning seriously enough. Creating false expectations. Pretending the virus would just disappear. I also made clear the mistakes that were made by blue-state governors, who locked down their states for far too long, causing severe economic distress, worsening mental health and domestic violence issues, and sacrificing nearly two years of our children's education, while not decreasing the death rates compared to states that took much more measured steps.

Both sides got it wrong.

I take the COVID pandemic very seriously. It is personal to me. I had COVID. I spent seven days in the intensive-care unit fighting for my life, and I feel very fortunate I am still here.

The Trump administration's greatest COVID triumph was Operation Warp Speed. Trump's early emphasis on vaccines as the silver bullet against the virus turned out to be exactly right. By committing tens of billions of dollars to the early purchase of vaccines not yet proven effective, he made a huge gamble but a smart one. Donald Trump, as we know, is a guy who's been taking gambles his entire career. In November 2020, when the Pfizer and Moderna companies announced that their vaccines were 90-plus percent effective, the American people finally saw light at the end of the tunnel. But even with this indisputably joyous news, Joe Biden, Kamala Harris, and the Democrats saw storm clouds overhead. Harris even vowed that she would not take a vaccine that was developed by the Trump administration. Biden urged caution about the medical trial results, which he claimed may have been influenced by Trump's political FDA. Democrats throughout Congress cast doubt on the effectiveness of the vaccines only because they were developed on the watch of Donald Trump.

That callous political behavior in the midst of a national crisis is still costing our country today, and I contend that it is a major contributor to vaccine hesitancy across the country. Those comments took a medical miracle and turned it into a partisan political football. It was that hesitancy that led to a major outbreak of the Delta variant in 2021.

This new twist on COVID was not a truly national pandemic. It was a national pandemic among the unvaccinated. While there have been some breakthrough infections among those who have gotten their shots, few of those folks have had to be hospitalized or faced the genuine prospect of dying. On the other hand, the unvaccinated were landing in hospitals in record numbers across the South and the Far West.

What should we do in light of these subsequent outbreaks?

First, we have to stop trying to guilt people into taking vaccines. As I have said often on TV, the unvaccinated do not want to be indoctrinated. They want to be educated. Their doubts about the vaccine can be explained in many different ways. Some people have a genuine suspicion of government. Some fear future complications caused by the vaccine. Some believe that if they have already had COVID, there is no need for them to get vaccinated against the new variants. Some just doubt the vaccine and its effectiveness based on the early doubts expressed by people like President Biden and Vice President Harris.

We do not need to close our country down again. We do not need universal mask mandates, especially for the vaccinated. We do not need mandates for vaccinations across the country. If we have learned anything over the years, it's that people will willingly break laws that they fundamentally disagree with. A law mandating everyone be vaccinated is unenforceable and would sow even more distrust among the doubters. The only way to defeat those doubts is to remind the doubters what a random killer the virus is and educate them on the effectiveness of the vaccines.

Why should we shut down again? More than half our nation is fully vaccinated. When those people got vaccinated, they were told they could go back to a life as close to normal as possible. To then shut down their businesses, their schools, and their leisure events would create enormous anger for little or no yield in public health benefits. We know that vaccinated people do not get seriously ill from the virus and we know they are much less likely to transmit it than the unvaccinated. So, no mandates of any kind for people who have already been vaccinated.

And why should we close our schools and return to distance learning?

Distance learning was and is a failure. Test results are already showing that our children fell behind as soon as they were sentenced to distance learning. Also, even more important, there is still no provable scientific evidence that children are more vulnerable to the virus in school.

All along, the mantra of President Biden and the Democrats has been *follow the science*. But there are exceptions to that rule when they want COVID mandates. My cynical view is that the Democrats believe that the more government is in control, the better off their party does politically. In this, they are always supported by their co-conspirators in the mainstream media, who always crave a crisis in order to draw eyeballs to their broadcasts. But none of these is an acceptable reason to drive our children back out of school, and in fact there are no provable scientific reasons to do it.

So what do we need to do to combat the Delta variants and other new ones undoubtedly coming at us from around the world? We need a relentless, ubiquitous education campaign for the American people from everyday medical professionals, not medical TV stars like Drs. Anthony Fauci and Scott Gottlieb. We also need to hear from COVID patients who have survived (like me) and the families of COVID patients who sadly didn't make it. They must tell the stories of the random, lethal nature of this terrible disease.

Those stories will move far more unvaccinated people to get vaccinated than all those testimonials from the public officeholders and the medical TV stars.

The COVID pandemic has already changed American life in every way since March 2020. Thankfully, we are almost through the crisis now. And we can go the rest of the way, not by taking away people's freedoms but by making people even freer to make the right choices. We can give them all the information they need from credible sources to get the vaccine and to end this deadly pandemic once and for all. Education always leads to freedom, even from this deadly virus. Government control leads to tyranny, even if done with good intentions. To me, the choice is easy.

CHAPTER 22

ON ELECTIONS

Elections have consequences," Barack Obama famously told congressional Republicans three days after he took office. Eric Cantor and others were up at the White House, complaining about the size of the new president's economic stimulus plan.

"At the end of the day," Obama added with a shrug, "I won."

The consequential nature of elections was something Republicans understood perfectly well during the Obama administration—but suddenly seemed to forget once Donald Trump came to town. For the first two years of the Trump administration, we had control over everything. We'd had majorities in the House since 2011 and the Senate since 2015. Now we also had the White House. Republicans were feeling like, *Okay, we've got the whole thing now.* There didn't seem to be any obvious threat on the horizon. We didn't feel any particular urgency. We forgot the old elections-have-consequences routine and started behaving like we had all the time in the world.

The Democrats had other ideas.

Have you noticed? Politics has a way of dragging you back to earth.

We lost the House in 2018. Two years later, we lost the Senate and the presidency. If there's ever been a period that reminds the

Republican Party of the kinds of consequences elections can bring, it's the first year of the Biden administration.

Joe Biden began his term by signing more executive orders than Donald Trump had, by at least a third. Most of those executive orders undid the actions that Trump had taken over the previous four years. And Biden started spending big. Really big. In Trump's final month in office, he and Congress had agreed on an additional $900 billion of COVID-related spending. Before that money was even out the door, Joe Biden advocated for another $1.9 trillion in COVID spending, much of which had been rejected under the previous deals because Republicans controlled the White House and the Senate. For instance, $350 billion was shipped out to the states when, in fact, most states weren't running deficits at all. They had surpluses. Disguised as COVID relief, this became a huge liberal boondoggle in all kinds of areas. The best example wasn't just the barrels of money that state governments didn't need. It was Biden's gargantuan infrastructure plan, a fat share of it funded with unspent COVID dollars. The Biden administration had to admit the money wasn't needed to combat the pandemic, even though that's exactly how Team Biden had advocated for it just a few months earlier.

Elections do indeed have consequences. Three trillion here. Six trillion there. Biden was just getting started, and the trillions kept adding up, all piled on top of each other. This was Joe Biden giving life to the entire Bernie Sanders/Elizabeth Warren radical liberal spending wish list.

Now, to be honest, Republicans don't have the cleanest hands on this issue anymore. We've lost some credibility on government spending. The Republican Congress, when there was such a thing, did not try very hard to restrain its own spending or the Trump administration's. That makes some people roll their eyes when we start lecturing on the perils of exorbitant government expenditures. That said, the spending restraint of the Republican Congress was downright Herculean, compared to the breathless orgy of spending that Biden and the Democratic Congress have quickly convened.

Two things we have to remember as the trillions go flying into the air: First, this money is being borrowed when interest rates are the lowest in modern American history. And second, all this spending is occurring in an American economy that is already recovering at overheated post-COVID growth rates. There are signs of inflation we haven't seen since the late Carter years. Yes, Joe Biden has said that Jimmy Carter is one of his favorite presidents. Get ready for real inflation, everyone, and a replay of the Carter economy.

By the way, while we are talking about the similarities between Joe Biden and his favorite president, Jimmy Carter, let's also remember their shared ineptitude in foreign policy execution. We all recall President Carter's failed attempt in 1979 to rescue the American hostages in Iran. That mission ended with disabled U.S. military equipment in the middle of the desert and the hostages no closer to home than when the rescue attempt began. Those images made America look incompetent and weak before the world.

Joe Biden's contribution to this history was his disastrous troop withdrawal from Afghanistan in the summer of 2021, and the images this time were just as horrific: our Afghan allies and supporters grasping on to the bottom of U.S. military transport planes as the planes took off and the panicked Afghanis desperately tried to escape the wrath of the Taliban.

Chilling.

People can debate the decision to withdraw from Afghanistan. I opposed it and believe that, because of our withdrawal, Afghanistan will once again become a safe harbor to terrorists plotting against the United States. But whatever you think about the overall decision, Biden completely botched the safe evacuation of those American civilians and our Afghani supporters. He missed the obvious strategy: Get the unarmed civilian personnel out before removing the armed U.S. soldiers. Keep Bagram Air Base open, not relying on the commercial airport in Kabul to withdraw Americans and our allies. We still don't know the full implications of that failure of leadership. But there's no denying it cost the lives of our innocent allies and thirteen American soldiers, and undermined America's reputation around the world. As with Carter in Iran, people are questioning our competence and commitment again. Those dreadful images undoubtedly brought great joy in the cities of Tehran, Beijing, and Moscow.

Ineptitude abroad, ineptitude at home.

With rising inflation will come rising interest rates. All that debt will get more and more expensive as we struggle to pay back money that's long been spent. That's why you and I try not to overload our credit cards. We understand: Spending big wads of borrowed money can be exhilarating, but all that extra debt is rarely a good long-term deal for anyone other than whoever you borrowed it from.

Republicans should reframe the discussion by making sure people understand: Tax increases are coming. They've already arrived at the state level, and they'll sweep through Washington soon enough if Joe Biden and the Democrats in Congress get their way. Individual tax increases. Corporate tax increases. New federal taxes and fees we've never seen before. Republicans need to stand up against this runaway government spending in one simple and direct way. Keep asking the American people: "Who do you trust more to spend your money? Your fellow citizens or the federal government?"

Boldly, clearly, repeatedly, Republicans must keep making the case that all this spending simply isn't sustainable, especially when we're competing in every sense with China. But heavy spending isn't Biden's only tool for changing the fabric of America. His deluge of executive orders is giving federal departments and agencies more and more control over all our daily lives. The IRS. The FTC. The SEC. The FDA. If it has initials and a Washington zip code, chances are it has a boatload of new regulations with you in mind.

Deciding whether or not you'll have an early termination fee in your Wi-Fi agreement. Deciding how much your solar panels or your next new car will cost. Deciding what the drugstore will charge for your next prescription, which will undoubtedly take the "warp speed" out of the next pharmaceutical miracle. It's no coincidence that the country that invented COVID vaccines is also the country that doesn't have price controls on prescription drugs. That's how we pay for the research and development that will save our lives with the next amazing treatment or cure.

Now, that's money well spent.

And it's not just health care. These Biden executive orders also seek to regulate every part of transportation—rail, road, and air. Every private sector workplace. Every law enforcement practice. Every classroom curriculum. Joe Biden, who ran as a moderate Democrat, is governing in a way that would make FDR blush. For those who care about social issues, Biden is showing what he really believes in: that the federal government is the solution to every problem, real or perceived. He wants to further restrict how nonprofits give out donated money to causes that need private philanthropy. For the first time in forty years, Biden wants to remove the Hyde Amendment, which prevents government funding of abortions. This is not a pro-choice position. It's a pro-abortion position that would put all taxpayers back in the business of paying for these procedures again. It's offensive not only to pro-life taxpayers. It should also be troubling to those who are pro-choice and believe that abortion should be rare and certainly not encouraged with government funding.

Meanwhile, Biden's appointing more liberals to the federal courts, judges who will attempt to make laws from the bench rather than merely interpret them. This is in an administration that will certainly get sued often as it keeps overreaching further into American life. All these issues will soon be heading into the federal courts. And while the Trump administration did its most admirable work appointing conservative judges and justices, Biden and his team are doing their very best to rebalance that in their favor—and they'll keep making headway as long as the Democrats control the U.S. Senate.

Another place where elections have consequences.

This is why it's so important for Republicans to stop talking about the past and get focused on the future.

While we're exhausting ourselves debating and "auditing" conspiracy theories from the 2020 election, Joe Biden and the liberal Democrats are laser focused on changing what America *is*. We have to fight for the future. We have to save our capitalist system. We have to be sure liberty and freedom prevail against expanding government control. We will not get help from the mainstream media, who will always be slanted against us. We will not get help from the titans of corporate America, who are now cowering in the corner from the threats of the progressive Left. Our only hope is to appeal directly, honestly, and strongly to the American people.

We have a message people are hungry for. There's a growing suspicion of this federal overreaching. There's already an anti-woke backlash in the air. Republicans have a road map that gives Americans a greater sense of confidence. We have policies that will put the nation back on track. But we'll never get a chance to share them if we continue to wallow in the past and our worst electoral loss since the days of Herbert Hoover.

CONCLUSION

As Republicans, what do we need to do? What exactly? Here's what:

• We need to stand up against the rise of China. It was the Republican Party under Ronald Reagan who brought down the Soviet Union, brought democracy to Eastern Europe and the former Soviet republics. The American people trust the Republican Party much more to push back against Communist China, if we show we have the integrity and are willing to tell the truth again, not toss bouquets at murdering, communist dictators.

• We must stand up for law and order and the rule of law. Let Democrats continue to flirt with the Black Lives Matter movement and defunding the police. Even Joe Biden has recognized the political toxicity of "defund the police." So, he tries to pretend he and the Democrats never said it. We know better. The majority of Americans will never buy that toxic idea, including people in tough neighborhoods who depend especially on police protection. It's no accident how quickly Biden backed away from that rhetoric, even attempting to say the Republicans are the ones who want to defund the police. To the contrary, Republicans should always be the party that stands up for public safety, smart policing, informed criminal justice reform, and the rule of law.

• We Republicans need to discredit and marginalize the conspiracy theorists and truth deniers. As we have said throughout this book, this is imperative for us to be taken seriously as a party by the voters we lost at the presidential level in the 2020 election.

• Republicans have to push back against the mainstream media, and we need our own persuasive messengers with the credibility to call out the falsehoods and biases of the corporate media. We have a winning message, but sometimes we just aren't being heard. There's only one way we can credibly tell it like it is: making sure we also push back against the conspiracy theories that have been wrecking our own credibility. The elite media are not on our side. Only if we tell the truth about *everything* will our media critique be believed. We need to be the party that questions and takes on the New York–Washington power structure. We need to stand up for the American people who are working for a living every day instead of those who want to just continue to dole out money in order to maintain power.

• We must be the party that supports innovation over regulation. When Joe Biden and his friends continue to say that more government regulation will help to solve climate change, our health-care needs, and our problems with Big Tech, we need to be the party that says it's not regulation, but innovation, that has always solved America's most difficult problems. We have to support an innovative pharmaceutical industry to help us cure and treat disease. We need to support innovation in tech so we can stay on the cutting edge of 5G and the next level of communication. We need to build a first-class twenty-first-century Navy to help keep the Chinese in check. Innovation is how America was built, not government regulation.

• We need to stand unabashedly for traditional values in our core American institutions. We do that by standing against the cancel culture, against critical race theory in our schools, and in support of the ideals that birthed American democracy: life, liberty, and the pursuit of happiness, supported by a capitalist system that rewards hard work and innovation and encourages people to believe that anyone in America with a worthy idea can become our next great business titan.

• Most important, we must give hope to the American people that government is not their only salvation. On this, even Ronald Reagan and Bill Clinton agreed. Reagan knew that "Government is not the solution to our problems. Government is the problem." Fifteen years later, Clinton declared, "The era of big government is over." Well, there's been some backsliding. We need Republicans like Ronald Reagan again and we need more Democrats who will recognize what Bill Clinton recognized rather than advocate for Joe Biden and Kamala Harris's dangerous policies, which only make the government bigger. We have to show that big government is the road to less freedom, less liberty, and less prosperity. By definition, when government is bigger, Americans are less free.

We do not have to change our policies to win again. Our support for traditional values and the opportunities of capitalism will attract Latino voters in ever-greater numbers if we campaign directly to them. I did this during my governorship and won 51 percent of the Latino vote in 2013. Our support for law and order and commonsense criminal justice reform with both the community and the police involved will lead to greater support for our party in urban areas being ravaged by violent crime. Our support for school choice and parental choice in public education will win back many of the suburban voters we lost in 2020 when they thought we didn't have their backs in the COVID crisis. We will keep everyday working-class Americans in our corner by standing up to Chinese trade and intellectual property abuses and bringing essential manufacturing back to the United States, making the phrase "America First" actually mean something more than tough talk sprinkled with praise for communist dictators. It will also mean creating even more good-paying jobs and making sure we never get held hostage to Chinese manufacturing in a crisis again. And that is just the beginning if we pull together and fight together for our country's future.

Now, let's get busy saving our party so we can save America by winning elections again.

ACKNOWLEDGMENTS

Writing this book has felt, in many ways, like executing an urgent mission. I love this country, and I am endlessly optimistic about its future. But I was raised by a strong Sicilian mother, the daughter of immigrants, who always taught me that nothing is accomplished without hard work and that there is nothing to be admired about standing on the sidelines. This book is my attempt to honor her admonitions for myself, my party, and my country.

When I thank people in my life, I always begin with my life partner of the past thirty-five years, my wife, Mary Pat. She has been a significant contributor to the conception of this book and to bringing it to life on these pages. Thanks for reading it as we were writing it, for your edits and observations, and for your love for me and your unending support for my feeling of duty to our country. My father, Bill Christie, continues to be an inspiration to me over his eighty-eight years with his work ethic and his love for life. Thanks for always encouraging me and rooting for me.

This book has been another joyful project with my literary collaborator, Ellis Henican. After *Let Me Finish* and now this book, we can actually finish each other's sentences and often do just that. Ellis is an extraordinarily talented writer with a wicked sense of humor and a sharp eye for authenticity. All of his skills and talents have made this book better than it ever could have been without him by my side. Once again, I enjoyed every minute of our time together.

My agents at WME have once again given me great guidance and wise representation. Jordan Bazant as the leader of "Team Christie" at WME and the incomparable Mel Berger as my literary agent took the concept of this book and quickly turned it into a reality. They are both real pros who have made my post-public-service life fun and interesting. Natasha Simons, my editor at Simon & Schuster, provided real support for this project from the beginning and genuine enthusiasm for the story as we wrote it. She challenged us to push as hard as we could to make this book reach its potential. Roberta Teer has once again played the role of researcher extraordinaire. She makes sure that the facts that Ellis or I are absolutely sure of actually are facts! Thanks once again to her. Our transcriber was also a repeat offender from *Let Me Finish*, Janis Spidle. She continues to know every one of my unfiltered thoughts on some very sensitive and important topics, and she transcribes them with trustworthiness and accuracy. An author cannot ask for anything more.

The advice, counsel, and honesty of good friends throughout the process of writing a book like this one has been invaluable. Thanks to Maria Comella, Bill Palatucci, Mike DuHaime, Chris Porrino, Phil Cox, and Austin Chambers for being regularly available to listen to my ideas and always telling it like it is. My team at Christie 55 Solutions have supported and indulged me by giving me the time it takes to write a book like this one. Thanks to my partner (and former chief of staff) Rich Bagger and to our fellow compatriots at Christie 55—Michele Brown, Bob Martin, and Megan Fielder. It is great to have a team like this to work with each and every day.

Thanks also to people in this business of public service who have inspired me and continue to inspire me about how important it is to try to make a difference in the lives of people you will probably never meet and certainly never know. To my political mentor in so many ways, the incomparable Governor Haley Barbour of Mississippi. So much of what I have learned about politics and governance came from the great example he has set and the wonderful conversations we have shared. I would not be here without him. To my political brother, Maryland governor Larry Hogan, who has been both a personal and professional inspiration to me since we first met in 2014. He has strength of principle and strength of character and has proven to be a great leader for the people of Maryland and a great friend to me. I am so glad I came to lunch in the summer of 2014. There is much more work to be done, my friend. To former West Virginia governor and current United States senator Joe Manchin. In 2009, he became my mentor governor and was a regular source of advice and confidence throughout my first year as governor of New Jersey. He then left for Washington's most exclusive club and the Senate's gain was the nation's governors' loss. Through the years, Mary Pat and I have been truly lucky to have Joe and Gayle as wonderful friends. America is seeing very clearly today what I learned twelve years ago—that Joe Manchin is a special leader. To one of my all-time favorite Jersey Girls, presidential counselor, and 2016 Trump for President winning campaign manager, Kellyanne Conway. She is one of the brightest political minds in our party and one of the most loyal friends you could ever be lucky enough to have. We rode the roller coaster of the last five years together, sometimes in the same car, and her advice and friendship was a regular source of strength and understanding. Thanks to her for her honesty and steadfastness in an arena that was often not known for either.

Finally, thanks to my colleagues at ABC News, my TV home since January 2018. Barbara Fedida, George Stephanopoulos, Jon Karl, Byron Pitts, Pierre Thomas, David Muir, Cecilia Vega, Linsey Davis, Donna Brazile, Sara Fagen, Yvette Simpson, and I have spent a lot of debate nights and election nights together over the past four years. It has been a pleasure to spend those special nights for democracy with you and our audience. Most of all, to my Democratic sparring partner and friend, Mayor Rahm Emanuel. And they said it wouldn't work? The last few years have been made even more special because of our worthy and spirited debates, both on and off the air. You are not only a worthy adversary but a very good friend. Until our next argument, I wish all the best for you and your wonderful family.